WORLD SOCCER
INFOGRAPHICS
The Beautiful Game in Vital Statistics

The World's Leading Football Data Provider

PUBLISHER'S NOTES

All European domestic league infographic data runs up until the end of the 2016–17 season.
All European team names printed in accordance with UEFA.

First published in the United States of America in 2018 by
UNIVERSE PUBLISHING
A Division of Rizzoli International Publications, Inc.
300 Park Avenue South
New York, NY 10010
www.rizzoliusa.com

Originally published in the United Kingdom in 2016 (updated in 2017) by
Carlton Books Limited

Infographic statistical data © Perform Media Channels Limited 2016, 2017
All other text, graphics, and design © Carlton Books Limited 2016, 2017

2018 2019 2020 2021 / 10 9 8 7 6 5 4 3 2 1

ISBN: 978-0-7893-3426-8
Library of Congress Control Number: 2017952765

Printed in China

Numbers, Statistics, and
Trends of the Players, Teams,
Stadiums, and more

WORLD SOCCER
INFOGRAPHICS
The Beautiful Game in Vital Statistics

opta

The World's Leading Football Data Provider

UNIVERSE

CONTENTS

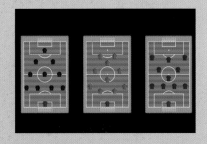

WORLD SOCCER

FIFA WORLD CUP

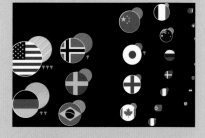

FIFA WOMEN'S WORLD CUP

DOMESTIC CLUB SOCCER

MISCELLANEOUS

CONTINENTAL CHAMPIONSHIPS

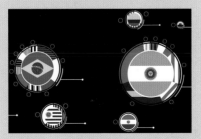

CONTINENTAL CLUB SOCCER

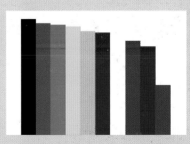

DOMESTIC CLUB SOCCER

opta

Foreword

It is now 20 years since Opta started collecting soccer data and in that time the popularity of the information produced has gone from being a curiosity in a newspaper or TV feature to an integral part of sports coverage in every type of media.

Data was long seen as the home of the stats geek, only accessible to those willing to pore through statistical tomes to find "interesting" snippets of information. Today it's consumed by ordinary soccer fans through a variety of methods. You'll still see tables of numbers and hear facts and figures spoken by commentators, pundits, or by people to their friends on their way to matches, but you're now just as likely to see a graphical interpretation of that information.

From pie charts and bar charts, to radars and word clouds, numbers are regularly turned into easily understandable graphics, where the viewer can see what you're trying to tell them instantly. Added to that, the positional and tracking data available within sports allows tactical insight to be communicated easily through heat maps, average formation graphics, or expected goals visualizations, which show at a glance the chance of scoring from a particular position on the pitch relative to other types of shots.

Infographics have become one of the most quickly developing trends in sports data analysis. As datasets become more complex, infographics are an invaluable way of displaying complex information in a clear, concise, attractive way. The unique infographics created for the second edition of this book, incorporating comparisons between players, teams, and leagues for almost every continent, showcases the mass of detailed data now available from right across the world of sports.

Enjoy the book,

Rob Bateman, Global Director of Content (@Orbinho)

Introduction

Statistics are an integral part of modern soccer—pored over by coaches, analysts, and armchair fans alike. Rarely though, have the thrills and skills, triumphs and trophies of the global game been transformed into such thought-provoking graphs, diagrams, and charts as those presented on the pages that follow. You'll be amazed at what emerges from these technicolor infographics. From the statistics that illuminate the Messi–Ronaldo rivalry to the evolution of team formations, right through to the different parts of the body used to score World Cup goals—it's all here… and more.

Our fascination with football takes many forms. We can admire the breathtaking skills of stars such as Mesut Özil, Eden Hazard, or Neymar; the performances of great teams like Bayern München and Real Madrid; and the strategies of coaches such as José Mourinho and Antonio Conte. However, in recent years, statistics, trends, and data collection have added to our interest in top-level soccer. And, where there are numbers, there can be infographics capable of unlocking the power of big data and presenting it in a brilliant, captivating way.

This invaluable book uses imaginative infographics to take a topical look at the trends and data in top-class soccer. It compares the top leagues and players across Europe and assesses the performances in the Champions League, Europa League, and Copa Libertadores. At the international level, we see the domination and surprises of the nation's tournaments around the world. And, of course, the greatest soccer show on earth, the FIFA World Cup, is represented in vibrant infographics that include analysis on goalkeepers, goal re-creations, and perfect penalty placements. Intriguing charts and maps also reveal other facets such as club rivalries, stadium sizes, MLS, the FIFA World Player of the Year and where to find the most shots from distance or dribbles.

Thanks to the rich and compelling information supplied by data providers such as Opta, soccer is no longer just a simple game of two halves. The doors have been blown open and the beautiful game is just a little bit more beautiful.

FIFA SOCCER NATIONS

FIFA's six confederations represent different regions of the world: UEFA (Europe), CAF (Africa), CONCACAF (North and Central America), CONMEBOL (South America), OFC (New Zealand and South Pacific island nations) and AFC (Asia). FIFA was founded on May 21, 1904 in Paris by delegates from Belgium, Denmark, France, the Netherlands, Spain, Sweden and Switzerland. It now has more member countries than the United Nations – 211 to the UN's 193. The British nations, acting in unison, had a checkered relationship with the world body in its early years, joining in 1906 but leaving on two occasions before re-joining permanently in 1946.

NATIONAL ASSOCIATIONS:
YEAR FOUNDED

- UEFA
- OFC
- AFC
- CONMEBOL
- CONCACAF
- CAF

Year	Nation
1863	England
1873	Scotland
1876	Wales
1880	Northern Ireland
1889	Denmark
1889	Netherlands
1891	New Zealand
1892	Singapore
1893	Argentina
1895	Belgium
1895	Chile
1895	Gibraltar
1895	Switzerland
1898	Italy
1900	Germany
1900	Malta
1900	Uruguay
1901	Czech Republic
1901	Hungary
1902	Guyana
1902	Norway
1904	Austria
1904	Haiti
1904	Sweden
1906	Paraguay
1907	Finland
1907	Phillipines
1908	Luxembourg
1908	Trinidad and Tobago
1909	Romania
1910	Barbados
1910	Jamaica
1912	Canada
1912	Croatia
1912	Russia
1913	Spain
1913	USA
1914	Brazil
1914	Hong Kong
1914	Kazakhstan
1914	Portugal
1916	Thailand
1919	Belgian Congo
1919	France
1919	Guatemala
1919	Poland
1919	Serbia
1920	Iran
1920	Slovenia
1920	Suriname
1921	Costa Rica
1921	Curaçao
1921	Egypt
1921	Estonia
1921	Japan
1921	Latvia
1921	Republic of Ireland
1922	Afghanistan
1922	Lithuania
1922	Peru
1923	Bulgaria
1923	Turkey
1924	China PR
1924	Colombia
1924	Cuba
1924	Grenada
1924	Uganda
1925	Bolivia
1925	Ecuador
1926	Greece
1926	Venezuela
1927	Mexico
1928	Antigua and Barbuda
1928	Bermuda
1928	Israel
1928	New Caledonia
1929	Zambia
1930	Albania
1930	Indonesia
1930	Tanzania
1931	Montenegro
1931	Nicaragua
1931	San Marino
1932	Aruba
1932	Lesotho
1932	St. Kitts and Nevis
1933	Cambodia
1933	Korea Republic
1933	Lebanon
1933	Malaysia
1934	Cyprus
1934	Liechtenstein
1934	Vanuatu
1935	El Salvador
1935	Honduras
1936	Chinese Tapei
1936	Liberia
1936	Sudan
1936	Syria
1936	Tajikistan
1937	India
1937	Panama
1938	Fiji
1938	Slovakia
1939	Macau
1939	Sri Lanka
1940	Puerto Rico
1943	Ethiopia
1945	Korea DPR
1945	Nigeria
1946	Kosovo

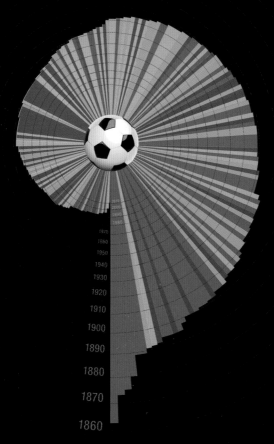

Year	Nation
1946	Uzbekistan
1947	Iceland
1947	Myanmar
1948	Burundi
1948	FYR Macedonia
1948	Iraq
1948	Pakistan
1949	Jordan
1951	Laos
1951	Nepal
1951	Somalia
1952	Gambia
1952	Kuwait
1952	Mauritius
1953	Dominican Republic
1955	Morocco
1956	Saudi Arabia
1957	Bahrain
1957	Equatorial Guinea
1957	Ghana
1957	Tunisia
1959	Brunei Darussalam
1959	Cameroon
1959	Mongolia
1960	Burkino Faso
1960	Côte D'ivoire
1960	Guinea
1960	Kenya
1960	Mali
1960	Qatar
1960	Senegal
1960	Sierra Leone
1960	Togo
1961	Australia
1961	Central African Republic
1961	Madagascar
1961	Mauritania
1961	Niger
1962	DR Congo
1962	Algeria
1962	Benin
1962	Chad
1962	Gabon
1962	Libya
1962	Palestine
1962	Papua New Guinea
1962	Vietnam
1962	Yemen
1965	Tonga
1965	Zimbabwe
1966	Cayman Islands
1966	Malawi
1967	Bahamas
1968	Samoa
1968	Swaziland
1970	Botswana
1970	Dominica
1971	Cook Islands
1971	United Arab Emirates
1972	Bangladesh
1972	Rwanda
1974	British Virgin Islands
1974	Guinea-Bissau
1975	Guam
1975	São Tomé e Príncipe
1976	Mozambique
1978	Oman
1978	Solomon Islands
1979	Angola
1979	Comoros
1979	Djibouti
1979	Faroe Islands
1979	Seychelles
1979	St. Lucia
1979	St. Vincent and the Grenadines
1980	Belize
1982	Cape Verde Islands
1982	Maldives
1983	Bhutan
1984	American Samoa
1989	Belarus
1989	Tahiti
1990	Anguilla
1990	Georgia
1990	Moldova
1990	Namibia
1991	South Africa
1991	Ukraine
1992	Armenia
1992	Azerbaijan
1992	Bosnia and Herzegovina
1992	Kyrgystan
1992	Turkmenistan
1992	US Virgin Islands
1994	Andorra
1994	Montserrat
1996	Eritrea
1996	Turks and Caicos Islands
2002	Timor-Leste
2011	South Sudan

NATIONAL ASSOCIATIONS: YEAR AFFILIATED WITH FIFA

🌐 **WORLD CUP**

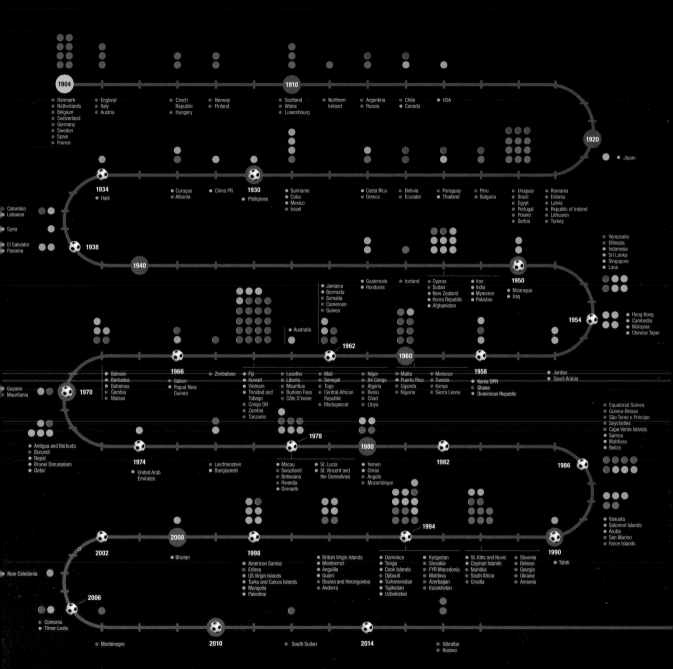

Source: Opta (June 2017)

SOCCER STADIUMS BY SIZE

The soccer world may still mourn the loss of iconic grounds such as Arsenal's Highbury stadium, Benfica's Estádio da Luz, and Athletic Bilbao's La Catedral at San Mamés, but the stadiums that replaced them and other new venues such as the Allianz Arena in Munich, Juventus' stadium in Turin, and Atlético Madrid's Wanda Metropolitano look set to join Camp Nou, Old Trafford, and La Bombonera on the list of the world's most hallowed grounds. This infographic illustrates the world's biggest soccer stadiums (on this page) and the homes of leading soccer clubs and major national teams (facing)—and, for comparison, includes two of the smallest.

Source: Google (May 2017)

RUNGRADO MAY DAY STADIUM
Pyongyang, North Korea

DPR KOREA NATIONAL FOOTBALL TEAM
150,000

CAMP NOU
Barcelona, Spain

BARCELONA
99,354

FNB STADIUM (SOCCER CITY)
Johannesburg, South Africa

SOUTH AFRICA NATIONAL TEAM,
KAIZER CHIEFS, 2010 WORLD CUP
94,736

WEMBLEY STADIUM
London, England

ENGLAND NATIONAL
FOOTBALL TEAM
90,000

ESTADIO AZTECA
Mexico City, Mexico

MEXICO NATIONAL FOOTBALL TEAM,
CLUB AMÉRICA
87,000

BORG EL ARAB STADIUM
Alexandria, Egypt

EGYPT NATIONAL
FOOTBALL TEAM
86,000

SALT LAKE STADIUM
Kolkata, India

INDIA NATIONAL
FOOTBALL TEAM
85,000

**SIGNAL IDUNA PARK
(WESTFALENSTADION)**
Dortmund, Germany
**BORUSSIA DORTMUND
81,359**

STADE DE FRANCE
Saint-Denis, France
**FRANCE NATIONAL FOOTBALL TEAM
81,338**

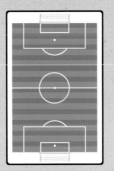

SANTIAGO BERNABÉU STADIUM
Madrid, Spain
**REAL MADRID
81,044**

LUZHNIKI STADIUM
Moscow, Russia
**RUSSIA NATIONAL FOOTBALL TEAM,
2018 WORLD CUP FINAL
81,000**

**STADIO GIUSEPPE MEAZZA
(SAN SIRO)**
Milan, Italy
**INTERNAZIONALE MILANO, AC MILAN
80,018**

MARACANÃ STADIUM
Rio De Janeiro, Brazil
**BRAZIL NATIONAL TEAM,
CR FLAMENGO, FLUMINENSE FC,
BOTAFOGO FR
78,383**

OLD TRAFFORD
Manchester, England
**MANCHESTER UNITED F.C.
75,643**

ALLIANZ ARENA
Munich, Germany
**BAYERN MÜNCHEN,
TSV 1860 MUNICH
75,024**

**PRINCIPALITY (MILLENNIUM)
STADIUM**
Cardiff, Wales
**WALES NATIONAL FOOTBALL TEAM
74,500**

STADIO OLIMPICO
Rome, Italy
**A.S. ROMA, S.S. LAZIO
72,630**

**OLYMPIC STADIUM ATHENS
(SPIROS LOUIS)**
Athens, Greece
**GREECE NATIONAL FOOTBALL TEAM,
AEK ATHENS, PANATHINAIKOS FC
69,618**

ESTÁDIO DA LUZ
Lisbon, Portugal
**S.L. BENFICA, UEFA EURO 2004 FINAL,
2014 UEFA CHAMPIONS LEAGUE FINAL
65,647**

CELTIC PARK
Glasgow, Scotland
**CELTIC FC
60,832**

EMIRATES STADIUM
London, England
**ARSENAL
60,432**

AMSTERDAM ARENA
Amsterdam, Netherlands
**AJAX, NETHERLANDS NATIONAL
FOOTBALL TEAM
54,033**

STADE LOUIS II
Monaco
**AS MONACO
18,500**

VICTORIA STADIUM
Gibraltar
**GIBRALTAR NATIONAL TEAM
5,000**

**ESTADI COMUNAL
D'ANDORRA LA VELLA**
La Vella, Andorra
**ANDORRA NATIONAL TEAM
1,300**

EVOLUTION OF FORMATIONS
1872–1967

Every team has 10 outfield players. What has proved critical over the years is not just how those players perform, but where. Formation is a key tactical element and, as these diagrams show, it is continually evolving. We can see the attack-heavy teams that dominated the early years of the game gradually becoming more balanced, with stronger midfields and defense.

1872

1-2-7 Formation
England

1889

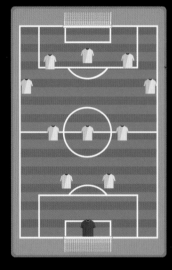

The Pyramid (2-3-5)
Preston North End

1930

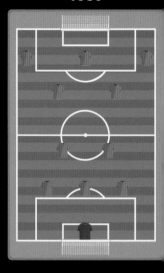

The WM Formation
Arsenal

> **" [Going behind] didn't bother us at all... We just knew we could turn the game around. "**
>
> Djalma Santos, Brazil's
> 1958 FIFA World Cup defender

Brazil's employment of a 4-2-4 formation helped them to victory in the 1958 FIFA World Cup

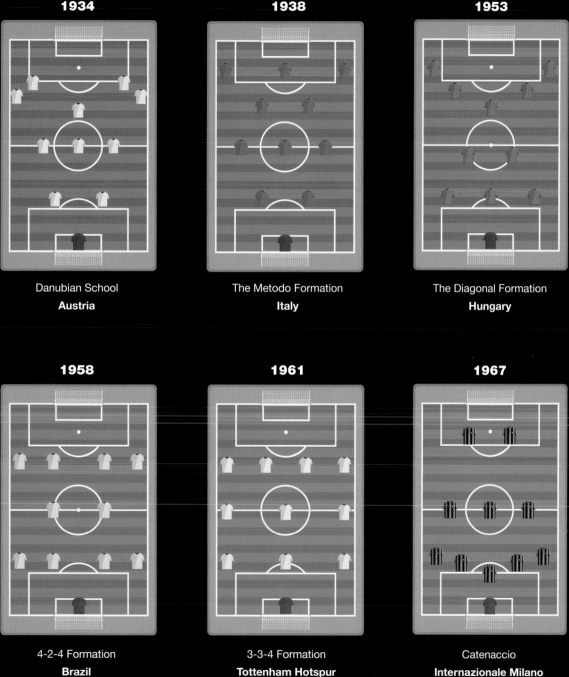

1934

Danubian School
Austria

1938

The Metodo Formation
Italy

1953

The Diagonal Formation
Hungary

1958

4-2-4 Formation
Brazil

1961

3-3-4 Formation
Tottenham Hotspur

1967

Catenaccio
Internazionale Milano

EVOLUTION OF FORMATIONS

1971–2017

1971

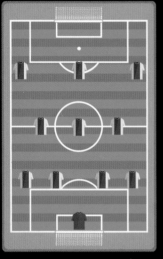

4-3-3 Formation

Ajax

1990

Wing-backs Formation

Germany

1998

4-4-2 Formation

Manchester United

2003

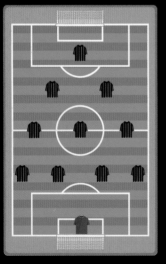

4-3-2-1 Christmas Tree

AC Milan

2006

Diamond Formation

Ghana

2012

The "False 9" Formation

Spain

From the 1970s onwards, the 4-4-2 formation became synonymous with the modern game. Here was a system that focused on passing and tackling in the central zones of the pitch and enabled increasingly fit midfielders to bolster both attacks and defenses. It seemed the evolution had reached its conclusion. However, the search for any slight advantage meant coaches kept on tinkering. "Wingless wonder" teams and fluid "total football" line-ups were followed by wing-backs, "false 9s", pyramids, and Christmas trees. Brazilian coach Carlos Alberto Parreira once predicted 4-6-0 as the "formation of the future"—and some might claim we are edging ever closer to that prophecy.

The pace and attacking skills of Tottenham Hotspur and England's Danny Rose (on left) were integral to the success of the club's wing-back formation in 2017.

2014

4-5-1 Formation

Chelsea

2017

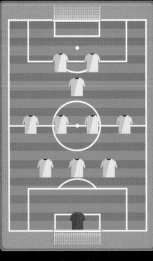

3-4-1-2 Formation

Tottenham Hotspur

" When you have full-backs like ours, Danny Rose or Kyle Walker, they can play forward as offensive players. We tried to put them in a better position to try and play more like wing-backs. That was our idea, and then to play with two strikers. "

Mauricio Pochettino, manager Tottenham Hotspur

FIFA WORLD CUP WINS BY COUNTRY

Brazil truly are the World Cup kings. Not only are they the most successful nation, they also top the chart of World Cup wins, have registered the most consecutive wins (from 2002 vs Turkey to 2006 vs Ghana) and they are the only team to have won all their matches in two tournaments (1970 and 2002). At the other end of the scale, Bulgaria failed to win in five finals from 1962 to 1986, before finally beating Greece in their second game in 1994.

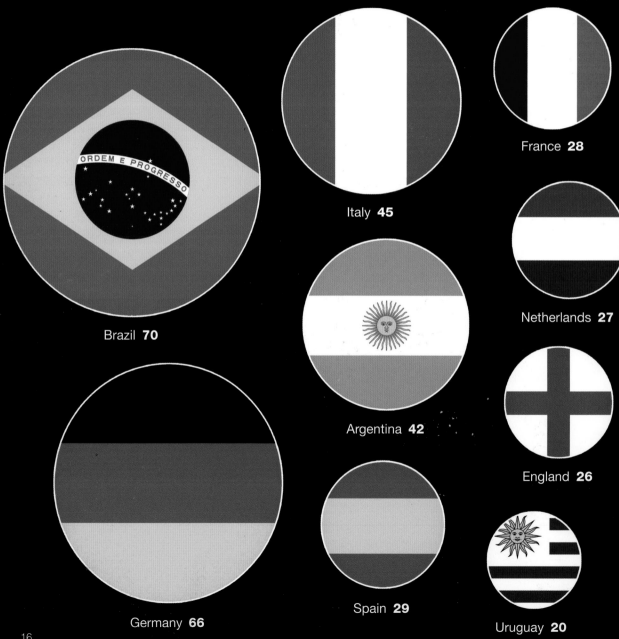

France **28**

Italy **45**

Netherlands **27**

Brazil **70**

Argentina **42**

England **26**

Germany **66**

Spain **29**

Uruguay **20**

Source: Opta (August 2015)
Data relates to individual games won per team, 1930–2014

 Yugoslavia **16**

 Sweden **16**

 Hungary **15**

 Poland **15**

 USSR **15**

 Belgium **14**

 Mexico **14**

 Portugal **13**

 Austria **12**

Chile **11**

Switzerland **11**

Czechoslovakia **11**

 Denmark **8**

 Romania **8**

 USA **8**

Colombia **7**

 Croatia **7**

 Paraguay **7**

Costa Rica **5**

Turkey **5**

 Korea Republic **5**

 Nigeria **5**

 Peru **4**

 Ghana **4**

 Japan **4**

 Ecuador **4**

 Scotland **4**

Cameroon **4**

Algeria **3**

 Ivory Coast **3**

 Bulgaria **3**

 Northern Ireland **3**

 Greece **2**

 Morocco **2**

Ukraine **2**

 Republic of Ireland **2**

 Senegal **2**

 Saudi Arabia **2**

 Russia **2**

 Norway **2**

 Australia **2**

 South Africa **2**

 East Germany **2**

Czech Republic **1**

 Tunisia **1**

 Jamaica **1**

 Slovenia **1**

 Bosnia and Herzegovina **1**

DPR Korea **1**

Cuba **1**

 Iran **1**

 Slovakia **1**

Wales **1**

 Serbia **1**

17

WORLD CUP FINALS RESULTS 1930–2014

The FIFA World Cup has grown from a small tournament comprising 13 teams from Europe and South America (US and Mexico participated, too) to 32 nations from five continents battling it out in the most widely followed sporting event in the world. There have been 20 to date, each one as spectacular as the last. Every tournament has had its amazing stories, controversies, moments that took our breath away, and heartbreak that saw us plunge into despair. Behind all these iconic events, what remains (apart from memories) are these simple facts—the statistics that mark each country's triumphs and disappointments in black and white. Make of these what you will…

Source: Google (October 2015)

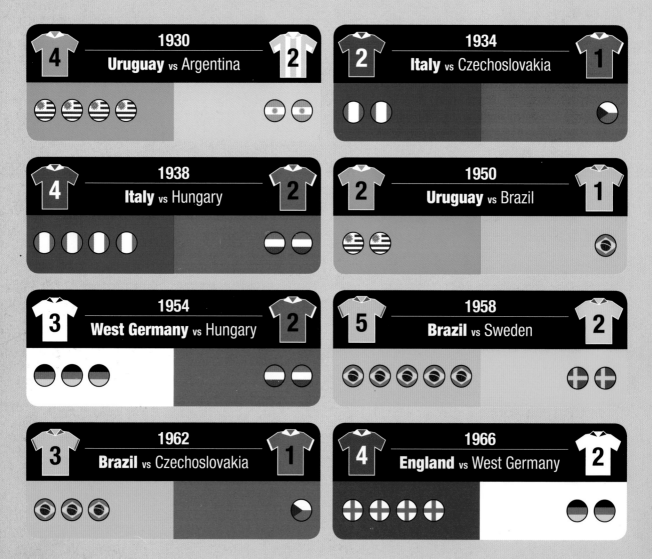

1930
Uruguay vs Argentina — 4 : 2

1934
Italy vs Czechoslovakia — 2 : 1

1938
Italy vs Hungary — 4 : 2

1950
Uruguay vs Brazil — 2 : 1

1954
West Germany vs Hungary — 3 : 2

1958
Brazil vs Sweden — 5 : 2

1962
Brazil vs Czechoslovakia — 3 : 1

1966
England vs West Germany — 4 : 2

1970 — **Brazil** vs Italy — 4 : 1

1974 — **West Germany** vs Netherlands — 2 : 1

1978 — **Argentina** vs Netherlands — 3 : 1

1982 — **Italy** vs West Germany — 3 : 1

1986 — **Argentina** vs West Germany — 3 : 2

1990 — **West Germany** vs Argentina — 1 : 0

1994 — **Brazil** vs Italy — 0 : 0 — PENALTIES

1998 — **France** vs Brazil — 3 : 0

2002 — **Brazil** vs Germany — 2 : 0

2006 — **Italy** vs France — 1 : 1 — PENALTIES

2010 — **Spain** vs Netherlands — 1 : 0

2014 — **Germany** vs Argentina — 1 : 0

WORLD CUP GOALSCORERS BY COUNTRY

It was Lucien Laurent, for France, who scored the first World Cup finals goal at the 1930 competition. Since then over 2,300 goals have been scored by 80 different countries in 20 finals tournaments. Germany and Brazil have both been tournament top scorers on four occasions,

GERMANY

Player	Goals
Miroslav Klose	16
Jürgen Klinsmann	11
Thomas Müller	10
Helmut Rahn	10
Uwe Seeler	9
Rudi Völler	8
Max Morlock	6
Helmut Haller	6
Gerd Müller	14
Karl-Heinz Rummenigge	9
Hans Schäfer	7
Lothar Matthäus	6
Lukas Podolski	5
Franz Beckenbauer	5

ITALY

Player	Goals
Roberto Baggio	9
Paolo Rossi	9
Salvatore Schillaci	6
Christian Vieri	9
Alessandro Altobelli	5
Silvio Piola	5

ARGENTINA

Player	Goals
Gabriel Batistuta	10
Diego Maradona	8
Mario Alberto Kempes	6
Guillermo Stábile	8
Lionel Messi	5
Gonzalo Higuaín	5

BRAZIL

Player	Goals
Ronaldo	15
Vavá	9
Rivaldo	8
Ademir	8
Jairzinho	9
Careca	7
Bebeto	6
Garrincha	5
Pelé	12
Leônidas da Silva	8
Rivellino	6
Zico	5
Romário	5

NETHERLANDS

Player	Goals
Wesley Sneijder	6
Robin van Persie	6
Johnny Rep	7
Dennis Bergkamp	6
Arjen Robben	6
Rob Rensenbrink	6
Johan Neeskens	5

Hungary have the highest strike rate at 2.72 goals scored per match (helped by their record 27 goals in 1954), while Canada, China, Dutch East Indies, Trinidad and Tobago, and Zaire all have reached the finals but failed to register a single goal—a notable achievement in itself.

Source: Opta (August 2015)

SPAIN

David Villa
9

Fernando Morientes
5

Fernando Hierro
5

Basora
5

Emilio Butragueño
5

Raúl
5

FRANCE

Just Fontaine
13

Thierry Henry
6

Michel Platini
5

Zinedine Zidane
5

HUNGARY

Sándor Kocsis
11

Lajos Tichy
7

György Sárosi
6

Gyula Zsengellér
5

URUGUAY

Óscar Míguez
8

Diego Forlán
6

ENGLAND

Gary Lineker
10

Geoff Hurst
5

CZECHOSLOVAKIA

Oldřich Nejedlý
7

Tomáš Skuhravý
5

AUSTRIA

Erich Probst
6

Hans Krankl
5

Juan Alberto Schiaffino
5

Luis Suárez
5

Pedro Cea
5

PERU

Teófilo Cubillas
10

BULGARIA

Hristo Stoichkov **6**

COLOMBIA

James Rodríguez **6**

CROATIA

Davor Šuker **6**

GHANA

Asamoah Gyan **6**

AUSTRALIA

Tim Cahill
5

BELGIUM

Marc Wilmots
5

CAMEROON

Roger Milla
5

POLAND

Grzegorz Lato
10

Andrzej Szarmach
7

SWEDEN

Henrik Larsson
5

Kennet Andersson
5

RUSSIA

Oleg Salenko **6**

DENMARK

Jon Dahl Tomasson **5**

USA

Landon Donovan **5**

PORTUGAL

Zbigniew Boniek **6**

Eusébio **9**

SWITZERLAND

Josef Hügi **6**

NORTHERN IRELAND

Peter McParland **5**

USSR

Valentin Ivanov **5**

THE PERFECT WORLD CUP PENALTY

To place or to blast? That is the question facing World Cup penalty-takers under the intense pressure of the glaring floodlights, thousands of expectant fans and their teammates unable to look away. In a World Cup tie the hopes of a nation lie on the quality of the execution. Some, like Andreas Brehme in 1990, have the steady composure to help their sides lift the Jules Rimet, whereas others, such as England's Chris Waddle's high-and-wide miss in 1990, led only to the shattering of millions of hearts. So where would you aim *your* penalty kick?

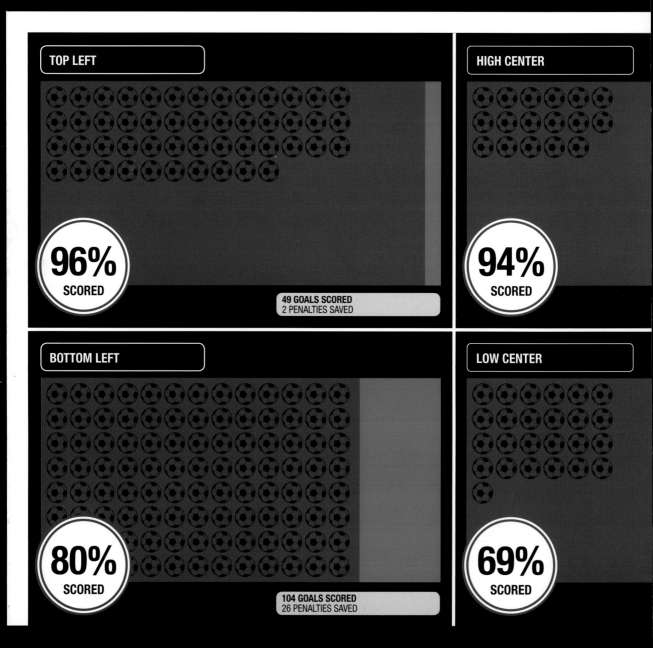

TOP LEFT

96% SCORED

49 GOALS SCORED
2 PENALTIES SAVED

HIGH CENTER

94% SCORED

BOTTOM LEFT

80% SCORED

104 GOALS SCORED
26 PENALTIES SAVED

LOW CENTER

69% SCORED

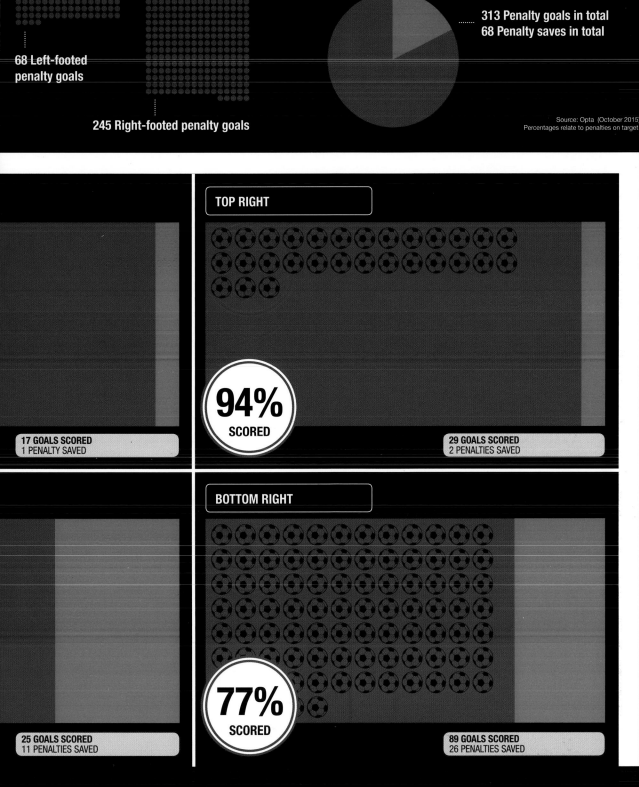

68 Left-footed
penalty goals

245 Right-footed penalty goals

313 Penalty goals in total
68 Penalty saves in total

Source: Opta (October 2015)
Percentages relate to penalties on target.

TOP RIGHT

94%
SCORED

17 GOALS SCORED
1 PENALTY SAVED

29 GOALS SCORED
2 PENALTIES SAVED

BOTTOM RIGHT

77%
SCORED

25 GOALS SCORED
11 PENALTIES SAVED

89 GOALS SCORED
26 PENALTIES SAVED

LONG-RANGE WORLD CUP GOALS

Everyone loves a shot at goal from far out, especially if it's on target and struck with an awesome power to match. In particular, long-range goals during World Cups are even more wondrous to behold because they instantly take on legendary status. Those long-rangers that live forever in the memory include Bobby Charlton's 25-yard strike against Mexico, which fired up England's 1966 campaign, Arie Haan's 40-yard lightning-bolt as the Netherlands defeated Italy in 1978, and James Rodríguez's sensational chest and volley against Uruguay in 2014. All excellent goals, but where do they map in the long-range pantheon?

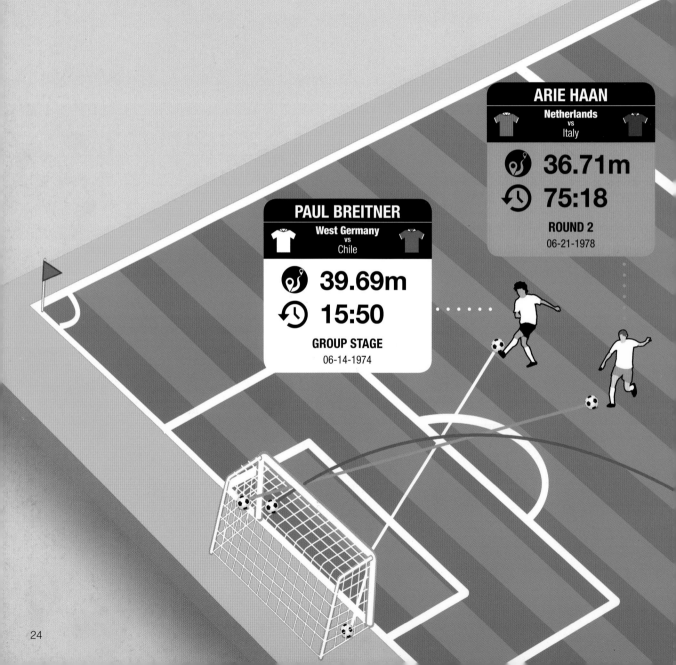

ARIE HAAN

Netherlands
vs
Italy

🌀 **36.71m**

🕐 **75:18**

ROUND 2
06-21-1978

PAUL BREITNER

West Germany
vs
Chile

🌀 **39.69m**

🕐 **15:50**

GROUP STAGE
06-14-1974

Source: Opta (October 2015)

LOTHAR MATTHÄUS

West Germany
vs
Yugoslavia

31.93m

62:51

GROUP STAGE
06-10-1990

ARIE HAAN

Netherlands
vs
West Germany

31.41m

26:40

ROUND 2
06-18-1978

JOE COLE

England
vs
Sweden

33.2m

33:04

GROUP STAGE
06-20-2006

RONALDINHO

Brazil
vs
England

40.08m

49:02

QUARTER-FINAL
06-21-2002

NELINHO

Brazil
vs
Italy

31.86m

63:35

3RD PLACE MATCH
06-24-1978

WORLD CUP GOALS BY BODY PART

"They all count!" It may be an old soccer cliché but it is as true in World Cup finals as it is anywhere else. For every exquisite shot curled in from the edge of the penalty area, there is a ricochet off the shin from two yards. For every perfectly timed scissor-kick, there is a vicious and ugly toe-punt just to make sure the ball goes in. When it comes down to the wire in a World Cup match, any goal will do.

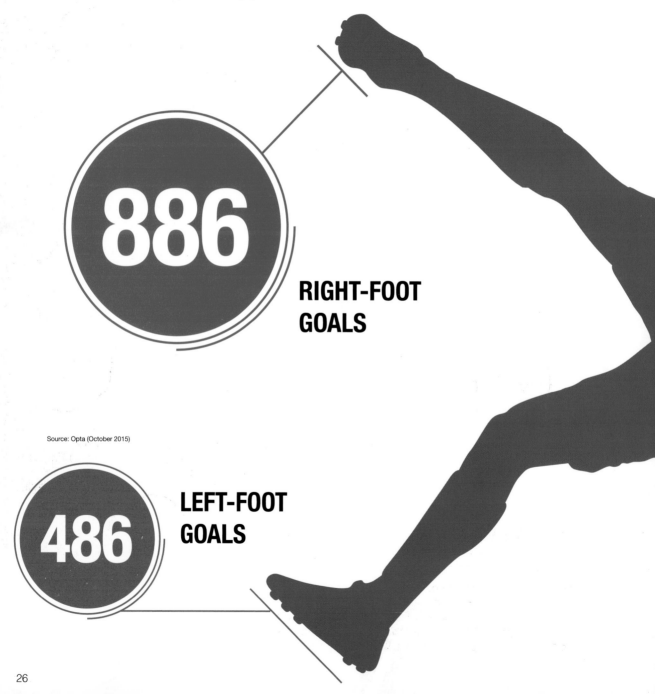

886

RIGHT-FOOT GOALS

Source: Opta (October 2015)

LEFT-FOOT GOALS

486

300 HEADED GOALS

10 OTHER GOALS

The most notorious scoring body part belongs to Maradona's "Hand of God" against England in 1986. Also worthy of a mention are Clint Dempsey's "Groin Goal" for the US against Portugal in 2014 and the great Jairzinho "chesting" the ball in to score Brazil's second goal in the 1970 final.

30 OWN GOALS

Of the 1,712 goals scored in the World Cup only 30 have been own goals—less than two percent. Perhaps the strangest own goal ever scored, so far, belongs to Greece's Vasilis Torosidis during the World Cup qualifying game against Romania in 2014, whose intended left-foot clearance from inside the penalty box ended up being fished out from the back of his own net.

WORLD CUP GOALKEEPERS

The Golden Glove Award, introduced in 1994 (and named the Yashin Award until 2010), is awarded to the best goalkeeper of the World Cup finals. Gianluigi Buffon, Iker Casillas, and Manuel Neuer are recent winners in 2006, 2010, and 2014, respectively. At the 2002 FIFA World Cup, German keeper Oliver Kahn became the first and so far only goalkeeper in the tournament's history to win the Golden Ball, the award given to the player voted as the most outstanding at the FIFA World Cup finals.

ARGENTINA

Ubaldo Fillol

53

1

AUSTRIA

Friedrich Koncilia

59

FRANCE

Joël Bats

1

BRAZIL

Leão

51

SWEDEN

Ronnie Hellström

52

USA

Brad Friedel

2

PARAGUAY

Justo Villar

1

USA

Tony Meola

42

1

GERMANY

Sepp Maier

61

SPAIN

Andoni Zubizarreta

62

SPAIN

Iker Casillas

40

2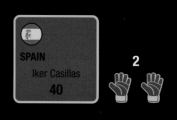

SERBIA

Vladimir Stojković

1

JAPAN

Yoshikatsu Kawaguchi

1

SAUDI ARABIA

Mohammed
Al-Deayea

54

USSR

Rinat Dasayev

41

SAVES

 PENALTY SAVES
(excluding penalty shootouts)

Source: Opta (October 2015)
All data from 1966–2014.

Source: Opta (October 2015)
All data from 1966–2014.

GHANA

Richard Kingson

42

POLAND

Jan Tomaszewski

2

NIGERIA

Vincent Enyeama

46

COLOMBIA

René Higuita

1

USA

Tim Howard

41

SWITZERLAND

Diego Benaglio

1

SWEDEN

Thomas Ravelli

42

ITALY

Dino Zoff

67

SWEDEN

Magnus Hedman

1

JAPAN

Eiji Kawashima

1

ITALY

Gianluigi Buffon

48

1

POLAND

Józef Młynarczyk

48

URUGUAY

Ladislao Mazurkiewicz

51

PERU

Ramón Quiroga

60

1

ENGLAND

Peter Shilton

55

GERMANY

Manuel Neuer

44

WORLD CUP FOULS AND CARDS

Behind these figures lie some of the most controversial and downright disgraceful moments in World Cup history. They include the South Africa vs Denmark tie in 1998, which resulted in seven yellow and three red cards, plus the three yellows in one match collected by Josip Šimunić for Croatia against Australia in 2006. If you thought that was bad, let's not forget the final itself, which saw two Argentinians sent off in 1990 and Zinedine Zidane seeing red after a confrontation with Marco Materazzi in 2006.

ARGENTINA 112	GERMANY 110	BRAZIL 95	ITALY 89	NETHERLANDS 89	MEXICO 67
SPAIN 65	URUGUAY 61	KOREA REPUBLIC 60	FRANCE 56	ENGLAND 50	USA 48
CAMEROON 45	CHILE 43	POLAND 40	PORTUGAL 40	PARAGUAY 39	SWEDEN 38
BELGIUM 37	GHANA 33	CROATIA 33	BULGARIA 33	ROMANIA 32	DENMARK 31
JAPAN 31	SWITZERLAND 31	COSTA RICA 30	TUNISIA 28	YUGOSLAVIA 27	NIGERIA 27
AUSTRIA 24	ECUADOR 23	AUSTRALIA 23	COLOMBIA 22	SAUDI ARABIA 22	USSR 21
SOUTH AFRICA 20	GREECE 19	SLOVENIA 19	MOROCCO 19	IVORY COAST 19	RUSSIA 19
IRAN 18	SERBIA 18	TURKEY 17	SCOTLAND 17	CZECHOSLOVAKIA 17	REPUBLIC OF IRELAND 16
ALGERIA 14	SENEGAL 14	HONDURAS 13	NORWAY 13	UKRAINE 12	SLOVAKIA 11
PERU 10	EAST GERMANY 10	ANGOLA 9	NORTHERN IRELAND 9	EL SALVADOR 9	TOGO 8
IRAQ 8	TRINIDAD AND TOBAGO 8	UNITED ARAB EMIRATES 6	BOLIVIA 6	NEW ZEALAND 6	CHINA PR 5
CZECH REPUBLIC 5	JAMAICA 4	EGYPT 4	HUNGARY 4	ISRAEL 4	HAITI 3
KUWAIT 3	BOSNIA AND HERZEGOVINA 3	DPR KOREA 2	ZAIRE 2	CANADA 1	

ARGENTINA 10   CAMEROON 8   URUGUAY 8   NETHERLANDS 7   ITALY 6   PORTUGAL 6

BRAZIL 6   MEXICO 6   FRANCE 6   GERMANY 5   CROATIA 4   USA 4

AUSTRALIA 4   ENGLAND 3   DENMARK 3   BELGIUM 3   BULGARIA 3   SWEDEN 3

SERBIA 3   ALGERIA 2   CHILE 2   TURKEY 2   KOREA REPUBLIC 2   BOLIVIA 2

PARAGUAY 2   HUNGARY 2   USSR 2   HONDURAS 2   CZECHOSLOVAKIA 2   SOUTH AFRICA 2

CZECH REPUBLIC 2   TUNISIA 1   CANADA 1   POLAND 1   JAMAICA 1   GREECE 1

SLOVENIA 1   TOGO 1   ANGOLA 1   UNITED ARAB EMIRATES 1   COSTA RICA 1   UKRAINE 1

IVORY COAST 1   SENEGAL 1   GHANA 1   IRAQ 1   YUGOSLAVIA 1   TRINIDAD AND TOBAGO 1

ZAIRE 1   SAUDI ARABIA 1   RUSSIA 1   ECUADOR 1   SCOTLAND 1   ROMANIA 1

SWITZERLAND 1   NORTHERN IRELAND 1   CHINA PR 1   AUSTRIA 1   NIGERIA 1   SPAIN 1

Total Fouls 1966–2014

GERMANY 1339	SWEDEN 467	SWITZERLAND 291	ALGERIA 205	TURKEY 117	TOGO 56
BRAZIL 1212	CAMEROON 438	COLOMBIA 284	MOROCCO 202	EL SALVADOR 109	EGYPT 52
ARGENTINA 1153	USSR 421	AUSTRIA 277	CZECHOSLOVAKIA 197	UKRAINE 108	CZECH REPUBLIC 52
ITALY 1147	PORTUGAL 399	ROMANIA 270	SAUDI ARABIA 184	SLOVENIA 103	ZAIRE 51
NETHERLANDS 996	USA 396	DENMARK 269	ECUADOR 184	SENEGAL 100	TRINIDAD AND TOBAGO 50
FRANCE 781	BULGARIA 383	COSTA RICA 252	SOUTH AFRICA 157	SERBIA 89	UNITED ARAB EMIRATES 48
ENGLAND 773	CHILE 357	AUSTRALIA 249	IVORY COAST 151	NEW ZEALAND 88	CANADA 45
SPAIN 735	PARAGUAY 348	IRAN 246	GREECE 150	DPR KOREA 86	BOSNIA AND HERZEGOVINA 41
MEXICO 683	YUGOSLAVIA 343	REPUBLIC OF IRELAND 238	NORTHERN IRELAND 150	ANGOLA 73	BOLIVIA 40
URUGUAY 652	JAPAN 319	TUNISIA 237	RUSSIA 141	SLOVAKIA 69	CHINA PR 40
BELGIUM 592	SCOTLAND 312	GHANA 233	HONDURAS 135	ISRAEL 68	HAITI 34
POLAND 574	NIGERIA 296	PERU 215	NORWAY 126	IRAQ 61	KUWAIT 32
KOREA REPUBLIC 516	CROATIA 291	HUNGARY 206	EAST GERMANY 119	JAMAICA 56	

1966 WORLD CUP GOALS

Many nations thought they had a chance of winning the World Cup in 1966: West Germany, Argentina, Brazil, and England were all confident it would be their turn to lift the Jules Rimet trophy. Despite being blighted by the barbaric treatment of Pelé and some controversial refereeing, the tournament was enlightened by the giant-slaying North Korea, the brilliance of Eusébio, and a nail-biting, but triumphant, final for the host nation. The 1966 World Cup also saw goals that would become legendary, including the lung-bursting run from West Germany's Franz Beckenbauer, an outside-of-the-foot free kick from Brazil's Garrincha, and Geoff Hurst's monumental hat trick in the final—the first ever in a World Cup final.

GEOFF HURST – England vs West Germany

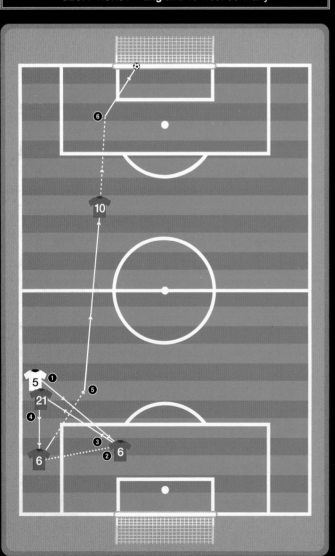

England's Geoff Hurst scores that famous fourth goal to put England 4–2 up against West Germany after extra time, July 30, 1966.

1. Pass (chipped, cross) **Schulz**
2. Ball recovery **Moore**
3. Pass **Moore**
4. Pass **Hunt**
5. Pass (chipped, long ball) **Moore**
6. Goal **Hurst**

KEY

Ball movement	Player with ball
Shot	Player without ball

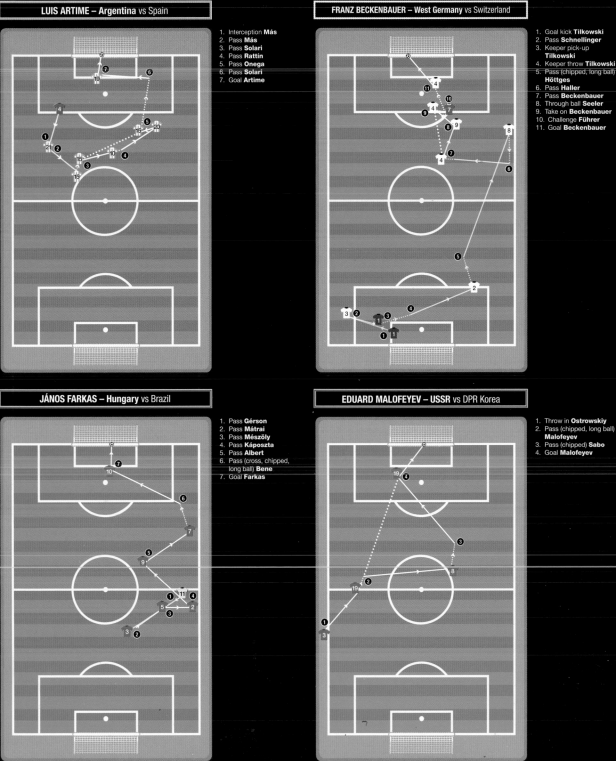

LUIS ARTIME – Argentina vs Spain

1. Interception **Más**
2. Pass **Más**
3. Pass **Solari**
4. Pass **Rattín**
5. Pass **Onega**
6. Pass **Solari**
7. Goal **Artime**

FRANZ BECKENBAUER – West Germany vs Switzerland

1. Goal kick **Tilkowski**
2. Pass **Schnellinger**
3. Keeper pick-up **Tilkowski**
4. Keeper throw **Tilkowski**
5. Pass (chipped, long ball) **Höttges**
6. Pass **Haller**
7. Pass **Beckenbauer**
8. Through ball **Seeler**
9. Take on **Beckenbauer**
10. Challenge **Führer**
11. Goal **Beckenbauer**

JÁNOS FARKAS – Hungary vs Brazil

1. Pass **Gérson**
2. Pass **Mátrai**
3. Pass **Mészöly**
4. Pass **Káposzta**
5. Pass **Albert**
6. Pass (cross, chipped, long ball) **Bene**
7. Goal **Farkas**

EDUARD MALOFEYEV – USSR vs DPR Korea

1. Throw in **Ostrowskiy**
2. Pass (chipped, long ball) **Malofeyev**
3. Pass (chipped) **Sabo**
4. Goal **Malofeyev**

1970 WORLD CUP GOALS

Many pundits, players, and fans still regard the 1970 World Cup in Mexico as the finest World Cup tournament of all. Reigning champions England played Brazil in a scintillating group game, Italy met Germany in the "Game of the Century"—Italy won 4–3 after five goals were scored in extra time, the only FIFA World Cup game when this has happened—and the final was a masterclass in demolition by the Brazilian squad. It was Carlos Alberto's perfect strike that was the nail in the coffin for Italy, and arguably one of the greatest goals ever scored, helping to create Brazil's glorious 4–1 win.

CARLOS ALBERTO – Brazil vs Italy

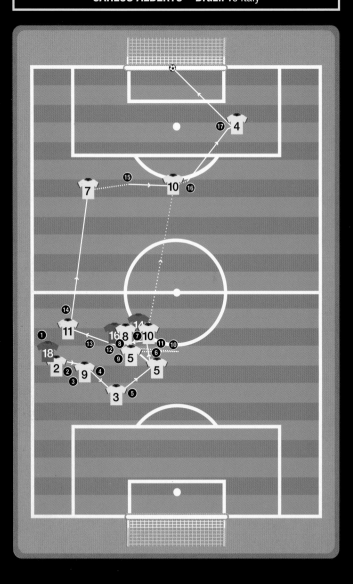

Brazil captain Carlos Alberto celebrates his team's fourth goal against Italy's goalkeeper Enrico Albertosi. Final score: Brazil 4 Italy 1, June 21, 1970.

1. Take on **Juliano**
2. Tackle **Brito**
3. Ball recovery **Tostão**
4. Pass **Tostão**
5. Pass **Piazza**
6. Pass **Clodoaldo**
7. Pass **Pelé**
8. Pass **Gérson**
9. Take on **Clodoaldo**
10. Good skill **Clodoaldo**
11. Challenge **Rivera**
12. Challenge **De Sisti**
13. Pass **Clodoaldo**
14. Pass **Rivelino**
15. Pass **Jairzinho**
16. Pass **Pelé**
17. Goal **Alberto**

KEY

Ball movement	━━━━	Player with ball	▪▪▪▪▪▪▪▪
Shot	━━━⚽	Player without ball	•••••••

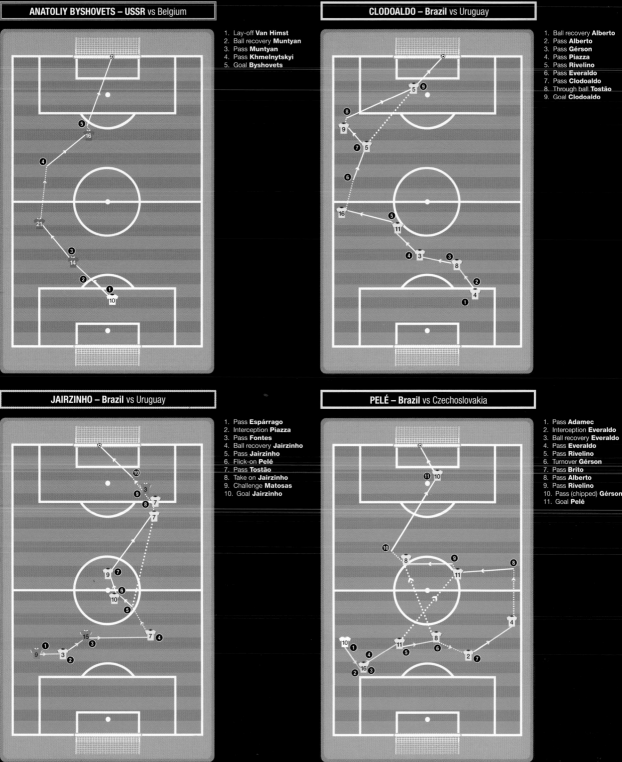

ANATOLIY BYSHOVETS – USSR vs Belgium

1. Lay-off **Van Himst**
2. Ball recovery **Muntyan**
3. Pass **Muntyan**
4. Pass **Khmelnytskyi**
5. Goal **Byshovets**

CLODOALDO – Brazil vs Uruguay

1. Ball recovery **Alberto**
2. Pass **Alberto**
3. Pass **Gérson**
4. Pass **Piazza**
5. Pass **Rivelino**
6. Pass **Everaldo**
7. Pass **Clodoaldo**
8. Through ball **Tostão**
9. Goal **Clodoaldo**

JAIRZINHO – Brazil vs Uruguay

1. Pass **Espárrago**
2. Interception **Piazza**
3. Pass **Fontes**
4. Ball recovery **Jairzinho**
5. Pass **Jairzinho**
6. Flick-on **Pelé**
7. Pass **Tostão**
8. Take on **Jairzinho**
9. Challenge **Matosas**
10. Goal **Jairzinho**

PELÉ – Brazil vs Czechoslovakia

1. Pass **Adamec**
2. Interception **Everaldo**
3. Ball recovery **Everaldo**
4. Pass **Everaldo**
5. Pass **Rivelino**
6. Turnover **Gérson**
7. Pass **Brito**
8. Pass **Alberto**
9. Pass **Rivelino**
10. Pass (chipped) **Gérson**
11. Goal **Pelé**

1974 WORLD CUP GOALS

In 1974, West Germany hosted (and won) a memorable World Cup that first gave us the Cruyff Turn, Zaire became the first African team to qualify, a Cold War classic between East and West Germany, and the "total soccer" displayed by the Netherlands. Goals came in all shapes and sizes, but we all remember the two belters from West Germany's Paul Breitner, Peter Lorimer's volley for Scotland against Zaire, Haiti's Emmanuel Sanon outpacing the Italian defense, and Johan Cruyff's stunner against Brazil—a goal that crowned the Dutchman Player of the Tournament.

JOHAN CRUYFF – Netherlands vs Brazil

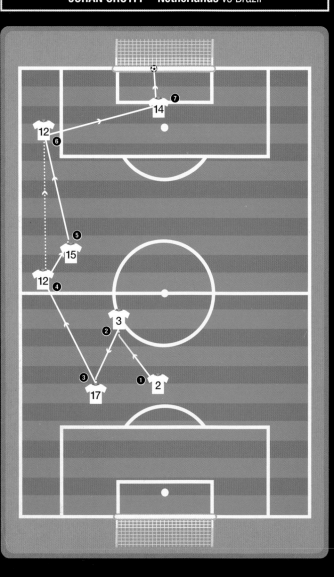

Fifty-two thousand fans watched Johan Cruyff score his second goal for the Netherlands against Brazil, July 3,1974.

1. Free kick taken **Haan**
2. Pass **van Hanegem**
3. Pass (chipped) **Rijsbergen**
4. Pass **Krol**
5. Pass **Rensenbrink**
6. Pass (cross, chipped, long ball) **Krol**
7. Goal **Cruyff**

KEY

Ball movement	Player with ball	
Shot	Player without ball	

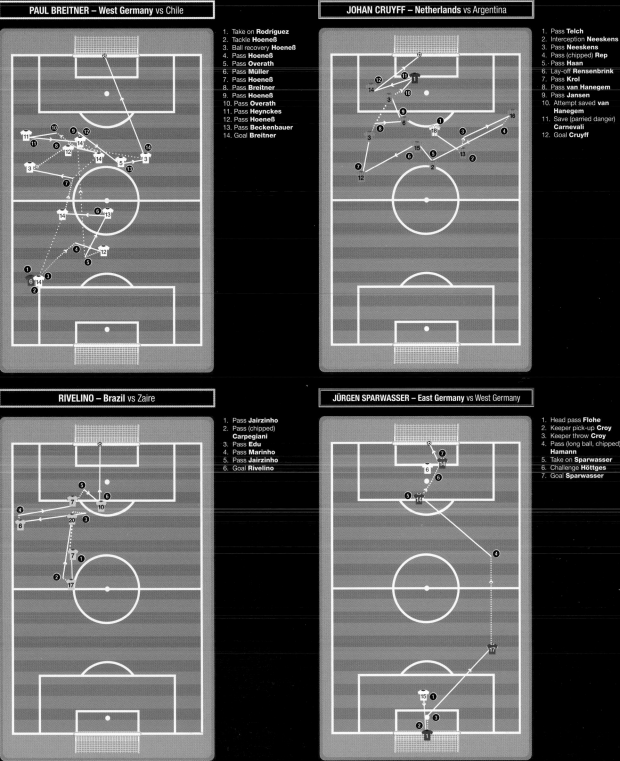

PAUL BREITNER – West Germany vs Chile

1. Take on **Rodríguez**
2. Tackle **Hoeneß**
3. Ball recovery **Hoeneß**
4. Pass **Hoeneß**
5. Pass **Overath**
6. Pass **Müller**
7. Pass **Hoeneß**
8. Pass **Breitner**
9. Pass **Hoeneß**
10. Pass **Overath**
11. Pass **Heynckes**
12. Pass **Hoeneß**
13. Pass **Beckenbauer**
14. Goal **Breitner**

JOHAN CRUYFF – Netherlands vs Argentina

1. Pass **Telch**
2. Interception **Neeskens**
3. Pass **Neeskens**
4. Pass (chipped) **Rep**
5. Pass **Haan**
6. Lay-off **Rensenbrink**
7. Pass **Krol**
8. Pass **van Hanegem**
9. Pass **Jansen**
10. Attempt saved **van Hanegem**
11. Save (parried danger) **Carnevali**
12. Goal **Cruyff**

RIVELINO – Brazil vs Zaire

1. Pass **Jairzinho**
2. Pass (chipped) **Carpegiani**
3. Pass **Edu**
4. Pass **Marinho**
5. Pass **Jairzinho**
6. Goal **Rivelino**

JÜRGEN SPARWASSER – East Germany vs West Germany

1. Head pass **Flohe**
2. Keeper pick-up **Croy**
3. Keeper throw **Croy**
4. Pass (long ball, chipped) **Hamann**
5. Take on **Sparwasser**
6. Challenge **Höttges**
7. Goal **Sparwasser**

1978 WORLD CUP GOALS

The "Tickertape Tournament" in 1978 was a bittersweet affair. It was set against an unsavory political background, boycotted by Johan Cruyff (rated as the world's best player at the time) and disgraced by Scotland's Willie Johnston, who was sent home after a positive drug test. However, the tournament also gave us some unforgettable goals, including a magical finish by Scotland's Archie Gemmill, screamers from the Netherlands' Arie Haan and Brazil's Nelinho, and a much-needed, morale-boosting triumph for the host nation, Argentina, when they defeated the Netherlands 3–1, thanks to the tournament's top scorer, Mario Kempes, and his second goal of the day.

ARIE HAAN – Netherlands vs West Germany

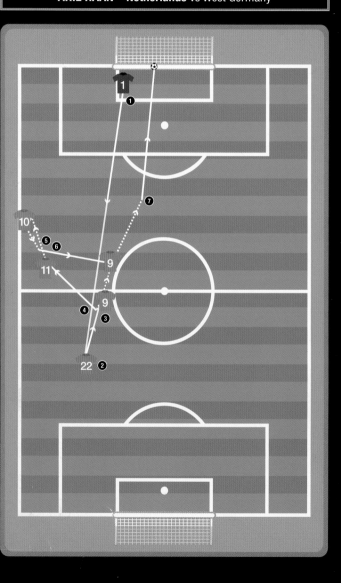

Arie Haan's goal against West Germany helped the Dutch national team reach the 1978 World Cup final, where they were beaten by Argentina 3–1 in extra time, June 18, 1978.

1. Goal kick (long ball) **Maier**
2. Head pass **Brandts**
3. Ball recovery **Haan**
4. Pass **Haan**
5. Pass **Willy van de Kerkhof**
6. Pass **René van de Kerkhof**
7. Goal **Haan**

KEY

Ball movement ━━━━ Player with ball ▪▪▪▪▪▪▪▪▪▪▪

Shot ━━━◉ Player without ball ••••••••••••••

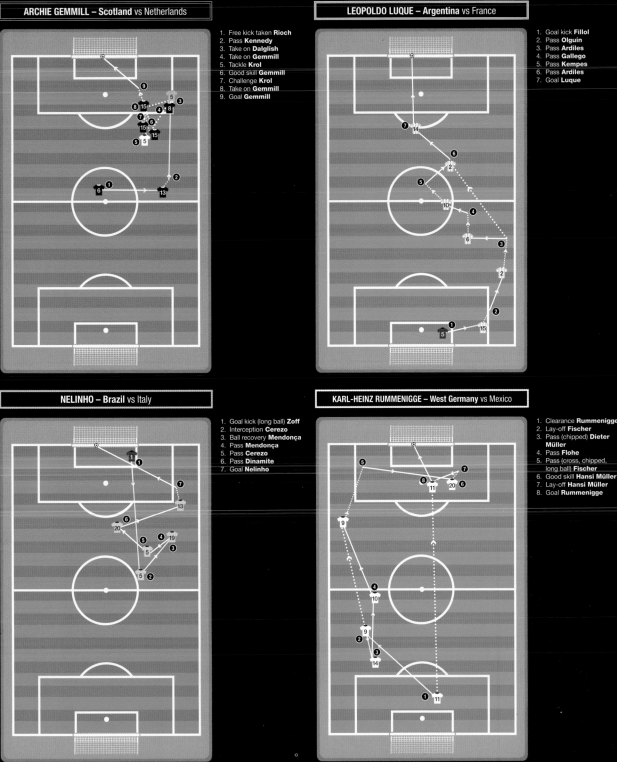

ARCHIE GEMMILL – Scotland vs Netherlands

1. Free kick taken **Rioch**
2. Pass **Kennedy**
3. Take on **Dalglish**
4. Take on **Gemmill**
5. Tackle **Krol**
6. Good skill **Gemmill**
7. Challenge **Krol**
8. Take on **Gemmill**
9. Goal **Gemmill**

LEOPOLDO LUQUE – Argentina vs France

1. Goal kick **Fillol**
2. Pass **Olguín**
3. Pass **Ardiles**
4. Pass **Gallego**
5. Pass **Kempes**
6. Pass **Ardiles**
7. Goal **Luque**

NELINHO – Brazil vs Italy

1. Goal kick (long ball) **Zoff**
2. Interception **Cerezo**
3. Ball recovery **Mendonça**
4. Pass **Mendonça**
5. Pass **Cerezo**
6. Pass **Dinamite**
7. Goal **Nelinho**

KARL-HEINZ RUMMENIGGE – West Germany vs Mexico

1. Clearance **Rummenigge**
2. Lay-off **Fischer**
3. Pass (chipped) **Dieter Müller**
4. Pass **Flohe**
5. Pass (cross, chipped, long ball) **Fischer**
6. Good skill **Hansi Müller**
7. Lay-off **Hansi Müller**
8. Goal **Rummenigge**

1982 WORLD CUP GOALS

Spain's 1982 World Cup finals saw 24 teams play in a format involving two group stages. It was never used again. The tournament became the battleground for two of the greatest matches ever played in World Cup history. Italy's Paolo Rossi hit a hat trick in an amazing 3–2 defeat of Brazil and, after a 3–3 draw, West Germany overcame France in the first ever World Cup penalty shootout. Memorable goals included an overhead bicycle kick by Germany's Klaus Fischer, a sublime chip from Brazil's Éder and a strike from his compatriot, Sócrates, which proved completely unstoppable. However, it was Tardelli's goal (and his celebration) against West Germany in the final that we all remember the most.

MARCO TARDELLI – **Italy** vs West Germany

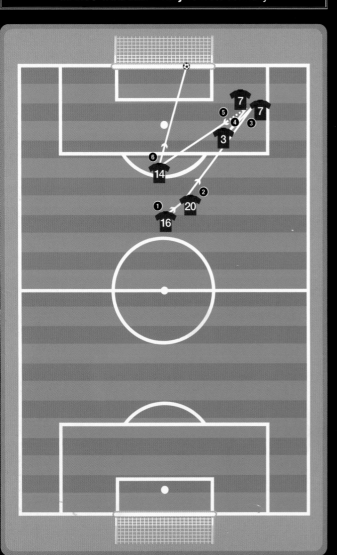

Italy's Marco Tardelli celebrates scoring his goal against West Germany during the 1982 World Cup final. Italy won the match 3–1, July 11, 1982.

1. Pass **Conti**
2. Pass **Rossi**
3. Pass **Scirea**
4. Pass **Bergomi**
5. Pass **Scirea**
6. Goal **Tardelli**

KEY

Ball movement	Player with ball
Shot	Player without ball

ZBIGNIEW BONIEK – Poland vs Belgium

1. Goal kick **Młynarczyk**
2. Pass **Janas**
3. Pass **Żmuda**
4. Pass **Buncol**
5. Pass **Majewski**
6. Pass (long ball) **Buncol**
7. Pass **Janas**
8. Pass (chipped, long ball) **Buncol**
9. Pass **Dziuba**
10. Take on **Lato**
11. Challenge **Millecamps**
12. Pull-back **Lato**
13. Goal **Boniek**

BRUNO CONTI – Italy vs Peru

KLAUS FISCHER – West Germany vs France

1. Corner taken **Kaltz**
2. Clearance **Platini**
3. Pass **Breitner**
4. Pass (chipped, cross) **Kaltz**
5. Head pass **Kaltz**
6. Pass (long ball) **Rummenigge**
7. Pass **Förster**
8. Pass (chipped, cross, long ball) **Littbarski**
9. Head pass **Rummenigge**
10. Goal **Fischer**

SÓCRATES – Brazil vs Italy

1986 WORLD CUP GOALS

Mexico may have hosted the 1986 World Cup, but the tournament was all about one man—Argentina's Diego Maradona. The 25-year-old's goals against England and Belgium were described by many pundits, players and fans alike as "pure genius". In the now famous quarterfinal match against England, Maradona's unforgettable "Hand of God" goal was (almost) forgotten when he scored his "Goal of the Century" just four minutes later. His achievements would dwarf the World Cup's other magical moments, which included six goals from England's Gary Lineker (the tournament's top scorer), a screamer from Brazil's Josimar and an ambitious scissor-kick from the Mexican player Manuel Negrete.

DIEGO MARADONA – Argentina vs England

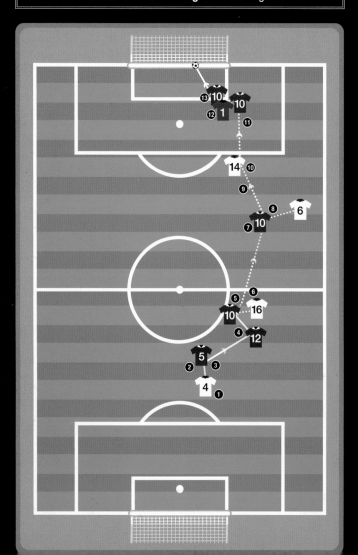

Diego Maradona dribbles the ball beyond England goalkeeper Peter Shilton to score the "Goal of the Century". Argentina won 2–1, June 22, 1986.

1. Pass **Hoddle**
2. Pass **Brown**
3. Ball recovery **Brown**
4. Pass **Enrique**
5. Take on **Maradona**
6. Challenge **Reid**
7. Take on **Maradona**
8. Challenge **Butcher**
9. Take on **Maradona**
10. Challenge **Fenwick**
11. Take on **Maradona**
12. Challenge **Shilton**
13. Goal **Maradona**

KEY

Ball movement	Player with ball
Shot	Player without ball

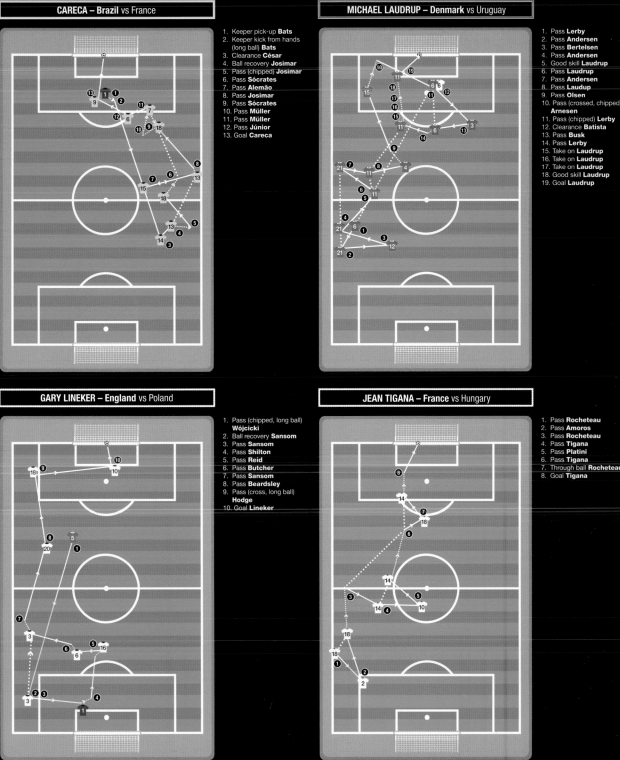

CARECA – Brazil vs France

1. Keeper pick-up **Bats**
2. Keeper kick from hands (long ball) **Bats**
3. Clearance **César**
4. Ball recovery **Josimar**
5. Pass (chipped) **Josimar**
6. Pass **Sócrates**
7. Pass **Alemão**
8. Pass **Josimar**
9. Pass **Sócrates**
10. Pass **Müller**
11. Pass **Müller**
12. Pass **Júnior**
13. Goal **Careca**

MICHAEL LAUDRUP – Denmark vs Uruguay

1. Pass **Lerby**
2. Pass **Andersen**
3. Pass **Bertelsen**
4. Pass **Andersen**
5. Good skill **Laudrup**
6. Pass **Laudrup**
7. Pass **Andersen**
8. Pass **Laudup**
9. Pass **Olsen**
10. Pass (crossed, chipped) **Arnesen**
11. Pass (chipped) **Lerby**
12. Clearance **Batista**
13. Pass **Busk**
14. Pass **Lerby**
15. Take on **Laudrup**
16. Take on **Laudrup**
17. Take on **Laudrup**
18. Good skill **Laudrup**
19. Goal **Laudrup**

GARY LINEKER – England vs Poland

1. Pass (chipped, long ball) **Wójcicki**
2. Ball recovery **Sansom**
3. Pass **Sansom**
4. Pass **Shilton**
5. Pass **Reid**
6. Pass **Butcher**
7. Pass **Sansom**
8. Pass **Beardsley**
9. Pass (cross, long ball) **Hodge**
10. Goal **Lineker**

JEAN TIGANA – France vs Hungary

1. Pass **Rocheteau**
2. Pass **Amoros**
3. Pass **Rocheteau**
4. Pass **Tigana**
5. Pass **Platini**
6. Pass **Tigana**
7. Through ball **Rocheteau**
8. Goal **Tigana**

1990 WORLD CUP GOALS

The negativity surrounding the soccer performances of the 1990 World Cup finals in Italy was alleviated by Luciano Pavarotti's singing of the tournament anthem "Nessun Dorma", the energy and spirit of Roger Milla and his Cameroon teammates, the passion and drama of England's Paul Gascoigne, and the superboots of Italy's Salvatore "Totò" Schillaci. There were outstanding goals galore too, including a surging run and knockout shot from Germany's Lothar Matthäus, an over-the-shoulder volley from England's David Platt, and virtuoso brilliance by Italy's one-and-only *Il Divin Codino* (The Divine Ponytail)—Roberto Baggio.

ROBERTO BAGGIO – Italy vs Czechoslovakia

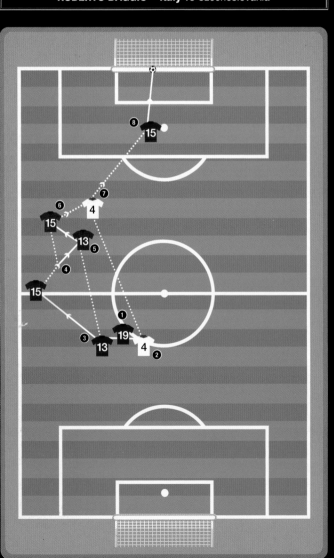

Roberto Baggio on his way to scoring Italy's second goal. Italy won 2–0 against Czechoslovakia, June 19, 1990.

1. Take on **Schillaci**
2. Tackle **Hašek**
3. Pass **Giannini**
4. Pass **Baggio**
5. Pass **Giannini**
6. Take on **Baggio**
7. Challenge **Hašek**
8. Goal **Baggio**

KEY

Ball movement	Player with ball
Shot	Player without ball

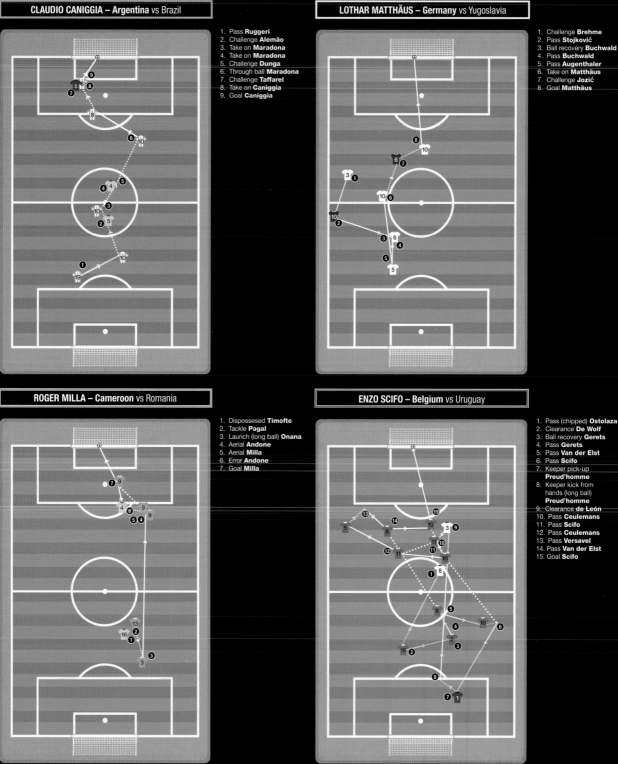

CLAUDIO CANIGGIA – Argentina vs Brazil

1. Pass **Ruggeri**
2. Challenge **Alemão**
3. Take on **Maradona**
4. Take on **Maradona**
5. Challenge **Dunga**
6. Through ball **Maradona**
7. Challenge **Taffarel**
8. Take on **Caniggia**
9. Goal **Caniggia**

LOTHAR MATTHÄUS – Germany vs Yugoslavia

1. Challenge **Brehme**
2. Pass **Stojković**
3. Ball recovery **Buchwald**
4. Pass **Buchwald**
5. Pass **Augenthaler**
6. Take on **Matthäus**
7. Challenge **Jozić**
8. Goal **Matthäus**

ROGER MILLA – Cameroon vs Romania

1. Dispossesed **Timofte**
2. Tackle **Pagal**
3. Launch (long ball) **Onana**
4. Aerial **Andone**
5. Aerial **Milla**
6. Error **Andone**
7. Goal **Milla**

ENZO SCIFO – Belgium vs Uruguay

1. Pass (chipped) **Ostolaza**
2. Clearance **De Wolf**
3. Ball recovery **Gerets**
4. Pass **Gerets**
5. Pass **Van der Elst**
6. Pass **Scifo**
7. Keeper pick-up **Preud'homme**
8. Keeper kick from hands (long ball) **Preud'homme**
9. Clearance **de León**
10. Pass **Ceulemans**
11. Pass **Scifo**
12. Pass **Ceulemans**
13. Pass **Versavel**
14. Pass **Van der Elst**
15. Goal **Scifo**

1994 WORLD CUP GOALS

Despite America's lack of a national top-level league, the 1994 World Cup is remembered for breaking average attendance records with almost 70,000 fans per game—a feat that still stands today. Played in nine cities across the US, this World Cup saw Italy lose 3–2 to Brazil in a penalty shootout—the first-ever World Cup final to be decided by penalties. Roberto Baggio's wild penalty miss will long be remembered. The flick, spin and volley by Germany's Jürgen Klinsmann, the 65-yard run to score by Saudi Arabia's Saeed Al-Owairan and the diving header by Bulgaria's Yordan Letchkov were all wonderful goals, but it's Hagi's strike against Colombia that we'll never forget...

GHEORGHE HAGI – Romania vs Colombia

Romania's Gheorghe Hagi celebrates after scoring his unforgettable left-foot lob over the top of Colombian keeper Óscar Córdoba, June 18, 199[*]

1. Tackle **Râducioiu**
2. Ball recovery **Petrescu**
3. Dispossesed **Rincón**
4. Pass **Petrescu**
5. Pass **Popescu**
6. Pass **Munteanu**
7. Goal **Hagi**

KEY

Ball movement	———	Player with ball	▪▪▪▪▪▪▪▪▪▪▪
Shot	——⚽	Player without ball	•••••••••••

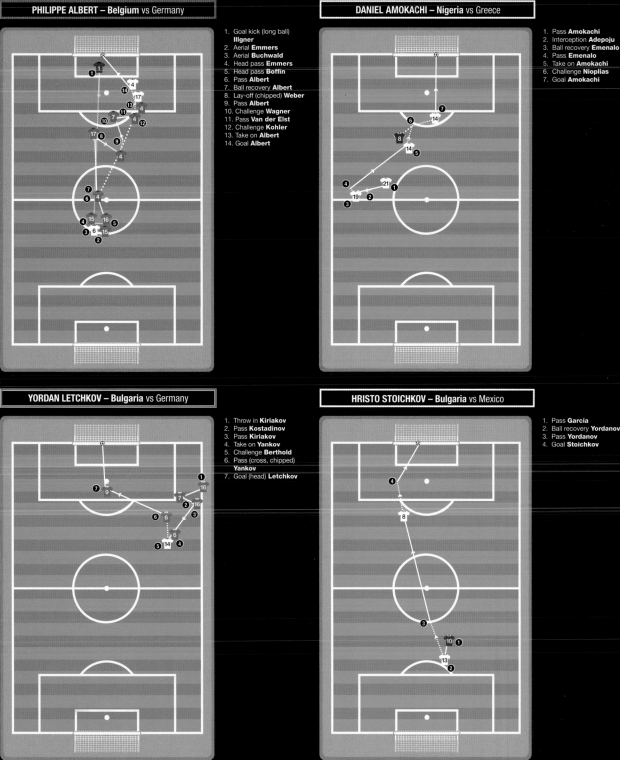

PHILIPPE ALBERT – Belgium vs Germany

1. Goal kick (long ball) **Illgner**
2. Aerial **Emmers**
3. Aerial **Buchwald**
4. Head pass **Emmers**
5. Head pass **Boffin**
6. Pass **Albert**
7. Ball recovery **Albert**
8. Lay-off (chipped) **Weber**
9. Pass **Albert**
10. Challenge **Wagner**
11. Pass **Van der Elst**
12. Challenge **Kohler**
13. Take on **Albert**
14. Goal **Albert**

DANIEL AMOKACHI – Nigeria vs Greece

1. Pass **Amokachi**
2. Interception **Adepoju**
3. Ball recovery **Emenalo**
4. Pass **Emenalo**
5. Take on **Amokachi**
6. Challenge **Nioplias**
7. Goal **Amokachi**

YORDAN LETCHKOV – Bulgaria vs Germany

1. Throw in **Kiriakov**
2. Pass **Kostadinov**
3. Pass **Kiriakov**
4. Take on **Yankov**
5. Challenge **Berthold**
6. Pass (cross, chipped) **Yankov**
7. Goal (head) **Letchkov**

HRISTO STOICHKOV – Bulgaria vs Mexico

1. Pass **García**
2. Ball recovery **Yordanov**
3. Pass **Yordanov**
4. Goal **Stoichkov**

1998 WORLD CUP GOALS

Host nation France lit up their own World Cup in 1998, and finished the tournament with the greatest triumph of all—defeating Ronaldo's Brazil in the final. England met Argentina in Saint-Étienne, unarguably the match of the tournament, while five goals secured the Golden Boot for Davor Šuker of Croatia. Rivaldo hit the winner as Brazil and Denmark shared five goals in a riveting quarterfinal, while goals such as Michael Owen's run-and-shoot, and Dennis Bergkamp's control-and-finish for the Netherlands—both against Argentina— highlighted that world-class soccer at its best can transcend any country's border.

DENNIS BERGKAMP – Netherlands vs Argentina

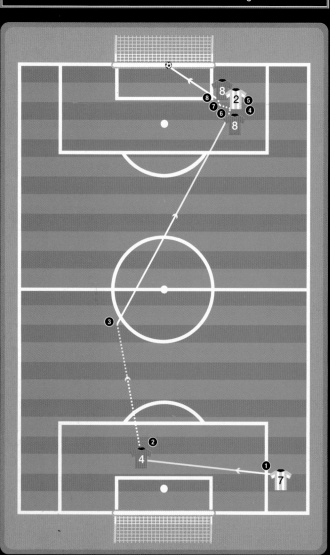

Dennis Bergkamp clips it beautifully past Argentinian goalkeeper Carlos Roa, July 4, 1998.

1. Pass (cross, long ball, chipped) **López**
2. Ball recovery **de Boer**
3. Pass (long ball, chipped) **de Boer**
4. Take on **Bergkamp**
5. Challenge **Ayala**
6. Good skill **Bergkamp**
7. Good skill **Bergkamp**
8. Goal **Bergkamp**

KEY

Ball movement	━━━━	Player with ball	•••••••••
Shot	━━━⚽	Player without ball	••••••••••

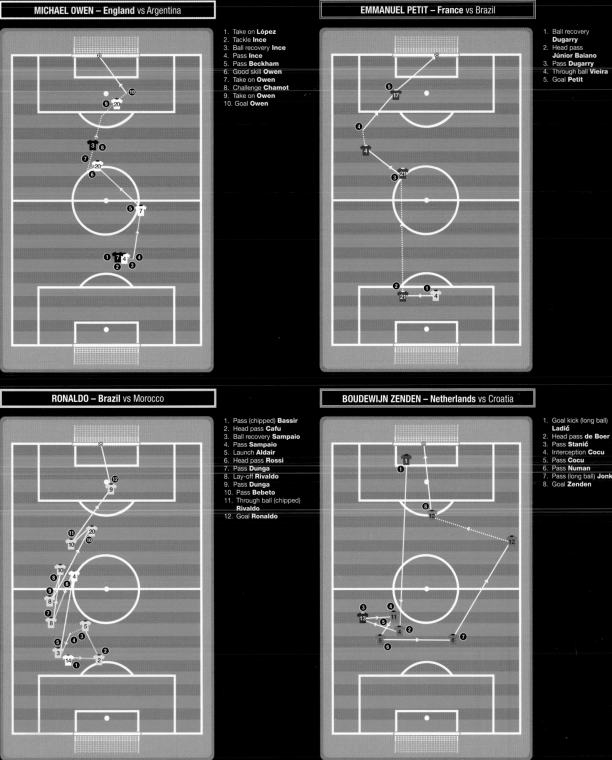

MICHAEL OWEN – England vs Argentina

1. Take on **López**
2. Tackle **Ince**
3. Ball recovery **Ince**
4. Pass **Ince**
5. Pass **Beckham**
6. Good skill **Owen**
7. Take on **Owen**
8. Challenge **Chamot**
9. Take on **Owen**
10. Goal **Owen**

EMMANUEL PETIT – France vs Brazil

1. Ball recovery **Dugarry**
2. Head pass **Júnior Baiano**
3. Pass **Dugarry**
4. Through ball **Vieira**
5. Goal **Petit**

RONALDO – Brazil vs Morocco

1. Pass (chipped) **Bassir**
2. Head pass **Cafu**
3. Ball recovery **Sampaio**
4. Pass **Sampaio**
5. Launch **Aldair**
6. Head pass **Rossi**
7. Pass **Dunga**
8. Lay-off **Rivaldo**
9. Pass **Dunga**
10. Pass **Bebeto**
11. Through ball (chipped) **Rivaldo**
12. Goal **Ronaldo**

BOUDEWIJN ZENDEN – Netherlands vs Croatia

1. Goal kick (long ball) **Ladić**
2. Head pass **de Boer**
3. Pass **Stanić**
4. Interception **Cocu**
5. Pass **Cocu**
6. Pass **Numan**
7. Pass (long ball) **Jonk**
8. Goal **Zenden**

2002 WORLD CUP GOALS

Japan and South Korea co-hosted Asia's first World Cup in 2002 and it is a tournament remembered for being full of surprises. Reigning champions France and preferred favorites Argentina went home after the group stage and South Korea beat Spain, Italy, and Portugal on their way to the semifinals. Few fans were shocked, however, by Brazil's clear run to victory, powered by a player at the top of his game—Ronaldo. The chest and volley by Uruguay's Diego Forlán, Matt Holland's superstrike for Ireland and the overhead kick by Brazil's Edmílson are goals also still regularly voted in World Cup Greatest Goals lists, along with these ones too...

JARED BORGETTI – Mexico vs Italy

Mexico's Jared Borgetti scored the first goal against Italy with a knockout strike past goalkeeper Gianluigi Buffon, June 13, 2002.

1. Clearance **Vidrio**
2. Tackle **Carmona**
3. Take on **Inzaghi**
4. Ball recovery **Torrado**
5. Pass **Torrado**
6. Pass **Márquez**
7. Pass **Luna**
8. Pass **Márquez**
9. Pass **Carmona**
10. Pass **Rodríguez**
11. Pass **Blanco**
12. Pass **Arellano**
13. Pass **Blanco**
14. Pass **Torrado**
15. Pass **Vidrio**
16. Pass (long ball) **Torrado**
17. Pass **Morales**
18. Pass **Luna**
19. Pass (chipped) **Blanco**
20. Goal **Borgetti**

KEY

Ball movement	Player with ball
Shot	Player without ball

SALIF DIAO – Senegal vs Denmark

1. Take on **Jørgenson**
2. Tackle **Camara**
3. Ball recovery **Camara**
4. Pass **Camara**
5. Pass **Diouf**
6. Pass (long ball) **Diao**
7. Through ball **Fadiga**
8. Goal **Diao**

EDMÍLSON – Brazil vs Costa Rica

1. Pass **Wanchope**
2. Interception **Silva**
3. Pass **Cafu**
4. Ball recovery **Cafu**
5. Pass **Cafu**
6. Pass **Juninho**
7. Pass **Cafu**
8. Pass **Edmílson**
9. Pass **Silva**
10. Pass **Edmílson**
11. Pass **Rivaldo**
12. Pass **Edmílson**
13. Pass (cross, chipped) **Júnior**
14. Goal **Edmílson**

RONALDINHO – Brazil vs England

1. Goal (free kick) **Ronaldinho**

CHRISTIAN VIERI – Italy vs Ecuador

1. Throw in **Panucci**
2. Pass **Totti**
3. Head pass **Di Biagio**
4. Pass **Tommasi**
5. Through ball **Totti**
6. Attempt saved **Vieri**
7. Save (parried danger) **Cevallos**
8. Clearance **Hurtado**
9. Head pass **Cannavaro**
10. Pass (long ball, chipped) **Tommasi**
11. Pass (long ball, chipped) **Panucci**
12. Pull back **Totti**
13. Goal **Vieri**

2006 WORLD CUP GOALS

The 2006 World Cup, hosted by Germany, will forever be dominated by one image: the world's greatest soccer player, Zinedine Zidane, playing his last game ever, headbutting Italy's Marco Materazzi in the chest. In a low-scoring tournament, five goals were enough to reward Germany's Miroslav Klose the Golden Boot, while Philipp Lahm's wonderstrike in the opening game, Bakari Koné's solo effort for the Ivory Coast and Argentina's Cambiasso finishing an exquisite 24-pass movement stood out as the tournament's best goals.

ESTEBAN CAMBIASSO – Argentina vs Serbia & Montenegro

Esteban Cambiasso celebrates in style after scoring the second goal against Serbia & Montenegro, June 16, 2006.

1. Dispossesed **Kežman**
2. Challenge **Mascherano**
3. Tackle **Rodríguez**
4. Ball recovery **Heinze**
5. Pass **Heinze**
6. Pass **Mascherano**
7. Pass **Riquelme**
8. Pass **Rodríguez**
9. Pass **Sorín**
10. Pass **Rodríguez**
11. Pass **Sorín**
12. Pass **Mascherano**
13. Pass **Riquelme**
14. Pass **Ayala**
15. Pass **Cambiasso**
16. Pass **Mascherano**
17. Pass **Rodríguez**
18. Pass **Sorín**
19. Pass **Rodríguez**
20. Pass **Cambiasso**
21. Pass **Riquelme**
22. Pass **Mascherano**
23. Pass **Mascherano**
24. Pass **Saviola**
25. Pass **Riquelme**
26. Pass **Saviola**
27. Pass **Cambiasso**
28. Pass **Crespo**
29. Goal **Cambiasso**

KEY

Ball movement

Shot

Player with ball

Player without ball

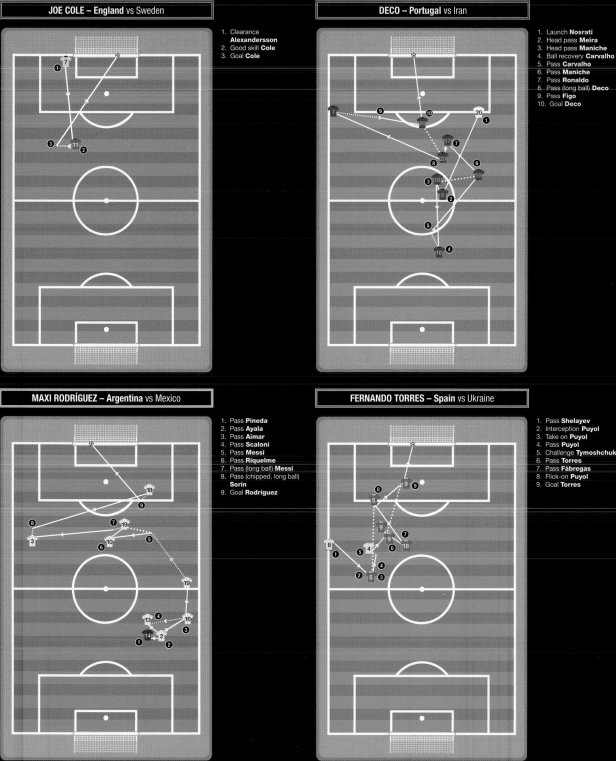

JOE COLE – England vs Sweden

1. Clearance **Alexandersson**
2. Good skill **Cole**
3. Goal **Cole**

DECO – Portugal vs Iran

1. Launch **Nosrati**
2. Head pass **Meira**
3. Head pass **Maniche**
4. Ball recovery **Carvalho**
5. Pass **Carvalho**
6. Pass **Maniche**
7. Pass **Ronaldo**
8. Pass (long ball) **Deco**
9. Pass **Figo**
10. Goal **Deco**

MAXI RODRÍGUEZ – Argentina vs Mexico

1. Pass **Pineda**
2. Pass **Ayala**
3. Pass **Aimar**
4. Pass **Scaloni**
5. Pass **Messi**
6. Pass **Riquelme**
7. Pass (long ball) **Messi**
8. Pass (chipped, long ball) **Sorín**
9. Goal **Rodríguez**

FERNANDO TORRES – Spain vs Ukraine

1. Pass **Shelayev**
2. Interception **Puyol**
3. Take on **Puyol**
4. Pass **Puyol**
5. Challenge **Tymoshchuk**
6. Pass **Torres**
7. Pass **Fàbregas**
8. Flick-on **Puyol**
9. Goal **Torres**

2010 WORLD CUP GOALS

The 2010 World Cup in South Africa was the first to be hosted on African soil. To the background blast of thousands of vuvuzelas, it was Ghana and Uruguay who were the surprise packages—separated only by penalties in the quarterfinal, after Luis Suárez's villainous last-minute handball save. Spain would triumph over the Netherlands in the final of a tournament illuminated by goals such as the incredible effort from an impossible angle by Brazil's Maicon, a precision chip from Italy's Fabio Quagliarella and, most memorable of all, the powerful left-foot punt from South Africa's Siphiwe Tshabalala...

SIPHIWE TSHABALALA – South Africa vs Mexico

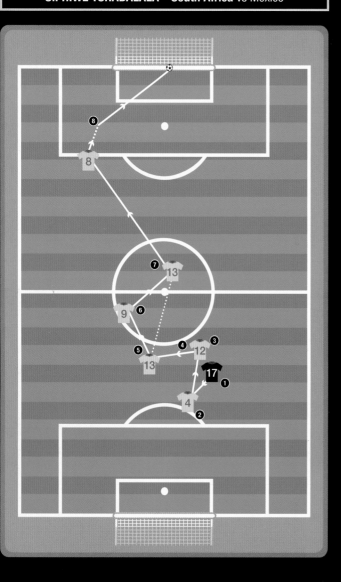

Siphiwe Tshabalala belts the ball hard from the 18-yard box to take South Africa into the lead against Mexico, June 11, 2010.

1. Flick-on **dos Santos**
2. Interception **Mokoena**
3. Ball recovery **Letsholonyane**
4. Pass **Letsholonyane**
5. Pass **Dikgacoi**
6. Pass **Mphela**
7. Through ball **Dikgacoi**
8. Goal **Tshabalala**

KEY

Ball movement	Player with ball
Shot	Player without ball

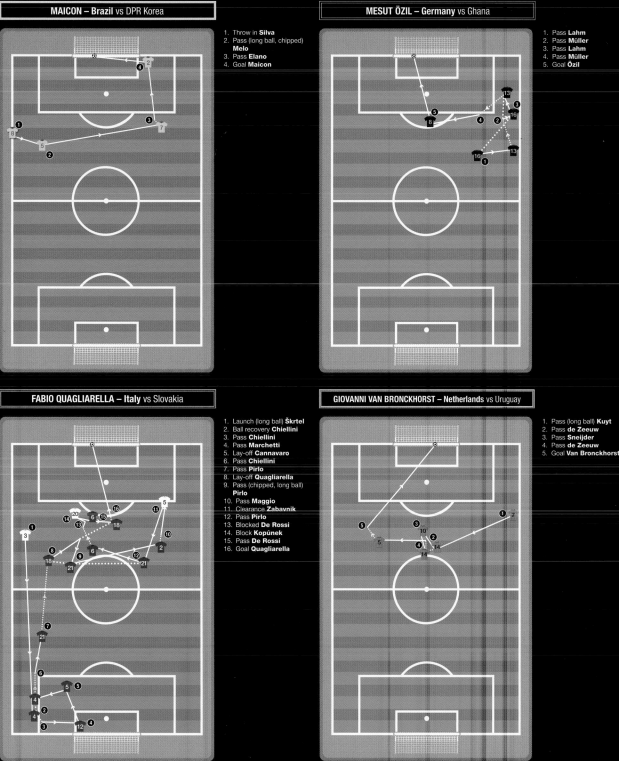

MAICON – Brazil vs DPR Korea

1. Throw in **Silva**
2. Pass (long ball, chipped) **Melo**
3. Pass **Elano**
4. Goal **Maicon**

MESUT ÖZIL – Germany vs Ghana

1. Pass **Lahm**
2. Pass **Müller**
3. Pass **Lahm**
4. Pass **Müller**
5. Goal **Özil**

FABIO QUAGLIARELLA – Italy vs Slovakia

1. Launch (long ball) **Škrtel**
2. Ball recovery **Chiellini**
3. Pass **Chiellini**
4. Pass **Marchetti**
5. Lay-off **Cannavaro**
6. Pass **Chiellini**
7. Pass **Pirlo**
8. Lay-off **Quagliarella**
9. Pass (chipped, long ball) **Pirlo**
10. Pass **Maggio**
11. Clearance **Zabavnik**
12. Pass **Pirlo**
13. Blocked **De Rossi**
14. Block **Kopúnek**
15. Pass **De Rossi**
16. Goal **Quagliarella**

GIOVANNI VAN BRONCKHORST – Netherlands vs Uruguay

1. Pass (long ball) **Kuyt**
2. Pass **de Zeeuw**
3. Pass **Sneijder**
4. Pass **de Zeeuw**
5. Goal **Van Bronckhorst**

2014 WORLD CUP GOALS

There were too many unforgettable stories in Brazil's 2014 World Cup: reigning champions Spain crashing out in the group stage; the attacking zest displayed by Mexico, Costa Rica, US, and Colombia; Brazil's semifinal capitulation; and the superb soccer played by worthy winners Germany. Miroslav Klose became the competition's all-time top scorer, Colombia's James Rodríguez scored from a top-class chest, swivel, and volley smash, Robin van Persie perfected a diving header, and Mario Götze hit a volley worthy of winning a World Cup final.

ROBIN VAN PERSIE – Netherlands vs Spain

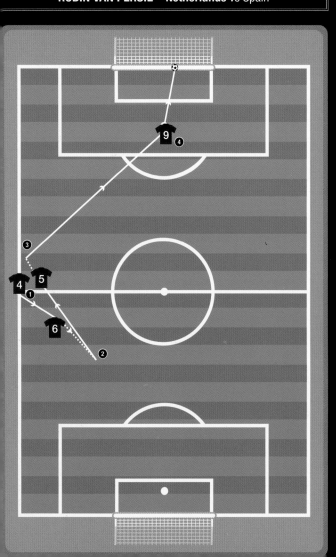

The Netherlands' Robin van Persie scores with his head to equalize in the match against Spain, June 13, 2014.

1. Throw in **Martins Indi**
2. Pass **De Jong**
3. Through ball (chipped, long ball) **Blind**
4. Goal (head) **Van Persie**

KEY

Ball movement	———	Player with ball	▪▪▪▪▪▪▪▪▪▪▪
Shot	———⚽	Player without ball	•••••••••••

MARIO GÖTZE – Germany vs Argentina

1. Free kick taken **Lahm**
2. Pass **Schweinsteiger**
3. Pass **Boateng**
4. Pass **Hummels**
5. Pass **Kroos**
6. Pass **Schürrle**
7. Pass **Kroos**
8. Pass (cross, chipped) **Schürrle**
9. Goal **Götze**

LIONEL MESSI – Argentina vs Bosnia

1. Free kick taken **Fernández**
2. Pass **Mascherano**
3. Pass **Di María**
4. Pass **Mascherano**
5. Pass **Gago**
6. Lay-off **Higuaín**
7. Pass **Messi**
8. Lay-off **Higuaín**
9. Take on **Messi**
10. Challenge **Bičakčić**
11. Goal **Messi**

JAMES RODRÍGUEZ – Colombia vs Uruguay

1. Pass **Armero**
2. Launch (long ball) **Ospina**
3. Head pass **González**
4. Pass (chipped, long ball) **Armero**
5. Head pass **Godín**
6. Pass (chipped) **Gutiérrez**
7. Pass **Aguilar**
8. Pass **Gutiérrez**
9. Pass **Cuadrado**
10. Pass **Zúñiga**
11. Pass **Gutiérrez**
12. Pass **Martínez**
13. Pass (cross, chipped) **Armero**
14. Head pass **Cuadrado**
15. Goal **Rodríguez**

DAVID VILLA – Spain vs Australia

1. Throw In (long ball) **McGowan**
2. Interception **Alonso**
3. Ball recovery **Iniesta**
4. Pass **Iniesta**
5. Pass **Torres**
6. Pass **Alonso**
7. Pass (long ball) **Cazorla**
8. Pass **Juanfran**
9. Pass **Iniesta**
10. Pass **Koke**
11. Pass **Alonso**
12. Pass **Cazorla**
13. Pass **Villa**
14. Pass (chipped, long ball) **Cazorla**
15. Pass **Juanfran**
16. Pass **Iniesta**
17. Pass **Juanfran**
18. Goal **Villa**

WOMEN'S WORLD CUP TROPHIES AND GOALS

The first official Women's World Cup took place in China in 1991. There were 12 teams but no winners' prize money and no sponsor, while the matches lasted just 80 minutes. Since then, the women's game and the competition have grown beyond recognition and, still played every four years, there have now been seven tournaments. In Canada, in 2015, the qualifying rounds saw 134 nations compete for 24 places; 26.7 million TV viewers made the final the most-watched soccer game in American history and the victorious US team won $2 million in prize money.

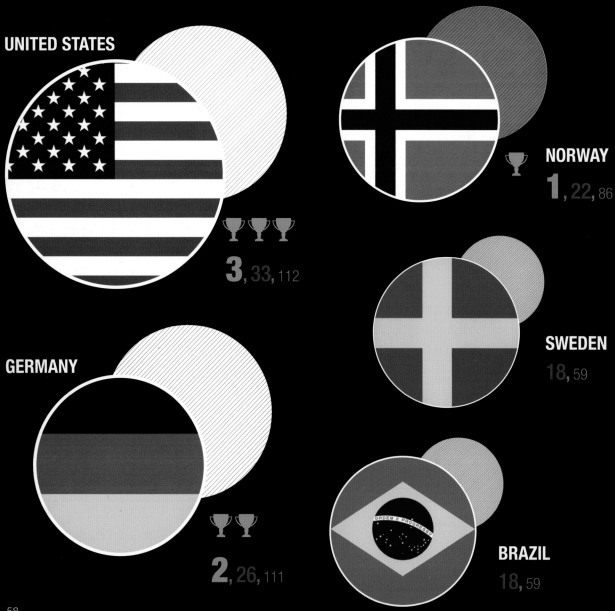

UNITED STATES

3, 33, 112

NORWAY

1, 22, 86

SWEDEN

18, 59

GERMANY

2, 26, 111

BRAZIL

18, 59

PR CHINA
15, 52

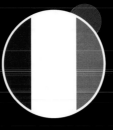
FRANCE
6, 22

 CAMEROON
2, 9

 SWITZERLAND
1, 11

AUSTRALIA
5, 29

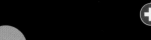 **GHANA**
1, 6

 JAPAN
1, 13, 36

RUSSIA
4, 16

 KOREA REPUBLIC
1, 5

 COLOMBIA
1, 4

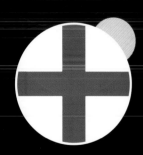
ENGLAND
10, 30

DENMARK
3, 19

 THAILAND
1, 3

NIGERIA
3, 18

 **NETHERLANDS**
1, 3

DPR KOREA
3, 12

 CHINESE TAIPEI
1, 2

CANADA
6, 30

ITALY
3, 11

 1 **TOURNAMENTS WON**
 1 MATCHES WON
 1 GOALS SCORED

59

WOMEN'S WORLD CUP GOALSCORERS

Since Chinese defender Ma Li scored the first goal in Women's World Cup history, 770 goals have been scored in the finals. Among these are memorable strikes such as the stunning volley by Germany's Birgit Prinz in 2003 and Brazilian Marta's unstoppable flick and finish in 2007. The 2015 World Cup competition was graced by fabulous long-range shots from

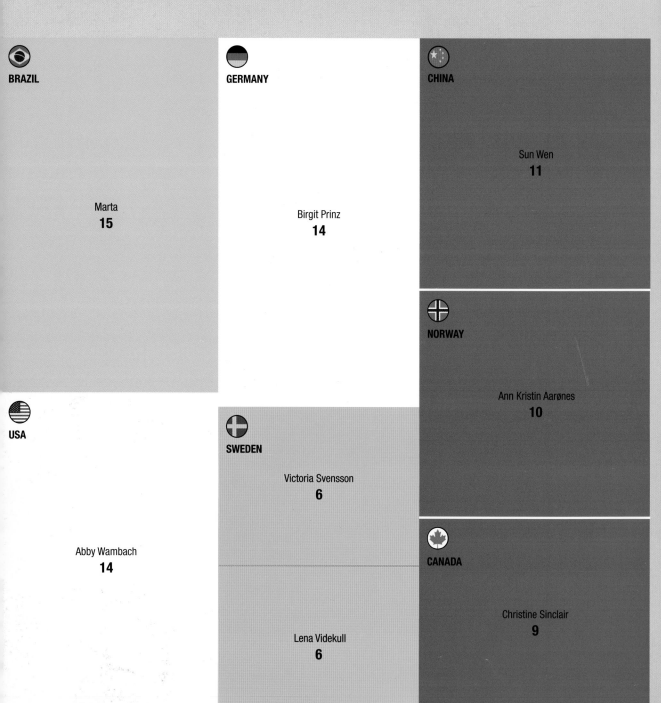

BRAZIL

Marta
15

GERMANY

Birgit Prinz
14

CHINA

Sun Wen
11

NORWAY

Ann Kristin Aarønes
10

USA

Abby Wambach
14

SWEDEN

Victoria Svensson
6

Lena Videkull
6

CANADA

Christine Sinclair
9

England's Lucy Bronze and France's Amandine Henry, but will surely be remembered most for the hat trick by the USA's Carli Lloyd in the final, capped by a sensational right-foot strike (and lob) from the halfway line. The goal was awarded Goal of the Tournament.

Source: Opta (August 2015)

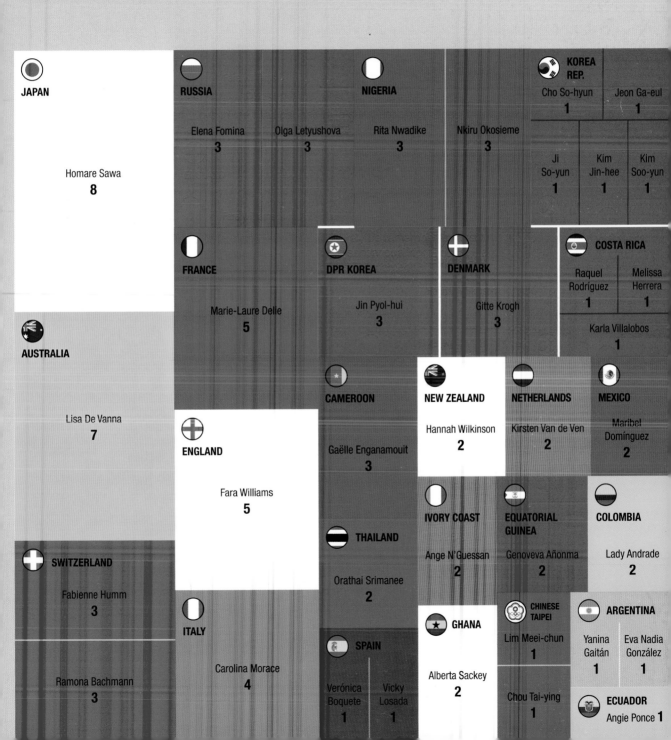

JAPAN
Homare Sawa
8

RUSSIA
Elena Fomina **3** Olga Letyushova **3**

NIGERIA
Rita Nwadike **3** Nkiru Okosieme **3**

KOREA REP.
Cho So-hyun **1** Jeon Ga-eul **1**
Ji So-yun **1** Kim Jin-hee **1** Kim Soo-yun **1**

FRANCE
Marie-Laure Delie **5**

DPR KOREA
Jin Pyol-hui **3**

DENMARK
Gitte Krogh **3**

COSTA RICA
Raquel Rodríguez **1** Melissa Herrera **1**
Karla Villalobos **1**

AUSTRALIA
Lisa De Vanna **7**

CAMEROON
Gaëlle Enganamouit **3**

NEW ZEALAND
Hannah Wilkinson **2**

NETHERLANDS
Kirsten Van de Ven **2**

MEXICO
Maribel Domínguez **2**

ENGLAND
Fara Williams **5**

THAILAND
Orathai Srimanee **2**

IVORY COAST
Ange N'Guessan **2**

EQUATORIAL GUINEA
Genoveva Añonma **2**

COLOMBIA
Lady Andrade **2**

SWITZERLAND
Fabienne Humm **3**

ITALY
Carolina Morace **4**

SPAIN
Verónica Boquete **1** Vicky Losada **1**

GHANA
Alberta Sackey **2**

CHINESE TAIPEI
Lim Meei-chun **1**
Chou Tai-ying **1**

ARGENTINA
Yanina Gaitán **1** Eva Nadia González **1**

ECUADOR
Angie Ponce **1**

Ramona Bachmann **3**

EUROPEAN CHAMPIONSHIP RECORDS BY NATION

Brainchild of Henri Delaunay, the secretary of the French Football Federation, the European Championship has been held every four years since 1960. Qualification for the first two finals was conducted on a home-and-away knockout basis, with the group qualification format beginning in 1968. Originally only four teams qualified for the finals. This was extended to eight teams in 1980, to 16 in 1996 and further expanded to include 24 nations in 2016. To mark 60 years of the tournament, the 2020 finals will be held in 13 different cities across the continent.

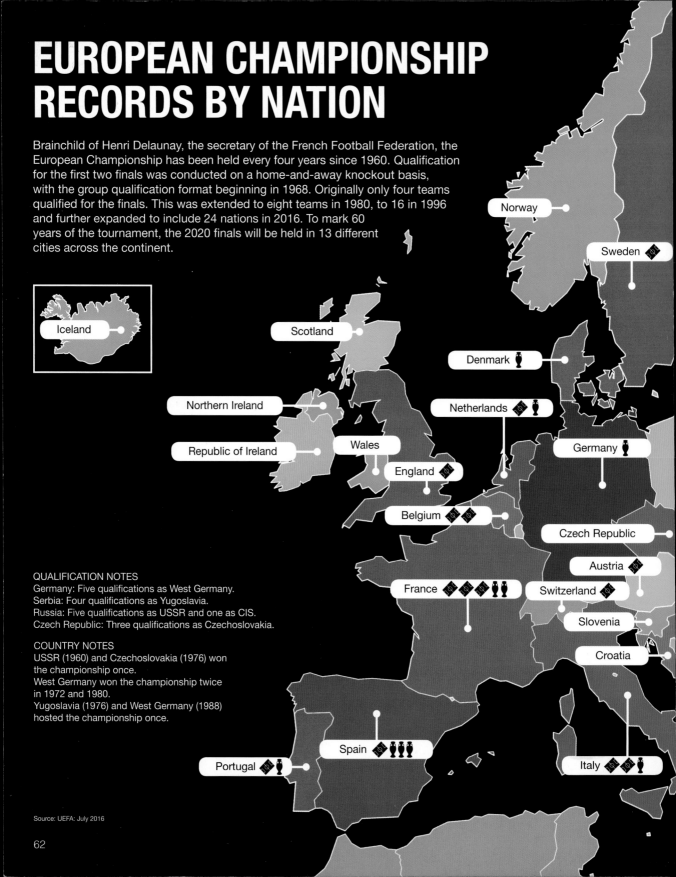

Norway

Sweden

Iceland

Scotland

Denmark

Northern Ireland

Netherlands

Germany

Republic of Ireland

Wales

England

Belgium

Czech Republic

Austria

France

Switzerland

Slovenia

Croatia

QUALIFICATION NOTES
Germany: Five qualifications as West Germany.
Serbia: Four qualifications as Yugoslavia.
Russia: Five qualifications as USSR and one as CIS.
Czech Republic: Three qualifications as Czechoslovakia.

COUNTRY NOTES
USSR (1960) and Czechoslovakia (1976) won the championship once.
West Germany won the championship twice in 1972 and 1980.
Yugoslavia (1976) and West Germany (1988) hosted the championship once.

Spain

Portugal

Italy

Source: UEFA: July 2016

EUROPEAN CHAMPIONSHIP TROPHIES, WINS, AND GOALS

It's an old soccer cliché, but it is certainly true that there have been no easy games in the European Championship. The format of this much-revered event has historically led to a select and elite group of nations reaching the finals, so this data is not distorted by easy wins and goal feasts. While Germany are top in the all-time Euro table, the other leading nations have similar records—except for England, whose lack of success in the competition is starkly obvious.

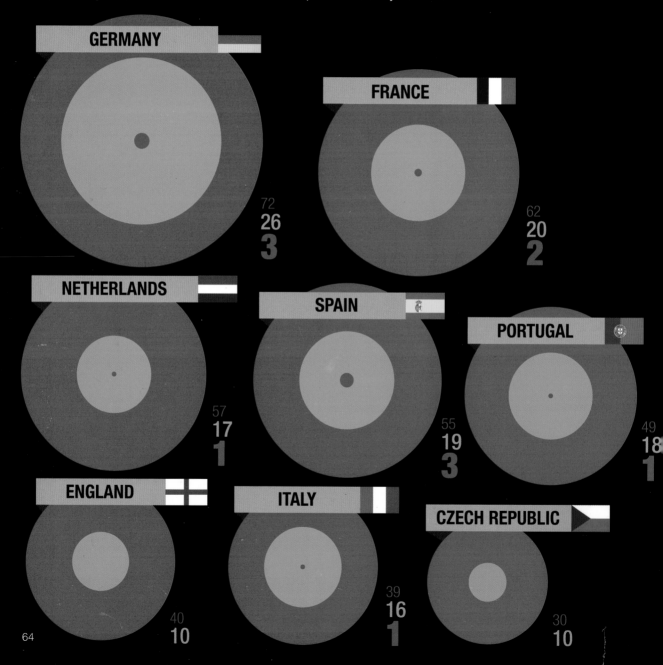

GERMANY
72
26
3

FRANCE
62
20
2

NETHERLANDS
57
17
1

SPAIN
55
19
3

PORTUGAL
49
18
1

ENGLAND
40
10

ITALY
39
16
1

CZECH REPUBLIC
30
10

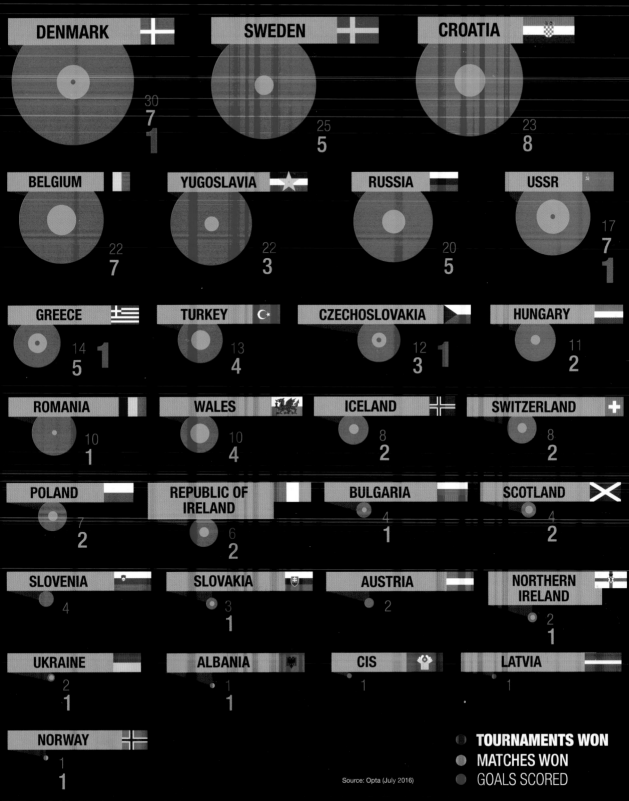

DENMARK

30
7
1

SWEDEN

25
5

CROATIA

23
8

BELGIUM

22
7

YUGOSLAVIA

22
3

RUSSIA

20
5

USSR

17
7
1

GREECE

14 **1**
5

TURKEY

13
4

CZECHOSLOVAKIA

12 **1**
3

HUNGARY

11
2

ROMANIA

10
1

WALES

10
4

ICELAND

8
2

SWITZERLAND

8
2

POLAND

7
2

REPUBLIC OF IRELAND

6
2

BULGARIA

4
1

SCOTLAND

4
2

SLOVENIA

4

SLOVAKIA

3
1

AUSTRIA

2

NORTHERN IRELAND

2
1

UKRAINE

2
1

ALBANIA

1
1

CIS

1

LATVIA

1

NORWAY

1
1

● **TOURNAMENTS WON**
● **MATCHES WON**
● GOALS SCORED

Source: Opta (July 2016)

65

UEFA EURO 2016 GOALS

Despite a record 108 goals being scored in the 2016 European Championship, the matches were not a feast of goals. With a ratio of just 2.12 a game, Euro 2016 was the lowest-scoring European Championship for 20 years. However, there certainly was drama: 18 goals (seven winners and three equalizers) were scored in the last five minutes or later, including Dimitri Payet's majestic 89th-minute winner against Romania in the opening game and Northern Ireland's Niall McGinn setting the record for latest goal ever in a European Championship at 96 minutes.

XHERDAN SHAQIRI – Switzerland vs Poland

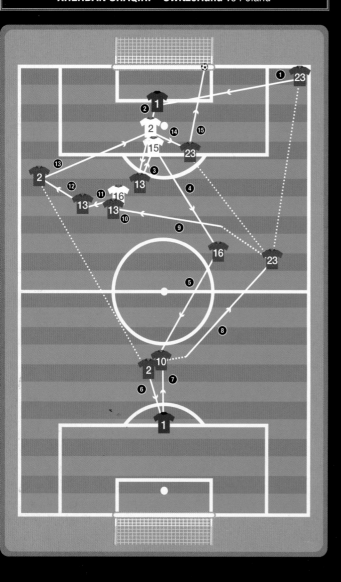

Many believed Xherdan Shaqiri's acrobatic strike for Switzerland in their last-16 match against Poland to be the Goal of the Tournament.

1. Corner kick **Shaqiri**
2. Punch **Fabianski**
3. Blocked shot **Rodriguez**
4. Defensive block **Glik**
5. Pass **Fernandes**
6. Pass **Lichtsteiner**
7. Pass **Sommer**
8. Pass **Xhaka**
9. Pass **Shaqiri**
10. Unsuccessful pass **Rodriguez**
11. Blocked pass **Blaszczykowski**
12. Pass **Rodriguez**
13. Unsuccessful pass **Lichtsteiner**
14. Clearance **Pazdan**
15. Goal **Shaqiri**

KEY

Ball movement	Player with ball	
Shot	Player without ball	

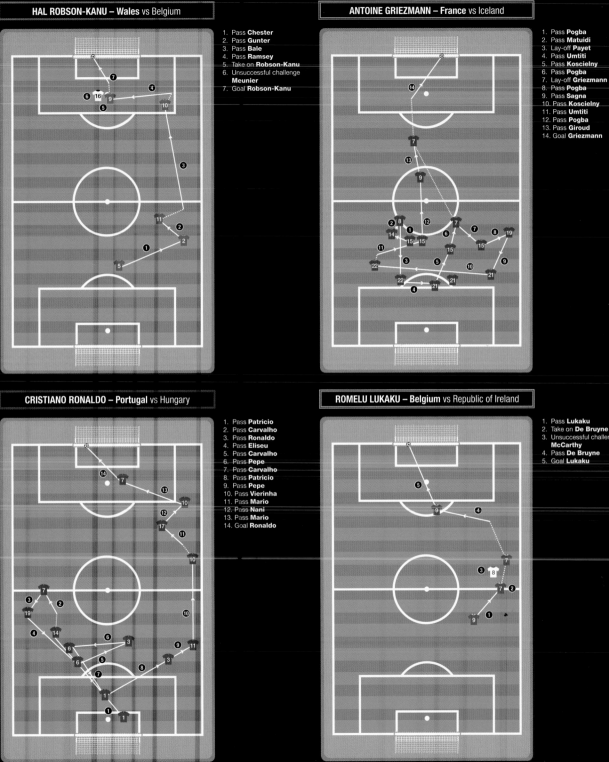

HAL ROBSON-KANU – Wales vs Belgium

1. Pass **Chester**
2. Pass **Gunter**
3. Pass **Bale**
4. Pass **Ramsey**
5. Take on **Robson-Kanu**
6. Unsuccessful challenge **Meunier**
7. Goal **Robson-Kanu**

ANTOINE GRIEZMANN – France vs Iceland

1. Pass **Pogba**
2. Pass **Matuidi**
3. Lay-off **Payet**
4. Pass **Umtiti**
5. Pass **Koscielny**
6. Pass **Pogba**
7. Lay-off **Griezmann**
8. Pass **Pogba**
9. Pass **Sagna**
10. Pass **Koscielny**
11. Pass **Umtiti**
12. Pass **Pogba**
13. Pass **Giroud**
14. Goal **Griezmann**

CRISTIANO RONALDO – Portugal vs Hungary

1. Pass **Patricio**
2. Pass **Carvalho**
3. Pass **Ronaldo**
4. Pass **Eliseu**
5. Pass **Carvalho**
6. Pass **Pepe**
7. Pass **Carvalho**
8. Pass **Patricio**
9. Pass **Pepe**
10. Pass **Vierinha**
11. Pass **Mario**
12. Pass **Nani**
13. Pass **Mario**
14. Goal **Ronaldo**

ROMELU LUKAKU – Belgium vs Republic of Ireland

1. Pass **Lukaku**
2. Take on **De Bruyne**
3. Unsuccessful challenge **McCarthy**
4. Pass **De Bruyne**
5. Goal **Lukaku**

COPA AMÉRICA
RECORDS BY NATION

The South American Football Championship is the oldest international continental soccer competition. The first event took place in Argentina in 1916 and was held annually (if sporadically) until 1967. The Copa América itself began in 1975 and, from 2007, has continued in a four-year cycle. It was originally contested by 10 teams, enlarged to 12 in 1993 and 16 (including the rest of the Americas) for a special 2016 centenary tournament in the US. After the 2019 tournament takes place in Brazil, the US will host a 2020 Copa América to move the competition to even-numbered years.

The 2019 Copa América will feature 16 teams: among the guest teams to have been invited – for the first time – are Spain, France and Italy.

QUALIFICATION NOTES
Also competed: Mexico (10), Costa Rica (5), United States (4), Jamaica (2), Haiti (1), Honduras (1), Japan (1). No host (3).

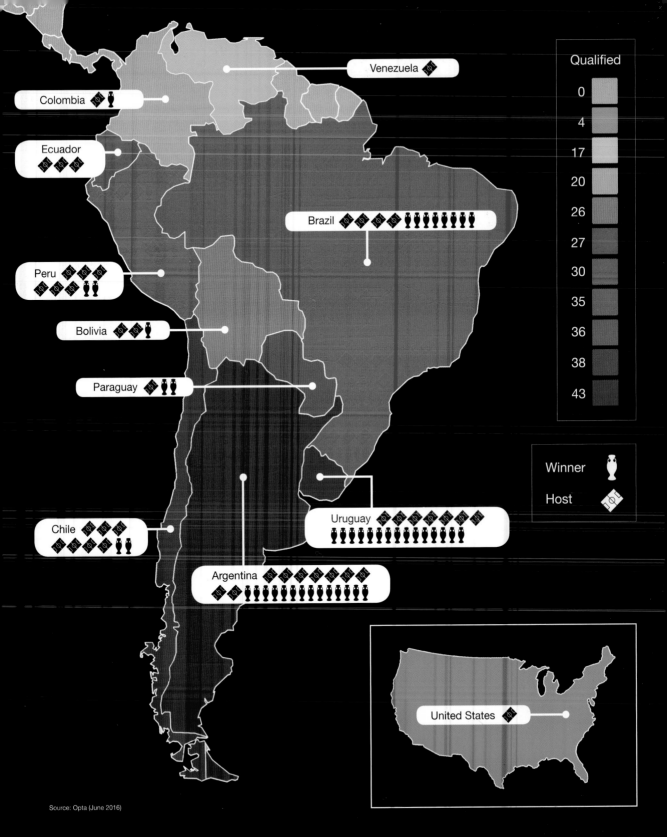

Qualified

0
4
17
20
26
27
30
35
36
38
43

Venezuela

Colombia

Ecuador

Brazil

Peru

Bolivia

Paraguay

Uruguay

Chile

Argentina

Winner

Host

United States

Source: Opta (June 2016)

COPA AMÉRICA TROPHIES, WINS, AND GOALS

The South American international tournament, Copa América is one of the most intensely fought competitions in world football. There have been 45 (often intermittent) tournaments in the Copa América's 100 years, in which all but Ecuador and Venezuela have been victors. Bolivia's sole victory came on high-altitude home soil in 1963, while Chile contested the most tournaments without a win until 2015, then won again in the centenary competition in 2016. Interestingly, both Pelé and Maradona—and their World Cup-winning teams—failed to secure a Copa América triumph.

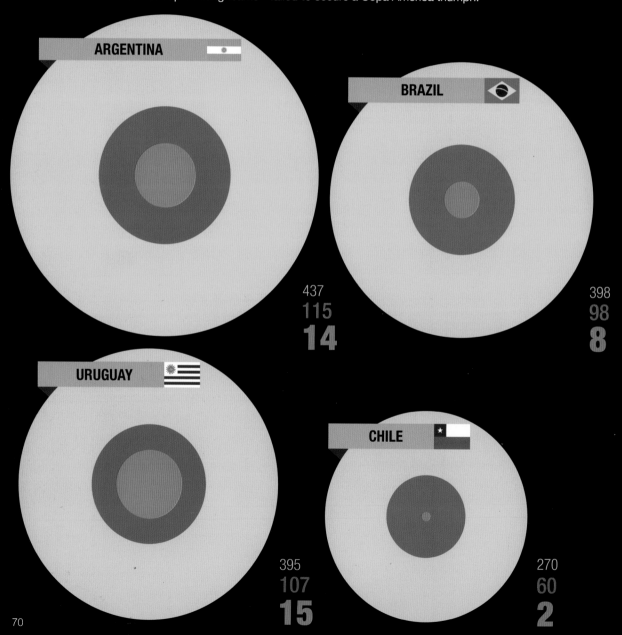

ARGENTINA
437
115
14

BRAZIL
398
98
8

URUGUAY
395
107
15

CHILE
270
60
2

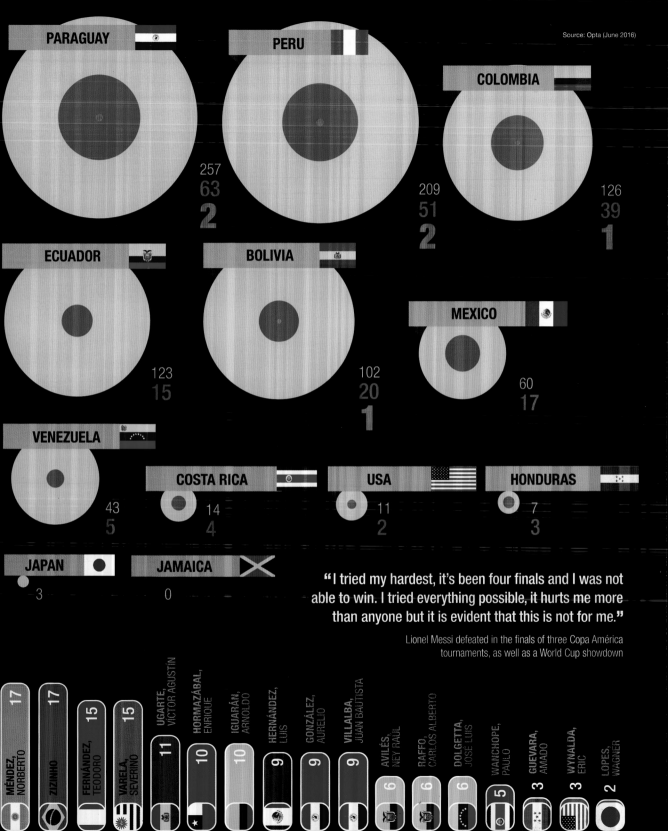

Source: Opta (June 2016)

PARAGUAY
257
63
2

PERU
209
51
2

COLOMBIA
126
39
1

ECUADOR
123
15

BOLIVIA
102
20
1

MEXICO
60
17

VENEZUELA
43
5

COSTA RICA
14
4

USA
11
2

HONDURAS
7
3

JAPAN
3

JAMAICA
0

"I tried my hardest, it's been four finals and I was not able to win. I tried everything possible, it hurts me more than anyone but it is evident that this is not for me."

Lionel Messi defeated in the finals of three Copa América tournaments, as well as a World Cup showdown

MÉNDEZ, NORBERTO — 17
ZIZINHO — 17
FERNÁNDEZ, TEODORO — 15
VARELA, SEVERINO — 15
UGARTE, VÍCTOR AGUSTÍN — 11
HORMAZÁBAL, ENRIQUE — 10
IGUARÁN, ARNOLDO — 10
HERNÁNDEZ, LUIS — 9
GONZÁLEZ, AURELIO — 9
VILLALBA, JUAN BAUTISTA — 9
AVILÉS, NEY RAÚL — 6
RAFFO, CARLOS ALBERTO — 6
DOLGETTA, JOSÉ LUIS — 6
WANCHOPE, PAULO — 5
GUEVARA, AMADO — 3
WYNALDA, ERIC — 3
LOPES, WAGNER — 2

AFRICA CUP OF NATIONS RECORDS BY NATION

The biennial Africa Cup of Nations tournament, contested by the nations of the Confederation of African Football, has been played since 1957. Just Egypt, Sudan, and Ethiopia played the first two tournaments before it was enlarged to include four (1962), six (1963), eight (1968), 12 (1992) and then 16 teams (1996). Because of its apartheid policy South Africa was excluded from the competition until 1996. The tournament moved to odd-numbered years from 2013 to avoid conflict with the World Cup; this meant there were tournaments in consecutive years.

Cameroon celebrate winning the 2017 Africa Cup of Nations after the Indomitable Lions *came from behind to beat Egypt 2–1 in Libreville, Gabon, to seal a fifth tournament victory*

Senegal

Guinea-Bissau

Guinea

Sierra Leone

Liberia

Cape Verde

Qualified		
0		12
1		13
2		14
3		15
4		16
5		17
6		18
7		19
8		20
9		21
10		22
11		23

Winner

Host

Morocco

Tunisia

Western Sahara

Algeria

Egypt

Libya

Mauritania

Mali

Niger

Chad

Sudan

Eritrea

Cameroon

Burkina Faso

Nigeria

Central African Republic

South Sudan

Ethiopia

Ivory Coast

Benin

Equatorial Guinea

Uganda

Somalia

Kenya

Togo

DR Congo

Rwanda

Tanzania

Ghana

Malawi

Congo

Angola

Zambia

Mauritius

Gabon

Zimbabwe

Mozambique

Botswana

Namibia

Madagascar

South Africa

Source: FIFA (February 2017)

73

AFRICA CUP OF NATIONS TROPHIES, WINS, AND GOALS

What began in 1957 with a three-team competition has developed 31 tournaments later into a month-long, 16-team extravaganza. The tournament has witnessed many great moments, including Benni McCarthy hitting four goals in 13 minutes against Namibia in 1998; Ivory Coast's second-choice keeper Boubacar Barry saving two penalties before hitting the winner in the shootout in 2015 and Vincent Aboubakar's sensational 88th-minute strike to win the trophy for Cameroon in 2017.

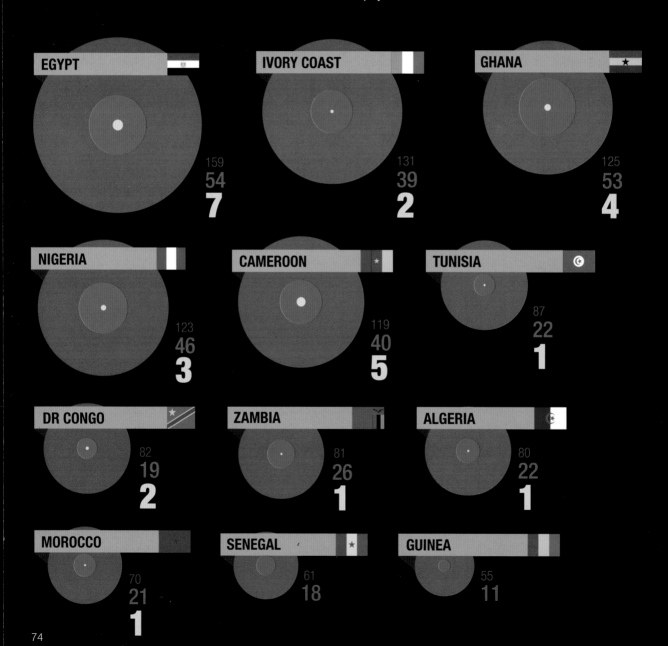

EGYPT
159
54
7

IVORY COAST
131
39
2

GHANA
125
53
4

NIGERIA
123
46
3

CAMEROON
119
40
5

TUNISIA
87
22
1

DR CONGO
82
19
2

ZAMBIA
81
26
1

ALGERIA
80
22
1

MOROCCO
70
21
1

SENEGAL
61
18

GUINEA
55
11

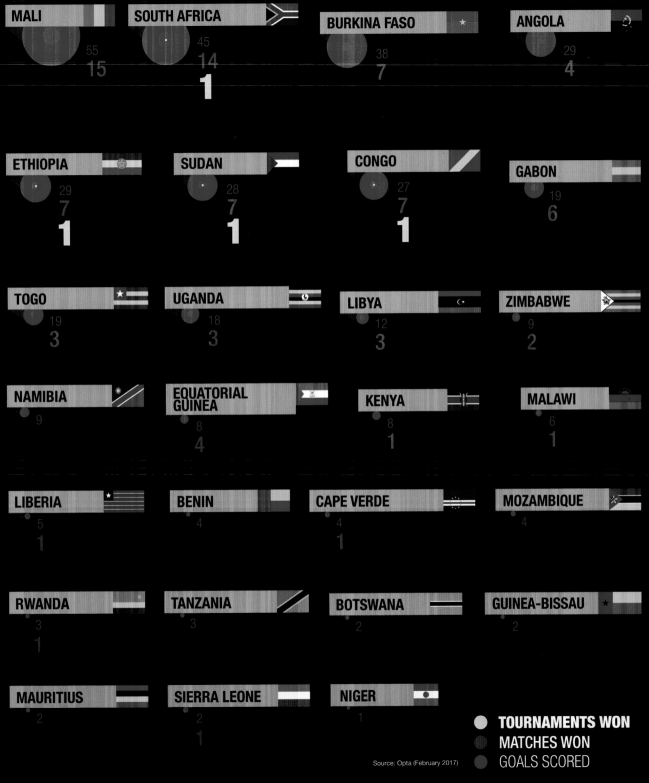

MALI
55
15

SOUTH AFRICA
45
14
1

BURKINA FASO
38
7

ANGOLA
29
4

ETHIOPIA
29
7
1

SUDAN
28
7
1

CONGO
27
7
1

GABON
19
6

TOGO
19
3

UGANDA
18
3

LIBYA
12
3

ZIMBABWE
9
2

NAMIBIA
9

EQUATORIAL GUINEA
8
4

KENYA
8
1

MALAWI
6
1

LIBERIA
5
1

BENIN
4

CAPE VERDE
4
1

MOZAMBIQUE
4

RWANDA
3
1

TANZANIA
3

BOTSWANA
2

GUINEA-BISSAU
2

MAURITIUS
2

SIERRA LEONE
2
1

NIGER
1

● **TOURNAMENTS WON**
● **MATCHES WON**
● **GOALS SCORED**

Source: Opta (February 2017)

ASIAN CUP RECORDS BY NATION AND REGION

The Asian Cup is contested by the nations and regions of the Asian Football Confederation, which stretches from the Middle East to Japan and Australia (who joined the AFC in 2006). It was held every four years from the inaugural 1956 tournament until 2004, then from 2007 (switching to avoid conflicting with the Olympics and European Championship). The number of nations competing in the finals increased from an original 4 to 12 in 1996, to 16 in 2004 and will increase to 24 in 2019.

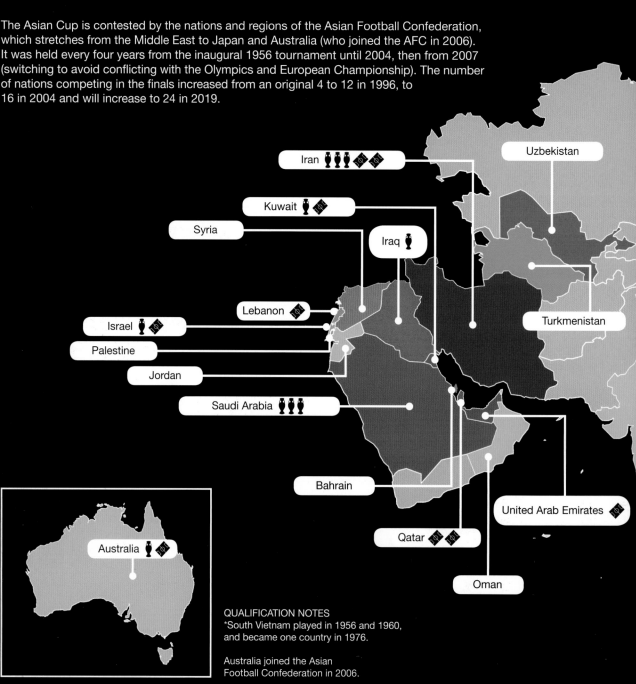

Iran
Uzbekistan
Kuwait
Syria
Iraq
Lebanon
Israel
Palestine
Jordan
Saudi Arabia
Turkmenistan
Bahrain
United Arab Emirates
Qatar
Oman
Australia

QUALIFICATION NOTES
*South Vietnam played in 1956 and 1960, and became one country in 1976.

Australia joined the Asian
Football Confederation in 2006.

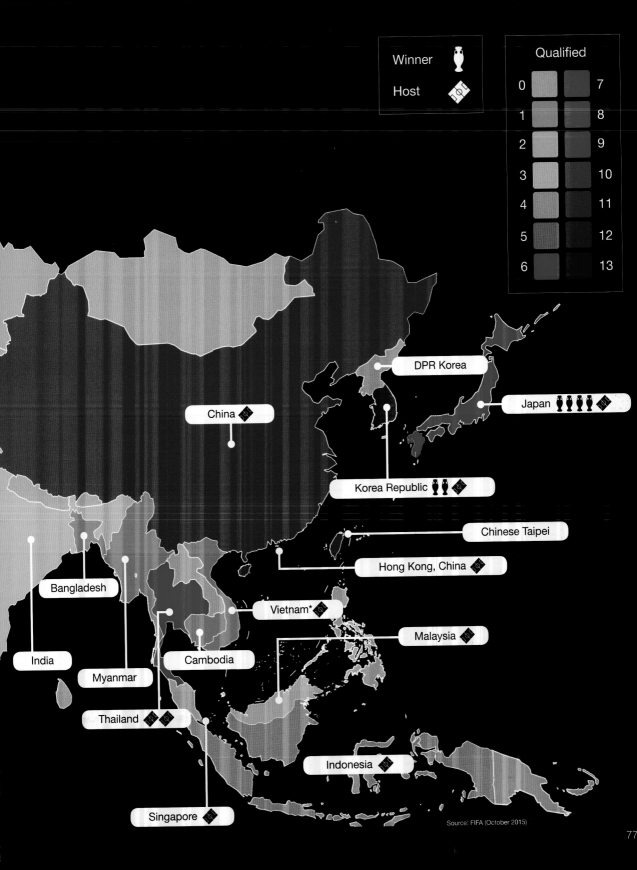

Winner

Host

Qualified

0	7
1	8
2	9
3	10
4	11
5	12
6	13

DPR Korea

Japan

China

Korea Republic

Chinese Taipei

Hong Kong, China

Bangladesh

Vietnam*

Malaysia

India

Cambodia

Myanmar

Thailand

Indonesia

Singapore

Source: FIFA (October 2015)

AFC ASIAN CUP
TROPHIES, WINS, AND GOALS

The most recent AFC Asian Cup in 2015 crowned host nation Australia the Champions of Asia after defeating the Republic of Korea 2–1 after extra time. The next tournament in 2019, which is to be hosted by the United Arab Emirates, will see the possible number of national teams expand from 16 to 24. The Asian Cup is the world's second oldest continental soccer championship, after Copa América, and the cup's most consistent side to date is Japan, who have triumphantly held the trophy aloft in four out of seven tournaments since 1992.

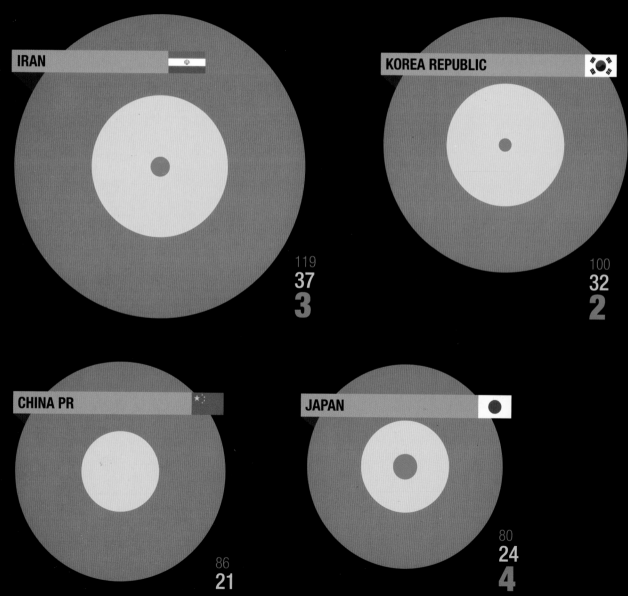

IRAN

119
37
3

KOREA REPUBLIC

100
32
2

CHINA PR

86
21

JAPAN

80
24
4

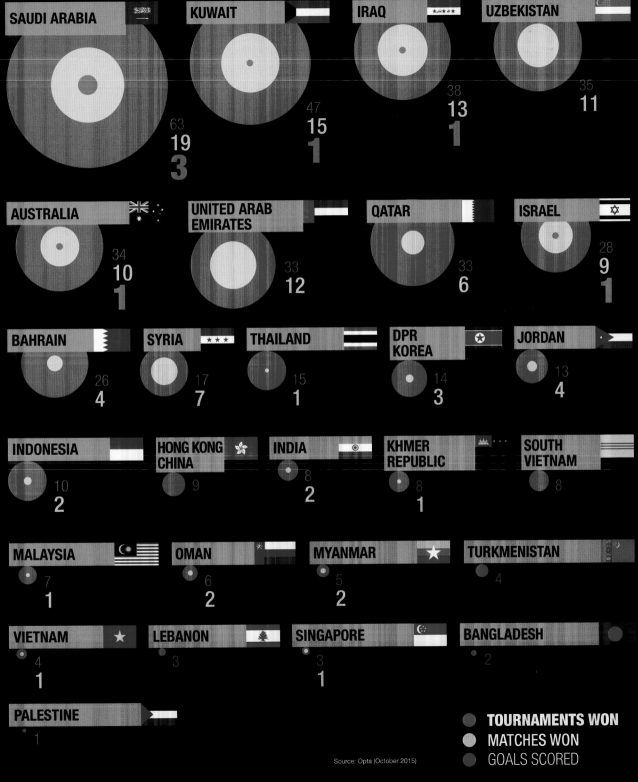

SAUDI ARABIA

KUWAIT

IRAQ

UZBEKISTAN

63
19
3

47
15
1

38
13
1

35
11

AUSTRALIA

UNITED ARAB EMIRATES

QATAR

ISRAEL

34
10
1

33
12

33
6

28
9
1

BAHRAIN

SYRIA

THAILAND

DPR KOREA

JORDAN

26
4

17
7

15
1

14
3

13
4

INDONESIA

HONG KONG CHINA

INDIA

KHMER REPUBLIC

SOUTH VIETNAM

10
2

9

8
2

8
1

8

MALAYSIA

OMAN

MYANMAR

TURKMENISTAN

7
1

6
2

5
2

4

VIETNAM

LEBANON

SINGAPORE

BANGLADESH

4
1

3

3
1

2

PALESTINE

1

TOURNAMENTS WON
MATCHES WON
GOALS SCORED

Source: Opta (October 2015)

CONCACAF GOLD CUP RECORDS BY NATION

The CONCACAF Gold Cup is a biennial competition for nations from North and Central America and the Caribbean. The six-team tournament was first held in 1963 and then every two years. Between 1973 and 1989, the competition was held every four years and doubled as a World Cup qualifying process. In 1991 it was expanded to eight teams and reverted to a biennial format and in 2001 it was enlarged to 12 nations. Between 1997 and 2003 guest teams, including Brazil and Colombia, also competed in the tournament. The most recent CONCACAF Gold Cup was hosted—and won—by the US in 2017.

QUALIFICATION NOTES
The color coding and winners and hosts icons are based only on the Gold Cup since 1991.

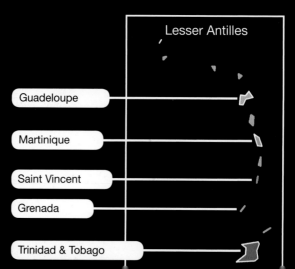

Mexico have won the CONCACAF Gold Cup a record 10 times.

Lesser Antilles

Guadeloupe

Martinique

Saint Vincent

Grenada

Trinidad & Tobago

Canada 🏆◈

Qualified

0
1
2
3
5
6
7
8
9
10
11
12
13
14

United States of America
◈◈◈◈◈◈◈◈◈◈
◈◈◈◈🏆🏆🏆🏆🏆

Source: FIFA (Ju

Mexico
🏆🏆🏆🏆🏆🏆🏆◈◈

Cuba

French Guia

Jamaica

Belize

Honduras

Haiti

Guatemala

Nicaragua

El Salvador

Panama

Costa Rica

Also competed: Brazil (3),
Colombia (3), Korea Republic
(2), Ecuador (1), Peru (1),
South Africa (1).

100 INTERNATIONAL CAPS

At Wembley Stadium, on April 11, 1959, England captain Billy Wright became the first soccer player to make 100 appearances for his country, but since then this feat has been repeated by many players around the world. The modern game's proliferation of matches (major nations play more games a year than their pre-1990s counterparts) and multiple substitution rules give today's players a better chance of becoming Centurions and also accounts for the absence in the list of such greats as Pelé (92 appearances), Diego Maradona (91), Eusébio (64) and Johan Cruyff (48).

Player	Caps	Player	Caps	Player	Caps	Player	Caps	Player	Caps	Player	Caps	Player	Caps	Player	Caps	Player	Caps
Ahmed Hassan (Egypt)	184	Hossam Hassan (Egypt)	178	Claudio Suárez (Mexico)	177	Mohamed Al-Deayea (Saudi Arabia)	172	Iván Hurtado (Ecuador)	168	Gianluigi Buffon (Italy)	168	Iker Casillas (Spain)	167	Vitalijs Astafjevs (Latvia)	165	Cobi Jones (United States)	164
Mohammed Al-Khilaiwi (Saudi Arabia)	163	Adnan Al-Talyani (United Arab Emirates)	161	Bader Al-Mutawa (Kuwait)	158	Landon Donovan (United States)	157	Sami Al-Jaber (Saudi Arabia)	156	Martin Reim (Estonia)	156	Essam El-Hadary (Egypt)	153	Yasuhito Endo (Japan)	152	Lothar Matthäus (West Germany / Germany)	150
Salman Isa (Bahrain)	149	Ali Daei (Iran)	149	Javad Nekounam (Iran)	148	Younis Mahmoud (Iraq)	148	Robbie Keane (Republic of Ireland)	146	Mohammed Husain (Bahrain)	145	Pável Pardo (Mexico)	145	Paulo da Silva (Paraguay)	144	Anatoliy Tymoshchuk (Ukraine)	144
Javier Zanetti (Argentina)	143	Gerado Torrado (Mexico)	143	Fawzi Doorbeen (Oman)	143	Thomas Ravelli (Sweden)	143	Anders Svensson (Sweden)	143	Cafu (Brazil)	142	Marko Kristal (Estonia)	142	Lilan Thuram (France)	142	Sergio Ramos (Spain)	142
Abdullah Zubromawi (Saudi Arabia)	141	Ahmed Mubarek (Oman)	140	Giorgos Karagounis (Greece)	139	Cristiano Ronaldo (Portugal)	138	Rigobert Song (Cameroon)	137	Jari Litmanen (Finland)	137	Miroslav Klose (Germany)	137	Amado Guevara (Honduras)	137	Hussein Saeed (Iraq)	137
Rafael Márquez (Mexico)	137	Javier Mascherano (Argentina)	136	Maynor Figueroa (Honduras)	136	Fabio Cannavaro (Italy)	136	Hong Myung-Bo (South Korea)	136	Walter Centeno (Costa Rica)	135	Noel Valladares (Honduras)	135	Amer Shafi (Jordan)	135	Waleed Ali Jumah (Kuwait)	135
Andrés Guardado (Mexico)	135	Daniel Bennett (Singapore)	135	Darijo Srna (Croatia)	134	Shay Given (Republic of Ireland)	134	Dorinel Munteanu (Romania)	134	Hussein Sulaimani (Saudi Arabia)	134	Shahril Bin Ishak (Singapore)	134	Jeff Agoos (United States)	134	Andres Oper (Estonia)	133
Carlos Ruiz (Guatemala)	133	Bashar Abdullah (Kuwait)	133	Saud Kariri (Saudi Arabia)	133	Xavi (Spain)	133	Andreas Isaksson (Sweden)	133	Clint Dempsey (United States)	132	Gabriel Gómez (Panama)	131	Kim Källström (Sweden)	131	Lee Woon-Jae (South Korea)	131
Kiatisuk Senamuang (Thailand)	131	Sargis Hovseyan (Armenia)	130	Lukas Podolski (Germany)	130	Edwin van der Sar (Netherlands)	130	Baihakki Bin Khaizan (Singapore)	130	Michael Bradley (United States)	130	Jorge Campos (Mexico)	130	Roberto Palacios (Peru)	129	Juan Arango (Venezuela)	128
Dennis Rommedahl (Denmark)	127	Ali Karimi (Iran)	127	Linval Dixon (Jamaica)	127	Luís Figo (Portugal)	127	Lee Young-Pyo (South Korea)	127	Marcelo Balboa (United States)	127	Luís Marin (Costa Rica)	127	Paolo Maldini (Italy)	126	Wesley Sneijder (Netherlands)	126
Ali Al-Habsi (Oman)	126	Andoni Zubizarreta (Spain)	126	Roberto Carlos (Brazil)	125	Ibrahim Hassan (Egypt)	125	Peter Shilton (England)	125	Musaed Neda (Kuwait)	125	Mario Fick (Liechtenstein)	125	Peter Jehle (Liechtenstein)	125	Petr Cech (Czech Republic)	124
Hany Ramzy (Egypt)	124	Ian Goodison (Jamaica)	124	Jaime Penedo (Panama)	124	Gheorghe Hagi (Romania)	124	DaMarcus Beasley (United States)	124	Thierry Henry (France)	123	Didier Zokora (Ivory Coast)	123	Michael Mifsud (Malta)	123	Server Djeparov (Uzbekistan)	123
Masami Ihara (Japan)	122	Carlos Salcido (Mexico)	122	Amad Al-Hosni (Oman)	122	Ismail Matar (United Arab Emirates)	122	Peter Schmeichel (Denmark)	121	Walter Ayoví (Ecuador)	121	Enar Jääger (Estonia)	121	Bastian Schweinsteiger (Germany)	121	Mohamed Abd Al-Jawad (Saudi Arabia)	121
Osama Al-Hawsawi (Saudi Arabia)	121	Aide Iskandar (Singapore)	121	Ahmed Fathi (Egypt)	120	Mart Poom (Estonia)	120	Sergei Ignashevich (Russia)	120	Yoo Sang-Chul (South Korea)	120	Rüstü Reçber (Turkey)	120	Subait Khater Al-Junaibi (United Arab Emirates)	120	Wayne Rooney (England)	119
Theodoros Zagorakis (Greece)	119	Boniek García (Honduras)	119	David Carabott (Malta)	119	Gilbert Agius (Malta)	119	Ramón Ramirez (Mexico)	119	Cuauhtémoc Blanco (Mexico)	119	Pat Jennings (Northern Ireland)	119	Justo Villar (Paraguay)	119	Cha-Bum-Kun (South Korea)	119
Timur Kapadze (Uzbekistan)	119	Heinz Hermann (Switzerland)	118	Geremi (Cameroon)	118	Samuel Eto'o (Cameroon)	118	Karel Poborský (Czech Republic)	118	Kolo Touré (Ivory Coast)	118	Maxi Pereira (Uruguay)	118	Lionel Messi (Argentina)	118	Amer Khalil (Jordan)	117
Sebastián Soria (Qatar)	117	Mohammed Al-Shalhoub (Saudi Arabia)	117	Olof Mellberg (Sweden)	117	Ragnar Klavan (Estonia)	117	Marcel Desailly (France)	116	Kostas Katsouranis (Greece)	116	Andrea Pirlo (Italy)	116	Theodore Whitmore (Jamaica)	116	Yoshikatsu Kawaguchi (Japan)	116
John O'Shea (Republic of Ireland)	116	Majed Abdullah (Saudi Arabia)	116	Ahmed Madani (Saudi Arabia)	116	Taisir Al-Jassim (Saudi Arabia)	116	Andrés Iniesta (Spain)	116	Roland Nilsson (Sweden)	116	Zlatan Ibrahimovic (Sweden)	116	Roberto Ayala (Argentina)	115	David Beckham (England)	115
Noureddine Naybet (Morocco)	115	Gheorghe Popescu (Romania)	115	Khairul Amri (Singapore)	115	Shunmugham Subramani (Singapore)	115	Abdulraheem Jumaa (United Arab Emirates)	115	Stipe Pletikosa (Croatia)	114	Steven Gerrard (England)	114	Kristen Viikmäe (Estonia)	114	Raio Piiroja (Estonia)	114

Source: Google (June 2017)

Nawaf Al-Khaldi, Kuwait — 114	Khaled Al-Muwallid, Saudi Arabia — 114	Indra Sahdan Daud, Singapore — 114	Björn Nordqvist, Sweden — 114	Abdulla Al-Mazooqi, Bahrain — 113	Viktor Onopko, CIS/Russia — 113	Philipp Lahm, Germany — 113	Ali Hussein Rehema, Iraq — 113	Andrejs Rubins, Latvia — 113
Martin Stocklasa, Liechtenstein — 113	Ahmad Al-Dossari, Saudi Arabia — 113	Xabi Alonso, Spain — 113	Angus Eve, Trinidad & Tobago — 113	Tim Howard, United States — 113	Alain Geiger, Switzerland — 112	Li Weifeng, PR China — 112	Yénier Márquez, Cuba — 112	Jón Dahl Tomasson, Denmark — 112
Édison Méndez, Ecuador — 112	Abdel-Zaher El-Saqua, Egypt — 112	Daniele De Rossi, Italy — 112	Dino Zoff, Italy — 112	Juris Laizans, Latvia — 112	Frank de Boer, Netherlands — 112	Roque Santa Cruz, Paraguay — 112	Claudio Bravo, Spain — 112	Wesam Abdulmajid, Qatar — 112
Yasser Al-Qahtani, Saudi Arabia — 112	Hakan Sükür, Turkey — 112	Zuhair Bakheet, United Arab Emirates — 112	Diego Forlán, Uruguay — 112	Carlos Valderrama, Colombia — 112	Hussain Ali Baba, Bahrain — 112	Rolando Fonseca, Costa Rica — 111	Odelín Molina, Cuba — 111	Wael Gomaa, Egypt — 111
Nashat Akram, Iraq — 111	Jarah Al-Ataiqi, Kuwait — 111	Blas Pérez, Panama — 111	Cesc Fàbregas, Spain — 111	David Silva, Spain — 111	Andriy Shevchenko, Ukraine — 111	Abdulsalam Jumaa, United Arab Emirates — 111	Claudio Reyna, United States — 111	Kennedy Mweene, Zambia — 111
Mehdi Mahdavikia, Iran — 110	Yuli Nakazawa, Japan — 110	Carmel Busuttil, Malta — 110	John Arne Riise, Norway — 110	Carlos Gamarra, Paraguay — 110	Fernando Couto, Portugal — 110	Kevin Kilbane, Republic of Ireland — 110	Fernando Torres, Spain — 110	Paul Caligiuri, United States — 110
Mark Schwarzer, Australia — 109	Sayed Mohammed Jaffer, Bahrain — 109	Mauricio Solís, Costa Rica — 109	Hawar Mulla Mohammed, Iraq — 109	Rafael van der Vaart, Netherlands — 109	Niclas Alexandersson, Sweden — 109	Totchtawan Sripan, Thailand — 109	José Rey, Venezuela — 109	Alexis Sanchez, Chile — 108
Álvaro Saborío, Costa Rica — 108	Thomas Helveg, Denmark — 108	Álex Aguinaga, Ecuador — 108	Zinedine Zidane, France — 108	Gábor Király, Hungary — 108	Nohayr Al-Mutairi, Kuwait — 108	Alberto García Aspe, Mexico — 108	Bilal Mohammed, Qatar — 108	Răzvan Raț, Romania — 108
Stern John, Trinidad & Tobago — 108	Diego Godin, Uruguay — 108	Carlos Bocanegra, United States — 108	Jürgen Klinsmann, West Germany/Germany — 108	Ahmed El-Kass, Egypt — 107	Bobby Moore, England — 107	Ashley Cole, England — 107	Joel Lindpere, Estonia — 107	Patrick Vieira, France — 107
Jalal Hosseini, Iran — 107	Jamal Mubarak, Kuwait — 107	Miroslav Karhan, Slovakia — 107	Aaron Mokoena, South Africa — 107	Henrik Larsson, Sweden — 107	Diego Simeone, Argentina — 106	Rashad Sadygov, Azerbaijan — 106	Ismail Abdul-Latif, Bahrain — 106	Fan Zhiyi, PR China — 106
Hao Haidong, PR China — 106	Frank Lampard, England — 106	Dmitri Kruglov, Estonia — 106	Guillermo Ramirez, Guatemala — 106	Shinji Okazaki, Japan — 106	Francisco Javier Rodriguez, Mexico — 106	Giovanni van Bronckhorst, Netherlands — 106	Nani, Portugal — 106	Muhsin Musabah, United Arab Emirates — 106
Eric Wynalda, United States — 106	Joseph Musonda, Zambia — 106	Ildefons Lima, Andorra — 105	Óscar Sonejee, Andorra — 105	Lúcio, Brazil — 105	Stiliyan Petrov, Bulgaria — 105	Tomáš Rosický, Czech Republic — 105	Bobby Charlton, England — 105	Jonatan Johansson, Finland — 105
Sami Hyypiä, Finland — 105	Imants Bleidelis, Latvia — 105	Franz Burgmeier, Liechtenstein — 105	Khamis Al-Dosari, Saudi Arabia — 105	Radhi Jaïdi, Tunisia — 105	Jürgen Kohler, West Germany / Germany — 105	Josip Šimunic, Croatia — 104	Nader El-Sayed, Egypt — 104	Billy Wright, England — 104
Per Mertesacker, Germany — 104	Gustavo Cabrera, Guatemala — 104	Didier Drogba, Ivory Coast — 104	Makoto Hasebe, Japan — 104	Mihails Zemļinskis, Latvia — 104	Dirk Kuyt, Netherlands — 104	Aaron Hughes, Northern Ireland — 104	Héctor Chumpitaz, Peru — 104	Kim Tae-Young, South Korea — 104
Stéphane Chapuisat, Switzerland — 103	Andreas Herzog, Austria — 103	Faouzi Aaish, Bahrain — 103	Ioannis Okkas, Cyprus — 103	Michael Laudrup, Denmark — 103	Indrek Zelinski, Estonia — 103	Didier Deschamps, France — 103	Mahdi Kareem, Iraq — 103	Máris Verpakovskis, Latvia — 103
Mohammed Al-Jahani, Saudi Arabia — 103	Hwang Sun-Hong, South Korea — 103	Lee Dong-Gook, South Korea — 103	Franz Beckenbauer, West Germany — 103	Mario Yepes, Colombia — 102	Ivica Olic, Croatia — 102	Martin Jørgensen, Denmark — 102	Aleksandr Dmitrijev, Estonia — 102	Joseph Kamwendo, Malawi — 102
Hani Al-Dhabit, Oman — 102	Román Torres, Panama — 102	Michał Żewłakow, Poland — 102	Steve Staunton, Republic of Ireland — 102	Kenny Dalglish, Scotland — 102	Raúl, Spain — 102	Bülent Korkmaz, Turkey — 102	Mohamed Omar, United Arab Emirates — 102	Jozy Altidore, USA — 102
Savo Milošević, Fr Yugoslavia/Serbia & Montenegro/Serbia — 102	Dejan Stankovic, Fr Yugoslavia/Serbia & Montenegro/Serbia — 102	Christopher Katongo, Zambia — 102	Husain Ahmed, Bahrain — 101	Alyaksandr Kulchy, Belarus — 101	Taffarel, Brazil — 101	Gonzalo Jara, Chile — 101	Leonel Álvarez, Colombia — 101	Thomas Häßler, West Germany / Germany — 101
Ulises De La Cruz, Ecuador — 101	Ahmed Shobair, Egypt — 101	József Bozsik, Hungary — 101	Andranik Teymourian, Iran — 101	Joe Brincat, Malta — 101	Phillip Cocu, Netherlands — 101	Robin van Persie, Netherlands — 101	Vincent Enyeama, Nigeria — 101	Joseph Yobo, Nigeria — 101
Thorbjørn Svensson, Norway — 101	Luis Tejada, Peru — 101	László Bölöni, Romania — 101	Vasiliy Berezutskiy, Russia — 101	Oleg Blokhin, Soviet Union — 101	Kasey Keller, United States — 101	Thomas Sørensen, Denmark — 101	Elijah Tana, Zambia — 101	Lakhdar Belloumi, Algeria — 100
Dani Alves, Brazil — 100	Robinho, Brazil — 100	Dario Šimic, Croatia — 100	Hans-Jurgen Dörner, East Germany — 100	Ulf Kirsten, East Germany / Germany — 100	Luis Capurro, Ecuador — 100	Mohamed Aboutrika, Egypt — 100	Ari Hjelm, Finland — 100	Didier Ovono, Gabon — 100
Levan Kobiashvili, Georgia — 100	Angelos Basinas, Greece — 100	Carlos Pavón, Honduras — 100	Rúnar Kristinsson, Iceland — 100	Emad Mohammed, Iraq — 100	Siaka Tiéné, Ivory Coast — 100	Yaya Toure, Ivory Coast — 100	Donovan Rcketts, Jamaica — 100	Fahad Awadh, Kuwait — 100
Igor Stepanovs, Latvia — 100	Goce Sedloski, Macedonia — 100	Henning Berg, Norway — 100	Román Torres, Panama — 100	Roberto Acuña, Paraguay — 100	Denis Caniza, Paraguay — 100	Jorge Soto, Peru — 100	Grzegorz Lato, Poland — 100	Damien Duff, Republic of Ireland — 100
Nazri Bin Nasir, Singapore — 100	Park Ji-Sung, South Korea — 100	Carles Puyol, Spain — 100	Piyapong Pue-on, Thailand — 100	Joe-Max Moore, United States — 100	Earnie Stewart, United States — 100	Tony Meola, United States — 100		

EUROPEAN CUP WINS BY NATION

The recent Champions League successes of Barcelona and Real Madrid have secured Spain's claim to be the most successful European nation. Real Madrid's consecutive triumphs in the European Cup's first five competitions help Spain top the list, although England have had more successful clubs and Italy have had more finalists. In later years, the concentration of financial might in Europe's major leagues has increased the dominance of those nations. The era of the Champions League (beginning in 1992) has seen Spain register 10 wins, followed by Italy (five), England (four) and Germany (three).

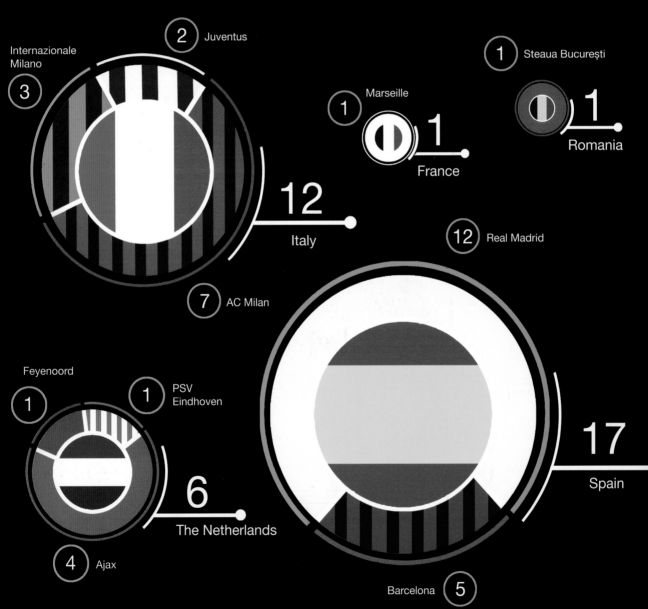

1 Chelsea

1 Aston Viilla

Nottingham
Forest

2

3

Manchester
United

12
England

5 Liverpool

1 Borussia Dortmund

Hamburger SV

1

1 Celtic

1
Scotland

7
Germany

5 Bayern München

Porto 2

4
Portugal

1 Red Star Belgrade

2 Benfica

1
Yugoslavia

Source: Opta (June 2017)

UEFA CHAMPIONS LEAGUE DECADE-BY-DECADE PERFORMANCE

England remains the supplier of the biggest number of clubs to reach the semifinals of the European Cup and Champions League. Ten teams from the English league have made the final four—Manchester United (12 times), Liverpool (9), Chelsea (7), Leeds United (3), Arsenal (2), Nottingham Forest (2), Derby County (1), Manchester City (1), Tottenham Hotspur (1), and Aston Villa (1). France and Germany have provided eight different clubs, while seven Spanish clubs, six different Italian teams, and five Scottish have also made the final hurdle.

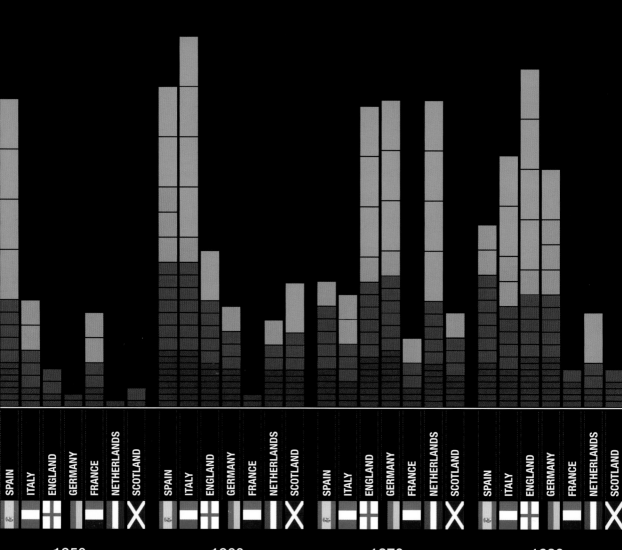

SPAIN	ITALY	ENGLAND	GERMANY	FRANCE	NETHERLANDS	SCOTLAND

1950s

SPAIN	ITALY	ENGLAND	GERMANY	FRANCE	NETHERLANDS	SCOTLAND

1960s

SPAIN	ITALY	ENGLAND	GERMANY	FRANCE	NETHERLANDS	SCOTLAND

1970s

SPAIN	ITALY	ENGLAND	GERMANY	FRANCE	NETHERLANDS	SCOTLAND

1980s

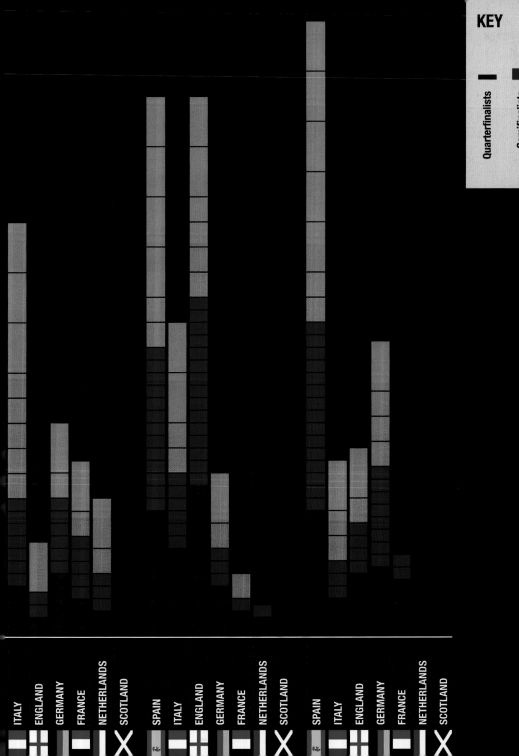

Source: Opta / June 201?

EUROPEAN CUP & CHAMPIONS LEAGUE RECORD GOALSCORERS

Real Madrid strikers have dominated the table of goalscorers in the Champions League and its forerunner, the European Cup. Legendary striker Alfredo di Stéfano led the table for many years before he was succeeded by Raúl in 2007. Barcelona's Lionel Messi managed to take the record in November 2014, only to be equaled by Cristiano Ronaldo a day later. The great rivals continue to spar for the crown, the Real striker scoring an astonishing nine goals in the 2017 knockout stages and notching his hundredth goal with a quarterfinal hat trick against Bayern München.

15 Manchester United
90 Real Madrid

1. Cristiano Ronaldo
105 Total goals scored

94 Barcelona

2. Lionel Messi
94 Total goals scored

5 Schalke
66 Real Madrid

3. Raúl
71 Total goals scored

13 Real Madrid 8 PSV
35 Manchester United

4. Ruud van Nistelrooy
56 Total goals scored

12 Lyon
39 Real Madrid

5. Karim Benzema
51 Total goals scored

8 Barcelona 7 Monaco
35 Arsenal

6. Thierry Henry
50 Total goals scored

49 Real Madrid

7. Alfredo Di Stéfano
49 Total goals scored

15 Dynamo Kiev 4 Chelsea
29 AC Milan

8. Andriy Shevchenko
48 Total goals scored

9 AC Milan 6 Inter
20 Paris Saint-Germain

6 Ajax

4 Barcelona
3 Juventus

9. Zlatan Ibrahimović
48 Total goals scored

EUROPEAN CUP & CHAMPIONS LEAGUE RECORD GOALSCORERS

42 Juventus

13. Alessandro Del Piero

42 Total goals scored

17 Borussia Dortmund

23 Bayern München

14. Robert Lewandowski

40 Total goals scored

39 Bayern München

15. Thomas Müller

39 Total goals scored

1 Honvéd

35 Real Madrid

16. Ferenc Puskás

36 Total goals scored

34 Bayern München

17. Gerd Müller

34 Total goals scored

9 Monaco

6 Valencia

17 Real Madrid

1 Liverpoo

18. Fernando Morientes

33 Total goals scored

5 Real Madrid

25 AC Milan

19. Kaká

30 Total Goals Scored

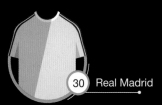

30 Real Madrid

19. Paco Gento

30 Total Goals Scored

30 Manchester United

19. Wayne Rooney

30 Total Goals Scored

10 Inter

3 Chelsea

16 Barcelona

1 Mallorca

19. Samuel Eto'o

30 Total goals scored

3 PSV

2 Chelsea

23 Bayern München

1 Real Madrid

23. Arjen Robben

29 Total goals scored

4 Monaco

25 Juventus

23. David Trezeguet

29 Total goals scored

23. Roy Makaay

12 Deportivo de La Coruña
17 Bayern München

29 Total goals scored

23. Patrick Kluivert

9 Ajax
20 Barcelona

29 Total goals scored

28 Manchester United

27. Ryan Giggs

28 Total goals scored

7 Milan
2 Bayern München
19 Marseille

27. Jean-Pierre Papin

28 Total goals scored

3 Olympiacos
2 AC Milan
22 Barcelona

29. Rivaldo

27 Total goals scored

5 Atlético de Madrid
22 Manchester City

29. Sergio Agüero

27 Total goals scored

"If he kicked the ball once, he scored two goals."

Zoltán Czibor on his International teammate Ferenc Puskás, scorer of a first-half

hat trick for Real Madrid in the 1962 UEFA European Cup Final

Source: Opta (June 2017)

Legendary Players

21 Liverpool
Steven Gerrard

18 Ajax
Johan Cruyff

17 Roma
Francesco Totti

17 Juventus
Michel Platini

9 Manchester United
George Best

UEFA CUP/EUROPA LEAGUE RECORDS BY NATION

The Europa League is UEFA's tournament for the continent's top teams who have failed to qualify for the Champions League, who have won their domestic cup or who have been eliminated in the early stages of the Champions League. It originated as the UEFA Cup in 1971–72 but, since 2009–10, the competition has been known as the UEFA Europa League. It now invites 177 different teams from 54 nations who enter the tournament at different stages. A team reaching the final from the first qualifying round would play a total of 23 matches. Atlético Madrid (2012) and Sevilla (2014) have both won the competition having began their journey in the third qualifying round.

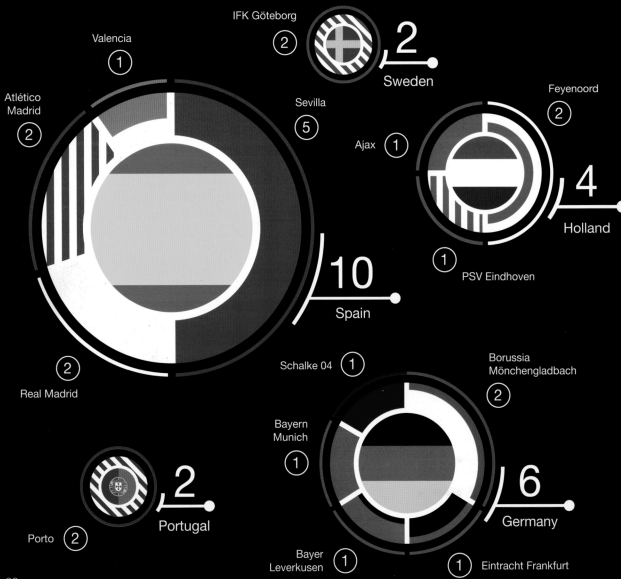

IFK Göteborg **2**

2 Sweden

Valencia **1**

Atlético Madrid **2**

Sevilla **5**

Ajax **1**

Feyenoord **2**

4 Holland

10 Spain

PSV Eindhoven **1**

Real Madrid **2**

Schalke 04 **1**

Borussia Mönchengladbach **2**

Bayern Munich **1**

6 Germany

Porto **2**

2 Portugal

Bayer Leverkusen **1**

1 Eintracht Frankfurt

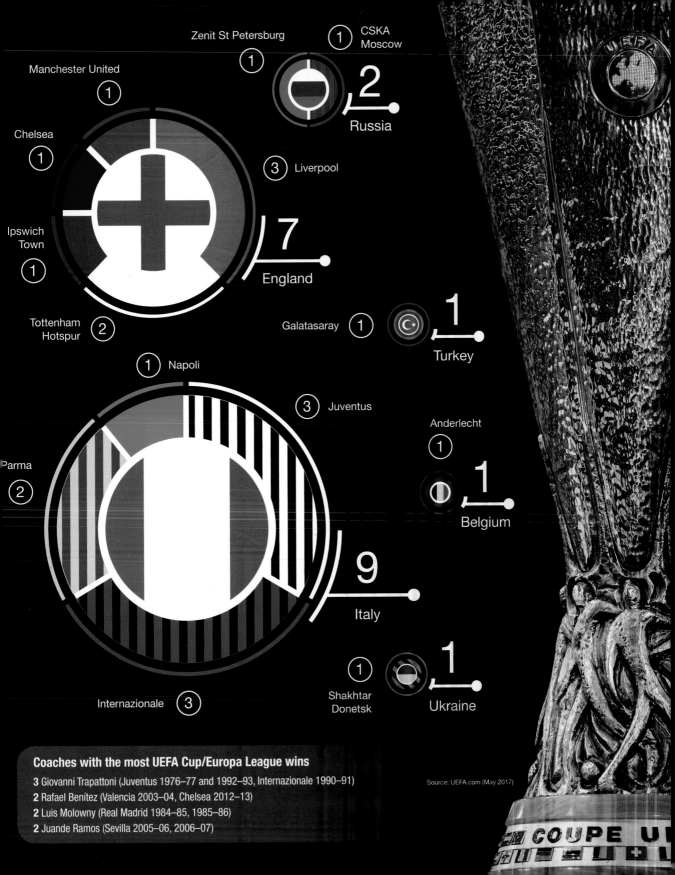

Zenit St Petersburg ① ① CSKA Moscow

Manchester United ①

2 Russia

Chelsea ①

③ Liverpool

Ipswich Town ①

7 England

Tottenham Hotspur ②

Galatasaray ① **1** Turkey

① Napoli

③ Juventus

Anderlecht ①

Parma ②

1 Belgium

9 Italy

① Shakhtar Donetsk **1** Ukraine

Internazionale ③

Coaches with the most UEFA Cup/Europa League wins
3 Giovanni Trapattoni (Juventus 1976–77 and 1992–93, Internazionale 1990–91)
2 Rafael Benítez (Valencia 2003–04, Chelsea 2012–13)
2 Luis Molowny (Real Madrid 1984–85, 1985–86)
2 Juande Ramos (Sevilla 2005–06, 2006–07)

Source: UEFA.com (May 2017)

COUPE U

MOST SUCCESSFUL EUROPEAN MANAGERS SINCE 1960

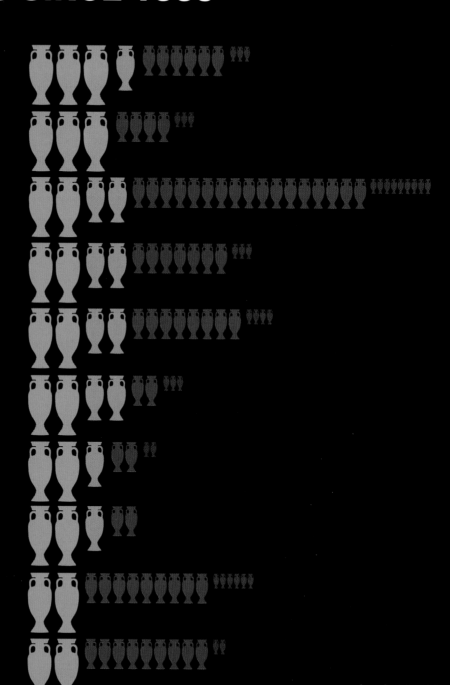

1	Bob Paisley	
2	Carlo Ancelotti	
3	Alex Ferguson	
4	Helenio Herrera	
5	José Mourinho	
6	Nereo Rocco	
7	José Villalonga	
8	Luis Carniglia	
9	Ottmar Hitzfeld	
10	Miguel Muñoz	

Source: Google (June 2017)
Super cups and careers outside Europe not included.

No matter how wealthy the club, it is a magnificent feat to guide a club to a league title. It is something else to take them to European success. Repeating the achievement takes a coach to legendary status. Separating the greatest from the great, however, is a tougher call. How do we rank Bob Paisley's European and League titles against Helenio Herrera's record? And, how much greater an achievement are the against-the-odds European triumphs of José Mourinho's Porto or Jock Stein's Celtic?

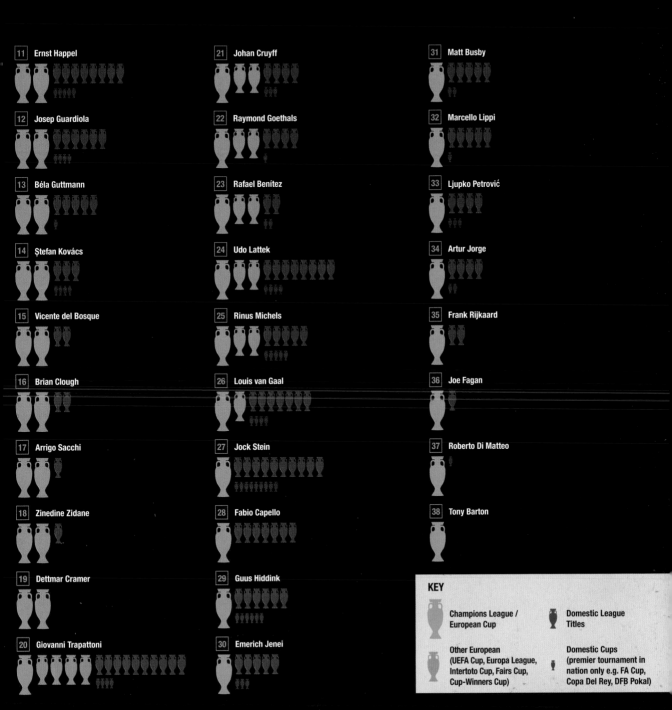

11 Ernst Happel

12 Josep Guardiola

13 Béla Guttmann

14 Ştefan Kovács

15 Vicente del Bosque

16 Brian Clough

17 Arrigo Sacchi

18 Zinedine Zidane

19 Dettmar Cramer

20 Giovanni Trapattoni

21 Johan Cruyff

22 Raymond Goethals

23 Rafael Benítez

24 Udo Lattek

25 Rinus Michels

26 Louis van Gaal

27 Jock Stein

28 Fabio Capello

29 Guus Hiddink

30 Emerich Jenei

31 Matt Busby

32 Marcello Lippi

33 Ljupko Petrović

34 Artur Jorge

35 Frank Rijkaard

36 Joe Fagan

37 Roberto Di Matteo

38 Tony Barton

KEY

Champions League / European Cup

Domestic League Titles

Other European (UEFA Cup, Europa League, Intertoto Cup, Fairs Cup, Cup-Winners Cup)

Domestic Cups (premier tournament in nation only e.g. FA Cup, Copa Del Rey, DFB Pokal)

COPA LIBERTADORES WINS BY NATION

Copa Libertadores de América is the most prestigious club tournament in South America. It is broadcast in over 130 countries and watched by more than a billion viewers. Played annually from February through qualifying, group stages and then a home and away knock-out stage, the tournament is now contested by 38 teams from 11 countries (including Mexican teams since 2000). At least three clubs from each country compete in the tournament with Argentina and Brazil each entitled to enter five teams.

   The 2016 final between Colombia's Atletico Nacional and Independiente del Valle of Ecuador was the first between teams from countries on South America's Pacific coast and also the first in 25 years not to feature Argentinian or Brazilian sides.

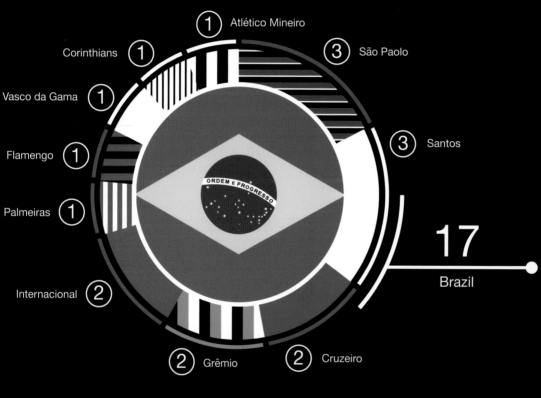

① Atlético Mineiro
① Corinthians
③ São Paolo
① Vasco da Gama
③ Santos
① Flamengo
① Palmeiras
17 Brazil
② Internacional
② Grêmio
② Cruzeiro

Colo-Colo
① **1** Chile

Nacional
③
⑤ Peñarol
8 Uruguay

① Once Caldas

② Atlético Nacional

3
Colombia

LDU Quito
① ⟶ **1**
Ecuador

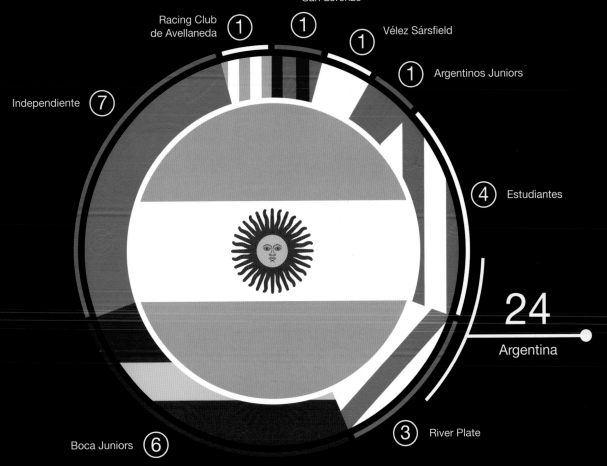

San Lorenzo

Racing Club de Avellaneda ①

①

① Vélez Sársfield

① Argentinos Juniors

Independiente ⑦

④ Estudiantes

24
Argentina

Boca Juniors ⑥

③ River Plate

Olimpia
③

3
Paraguay

Source: Opta (July 2016)

SOCCER RIVALRIES: PART 1

History, tradition, passion, and pride—these are the elements that come to the fore when great soccer rivals collide. Every nation has its rival teams. Some, such as Tottenham Hotspur and Arsenal, are born from geographical proximity—they're based four miles apart. France's Olympique de Marseille and Paris Saint-Germain may reside further apart, but the rivalry between the North and South, and the country's two biggest cities, makes the "Le Classique" derby just as bitterly fought.

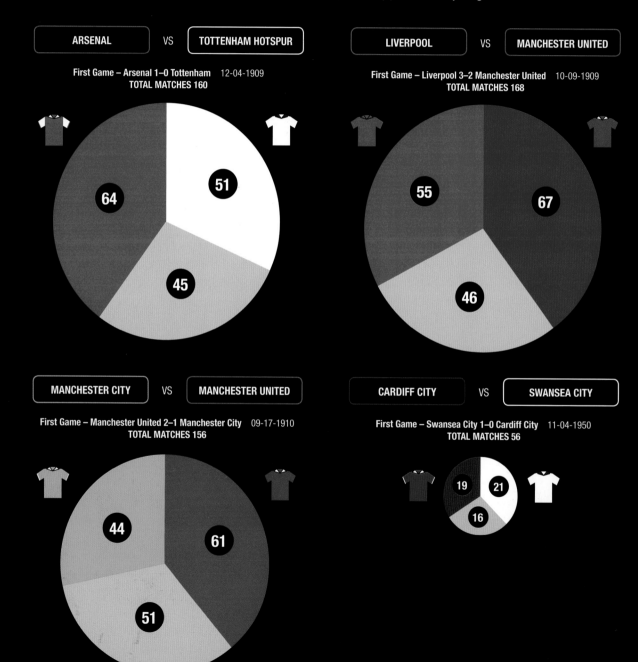

ARSENAL VS **TOTTENHAM HOTSPUR**

First Game – Arsenal 1–0 Tottenham   12-04-1909
TOTAL MATCHES 160

64 / 51 / 45

LIVERPOOL VS **MANCHESTER UNITED**

First Game – Liverpool 3–2 Manchester United   10-09-1909
TOTAL MATCHES 168

55 / 67 / 46

MANCHESTER CITY VS **MANCHESTER UNITED**

First Game – Manchester United 2–1 Manchester City   09-17-1910
TOTAL MATCHES 156

44 / 61 / 51

CARDIFF CITY VS **SWANSEA CITY**

First Game – Swansea City 1–0 Cardiff City   11-04-1950
TOTAL MATCHES 56

19 / 21 / 16

HAMBURGER SV VS BAYERN MÜNCHEN

First Game – Hamburger SV 0–4 Bayern München   10-20-1965
TOTAL MATCHES 104

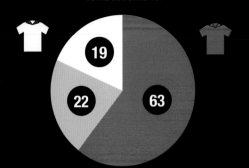

BAYERN MÜNCHEN VS BORUSSIA DORTMUND

First Game – Borussia Dortmund 2–0 Bayern München   10-16-1965
TOTAL MATCHES 96

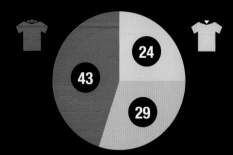

OLYMPIQUE DE MARSEILLE VS SAINT-ÉTIENNE

First Game – Saint-Étienne 1–0 Olympique de Marseille   11-06-1938
TOTAL MATCHES 104

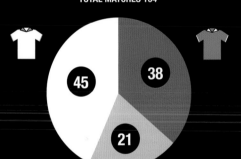

OLYMPIQUE LYONNAIS VS OLYMPIQUE DE MARSEILLE

First Game – Olympique Lyonnais 2–2 Olympique de Marseille   11-11-1951
TOTAL MATCHES 94

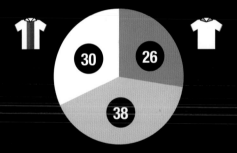

OLYMPIQUE DE MARSEILLE VS PARIS SAINT-GERMAIN

First Game – Olympique de Marseille 4–2 Paris Saint-Germain   12-12-1971
TOTAL MATCHES 76

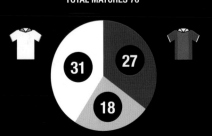

" On derby day in Manchester the city is cut in two. The Blues and the Reds invade the street and if your team wins the city belongs to you. "

Eric Cantona, Manchester United

Source: Opta (May 2017)

SOCCER RIVALRIES: PART 2

"The Derby" is an unofficial competition recognized across the soccer world. It signifies a two-match battle between two rival teams each season, where the victorious side wins hometown pride and temporary bragging rights over the other. Italy plays host to some of the sport's more heated rivalries, the oldest being the *Derby della Lanterna* in which Genoa duel Sampdoria, while *Derby d'Italia* brings together Internazionale Milano and Juventus. Meanwhile, in Spain's La Liga, the dominance of powerhouses Barcelona and Real Madrid has fired *El Clásico*, a rivalry constantly simmering through decades of interconnected history, politics, and geography.

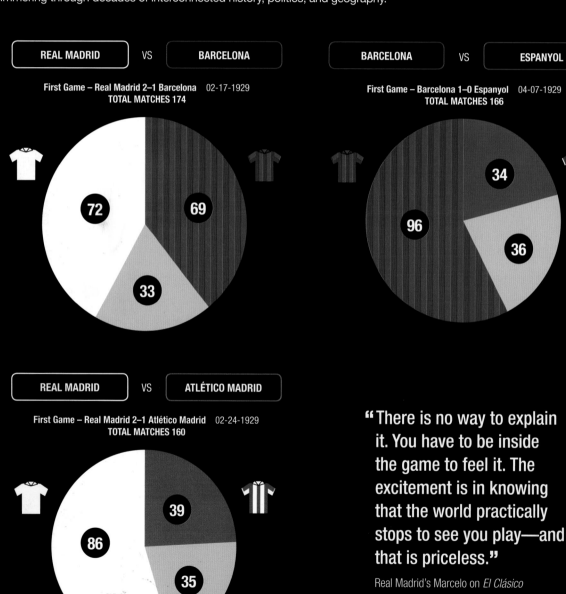

| REAL MADRID | VS | BARCELONA |

First Game – Real Madrid 2–1 Barcelona   02-17-1929
TOTAL MATCHES 174

72   69   33

| BARCELONA | VS | ESPANYOL |

First Game – Barcelona 1–0 Espanyol   04-07-1929
TOTAL MATCHES 166

34   96   36

| REAL MADRID | VS | ATLÉTICO MADRID |

First Game – Real Madrid 2–1 Atlético Madrid   02-24-1929
TOTAL MATCHES 160

86   39   35

" There is no way to explain it. You have to be inside the game to feel it. The excitement is in knowing that the world practically stops to see you play—and that is priceless."

Real Madrid's Marcelo on *El Clásico*

INTERNAZIONALE MILANO	VS	JUVENTUS

First Game – Internazionale Milano 2–1 Juventus   02-02-1930
TOTAL MATCHES 168

INTERNAZIONALE MILANO	VS	AC MILAN

First Game – Internazionale Milano 2–1 AC Milan   11-10-1929
TOTAL MATCHES 166

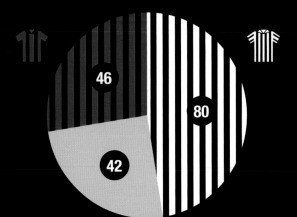

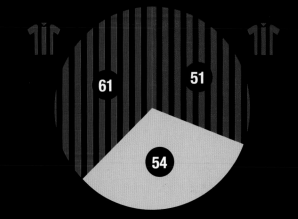

SS LAZIO	VS	AS ROMA

First Game – AS Roma 1–0 SS Lazio   12-08-1929
TOTAL MATCHES 146

JUVENTUS	VS	TORINO FC

First Game – Juventus 0–0 Torino FC   11-24-1929
TOTAL MATCHES 144

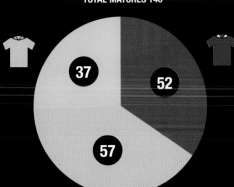

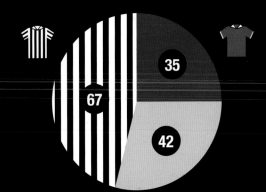

GENOA	VS	UC SAMPDORIA

First Game – Genoa 2–1 UC Sampdoria   10-06-1935
TOTAL MATCHES 68

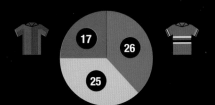

Source: Opta (May 2017)

SOCCER RIVALRIES: PART 3

Soccer fans know that it's the tough and tense matches between fierce rivals that really heighten their emotions during a season. AFC Ajax vs Feyenoord, for example, has become the most ferocious game in the Netherlands as the capital's city slickers do battle with the working-class port laborers. In Turkey's capital Istanbul, neighbors Fenerbahçe S.K. and Galatasaray S.K. continue a rivalry more than 100 years old. Across the Atlantic Ocean, it is New York City FC and the New York Red Bulls that have developed a more recent mutual antagonism after just a handful of matches.

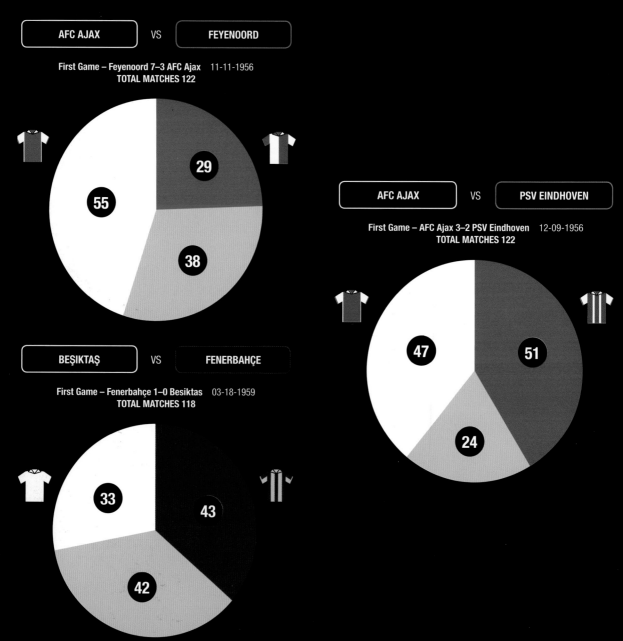

AFC AJAX VS **FEYENOORD**

First Game – Feyenoord 7–3 AFC Ajax   11-11-1956
TOTAL MATCHES 122

55   29   38

AFC AJAX VS **PSV EINDHOVEN**

First Game – AFC Ajax 3–2 PSV Eindhoven   12-09-1956
TOTAL MATCHES 122

47   51   24

BEŞİKTAŞ VS **FENERBAHÇE**

First Game – Fenerbahçe 1–0 Besiktas   03-18-1959
TOTAL MATCHES 118

33   43   42

It's nowhere near as steeped in history as El Clasico or the Old Firm Derby, but New York is growing its own bitterly fought rivalry. The Hudson River Derby pitches the New York Red Bulls, who play in NJ, against their neighbors NYCFC, who set up home in Yankee Stadium in the Bronx. New York Red Bulls had been established for nearly 20 years (with sworn enemies in Washington's DC United) before neighbors NYCFC arrived in 2015. They dealt out four beatings before the newcomers finally tasted victory.

| FENERBAHÇE | VS | GALATASARAY |

First Game – Fenerbahçe 1–0 Galatasaray 12-17-1959
TOTAL MATCHES 120

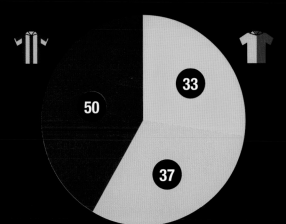

| BEŞİKTAŞ | VS | GALATASARAY |

First Game – Besiktas 1–0 Galatasaray 12-02-1959
TOTAL MATCHES 118

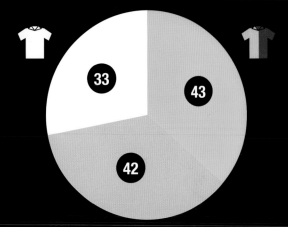

| LA GALAXY | VS | SAN JOSE EARTHQUAKES |

First Game – LA Galaxy 2–0 San Jose Earthquakes 04-03-2008
TOTAL MATCHES 27

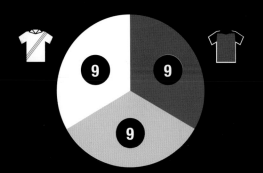

| NEW YORK CITY FC | VS | NEW YORK RED BULLS |

First Game – New York Red Bulls 2–1 New York City FC 05-10-2015
TOTAL MATCHES 7

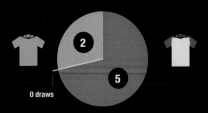

0 draws

Source: Opta (May 2017)

PREMIER LEAGUE TITLE WINNERS

The Premier League was formed in 1992. It is far and away the wealthiest league, most of the clubs featuring among the top-50 richest soccer brands in the world. Since its formation, the Premier League has been contested by 47 clubs, and games are broadcast in more than 200 countries. For many years the title was fought over by the "big four"—Manchester United, Arsenal, Chelsea, and Liverpool—but Manchester City and, more recently, Tottenham Hotspur have joined them. Even more surprising, then, was Leicester City's triumph against all odds in 2016.

Note: For the first three seasons of its existence, the Premier League comprised 22 teams rather than 20, as became the norm.

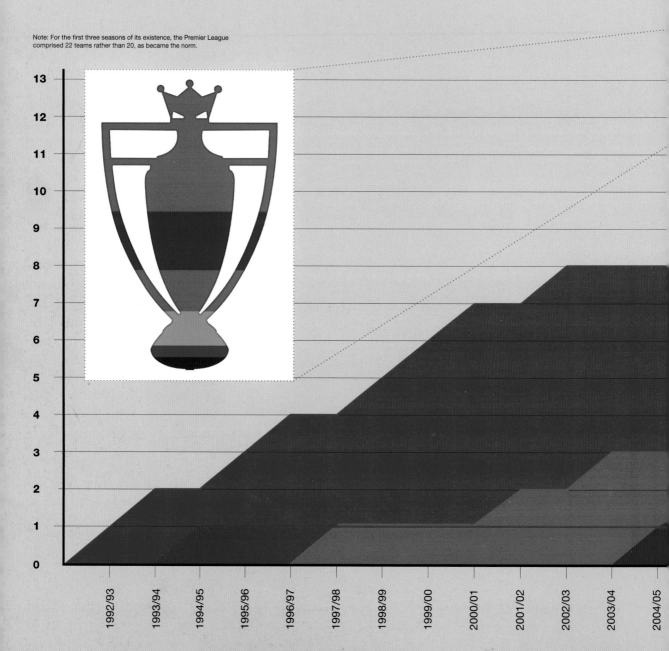

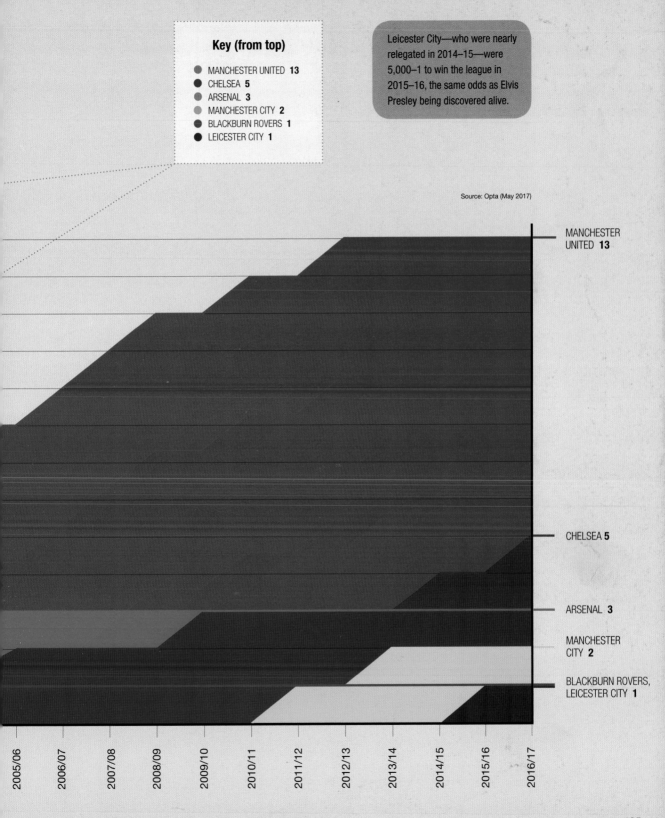

Key (from top)

- MANCHESTER UNITED **13**
- CHELSEA **5**
- ARSENAL **3**
- MANCHESTER CITY **2**
- BLACKBURN ROVERS **1**
- LEICESTER CITY **1**

Leicester City—who were nearly relegated in 2014–15—were 5,000–1 to win the league in 2015–16, the same odds as Elvis Presley being discovered alive.

Source: Opta (May 2017)

MANCHESTER UNITED **13**

CHELSEA **5**

ARSENAL **3**

MANCHESTER CITY **2**

BLACKBURN ROVERS, LEICESTER CITY **1**

2005/06 | 2006/07 | 2007/08 | 2008/09 | 2009/10 | 2010/11 | 2011/12 | 2012/13 | 2013/14 | 2014/15 | 2015/16 | 2016/17

PREMIER LEAGUE EVER-PRESENTS

The relegation of Aston Villa to the Championship in 2016 reduced the survivors from the founding season of the Premier League to six. Of the 47 teams that have played in the top league, all but these six have spent time in lower leagues—Coventry City, Swindon Town, Blackpool, Portsmouth, and Bradford City have all subsequently fallen as far as the fourth tier. Brighton & Hove Albion and Huddersfield Town's 2017 promotion to the top flight will make them the 48th and 49th clubs to play in the Premier League.

Source: Opta (May 2017)

LEAGUE POSITION AT END OF SEASON

YEAR (END OF SEASON)

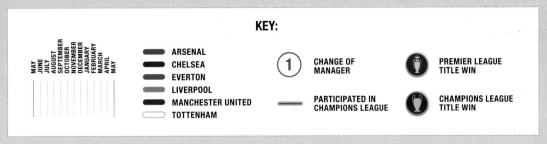

KEY:

MAY
JUNE
JULY
AUGUST
SEPTEMBER
OCTOBER
NOVEMBER
DECEMBER
JANUARY
FEBRUARY
MARCH
APRIL
MAY

ARSENAL
CHELSEA
EVERTON
LIVERPOOL
MANCHESTER UNITED
TOTTENHAM

(1) CHANGE OF MANAGER

PARTICIPATED IN CHAMPIONS LEAGUE

PREMIER LEAGUE TITLE WIN

CHAMPIONS LEAGUE TITLE WIN

Source: Opta May 2017

Note: For the first three seasons of its existence, the Premier League comprised 22 teams rather than 20, as became the established contingent.

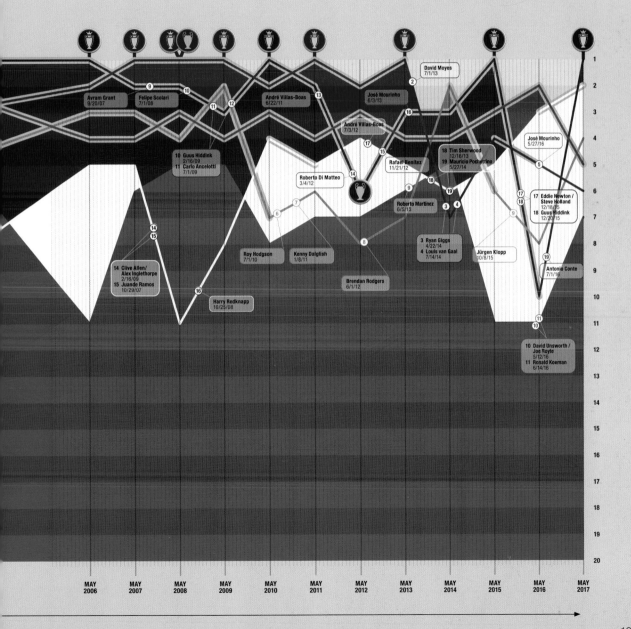

Avram Grant
9/20/07

Felipe Scolari
7/1/08

André Villas-Boas
6/22/11

José Mourinho
6/3/13

David Moyes
7/1/13

André Villas-Boas
7/3/12

José Mourinho
5/27/16

10 Guus Hiddink
2/16/09
11 Carlo Ancelotti
7/1/09

Rafael Benítez
11/21/12

18 Tim Sherwood
12/16/13
19 Mauricio Pochettino
5/27/14

Roberto Di Matteo
3/4/12

17 Eddie Newton /
Steve Holland
12/18/15
18 Guus Hiddink
12/20/15

Roberto Martinez
6/5/13

14 Clive Allen/
Alex Inglethorpe
15 Juande Ramos
10/29/07

Roy Hodgson
7/1/10

Kenny Dalglish
1/8/11

3 Ryan Giggs
4/22/14
4 Louis van Gaal
7/14/14

Jürgen Klopp
10/8/15

Antonio Conte
7/1/16

Harry Redknapp
10/25/08

Brendan Rodgers
6/1/12

10 David Unsworth /
Joe Royle
5/12/16
11 Ronald Koeman
6/14/16

MAY 2006
MAY 2007
MAY 2008
MAY 2009
MAY 2010
MAY 2011
MAY 2012
MAY 2013
MAY 2014
MAY 2015
MAY 2016
MAY 2017

PREMIER LEAGUE GAME WINS PER CLUB

The Premier League thrives on the ability of any of its teams to beat another. Although the elite teams generally dominate the top of the table, they cannot be sure of winning every game. The league winners collect around 27 wins in a season, Chelsea holding the record with 30 wins (2016–17). Consecutive runs of eight or more victories are rare, Arsenal setting the bar at 14 in 2002.

Source: Opta (May 2017)

- IPSWICH TOWN **57**
- NOTTINGHAM FOREST **60**
- DERBY COUNTY **68**
- BIRMINGHAM CITY **73**
- SWANSEA CITY **74**
- PORTSMOUTH **79**
- QUEENS PARK RANGERS **81**
- WIGAN ATHLETIC **85**
- CRYSTAL PALACE **86**
- NORWICH CITY **89**
- CHARLTON ATHLETIC **93**
- WIMBLEDON **99**
- COVENTRY CITY **99**
- SHEFFIELD WEDNESDAY **101**
- WEST BROMWICH ALBION **106**
- STOKE CITY **109**
- LEICESTER CITY **130**
- BOLTON WANDERERS **149**
- FULHAM **150**
- SUNDERLAND **138**
- MIDDLESBROUGH **165**
- LEEDS UNITED **189**
- SOUTHAMPTON **222**
- BLACKBURN ROVERS **262**
- WEST HAM UNITED **265**
- ASTON VILLA **316**

Under 50 Wins

HULL CITY **41**	OLDHAM ATHLETIC **22**
WATFORD **34**	BRADFORD CITY **14**
WOLVERHAMPTON WANDERERS **32**	BLACKPOOL **10**
READING **32**	BARNSLEY **10**
SHEFFIELD UNITED **32**	CARDIFF CITY **7**
BURNLEY **26**	SWINDON TOWN **5**
BOURNEMOUTH **23**	

NEWCASTLE UNITED **322**
MANCHESTER CITY **327**
EVERTON **349**
TOTTENHAM HOTSPUR **400**
LIVERPOOL **478**
CHELSEA **516**
ARSENAL **525**
MANCHESTER UNITED **604**

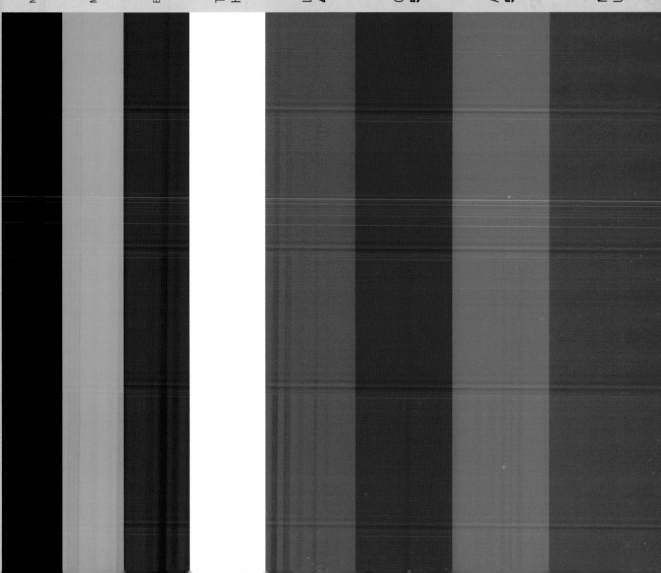

PREMIER LEAGUE GOALS PER CLUB

The elite list of Premier League goalscorers changes very slowly—very few of the 100 goal club are still playing. But there are some exceptions. Jermain Defoe moved into the top 10 with his Indian summer at Sunderland, Peter Crouch hit his 100th goal in February 2017 and Sergio Agüero surged up the list with 44 goals in two seasons (2015–16 to 2016–17). Who might be next to join them? The smart money is on Romelu Lukaku (85), Harry Kane (78), or Christian Benteke (66).

> " Alan Shearer is the greatest English center-forward there has ever been without a shadow of a doubt; he's a very, very special player. He makes average balls into great balls. He's the scorer of every type of goal going."
>
> Graeme Souness

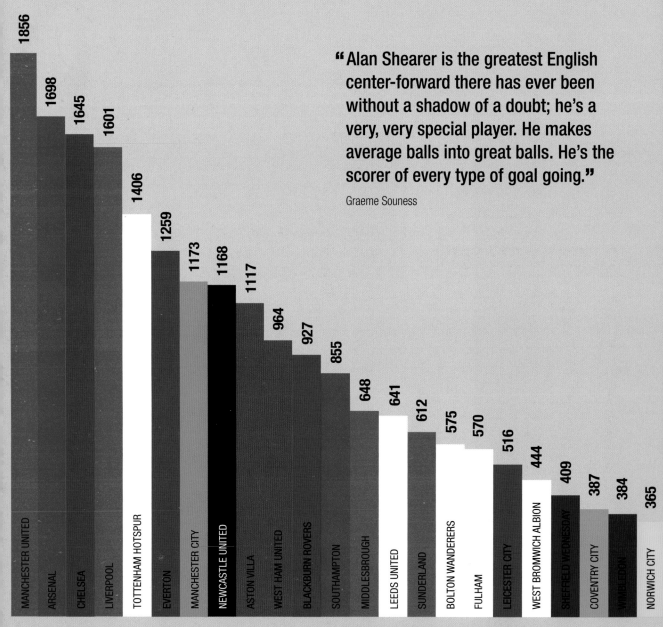

Club	Goals
MANCHESTER UNITED	1856
ARSENAL	1698
CHELSEA	1645
LIVERPOOL	1601
TOTTENHAM HOTSPUR	1406
EVERTON	1259
MANCHESTER CITY	1173
NEWCASTLE UNITED	1168
ASTON VILLA	1117
WEST HAM UNITED	964
BLACKBURN ROVERS	927
SOUTHAMPTON	855
MIDDLESBROUGH	648
LEEDS UNITED	641
SUNDERLAND	612
BOLTON WANDERERS	575
FULHAM	570
LEICESTER CITY	516
WEST BROMWICH ALBION	444
SHEFFIELD WEDNESDAY	409
COVENTRY CITY	387
WIMBLEDON	384
NORWICH CITY	365

ALAN SHEARER 260
THIERRY HENRY 175
LES FERDINAND 149
ROBBIE KEANE 126
STEVEN GERRARD 120
RYAN GIGGS 109
PETER CROUCH 103
RUUD VAN NISTELROOY 95
OLE GUNNAR SOLSKJAER 91
FERNANDO TORRES 85
CRISTIANO RONALDO 84
GARY SPEED 80

WAYNE ROONEY 198
ROBBIE FOWLER 163
TEDDY SHERINGHAM 146
NICOLAS ANELKA 125
IAN WRIGHT 113
PAUL SCHOLES 107
MATTHEW LE TISSIER 100
DIMITAR BERBATOV 94
JAMES BEATTIE 91
LOUIS SAHA 85
KEVIN CAMPBELL 83
TONY COTTEE 78

ANDREW COLE 187
JERMAIN DEFOE 158
ROBIN VAN PERSIE 144
DWIGHT YORKE 123
DION DUBLIN 111
DARREN BENT 106
EMMANUEL ADEBAYOR 97
MARK VIDUKA 92
KEVIN DAVIES 88
ROMELU LUKAKU 85
CHRIS SUTTON 83
HARRY KANE 78

FRANK LAMPARD 177
MICHAEL OWEN 150
JIMMY FLOYD HASSELBAINK 127
SERGIO AGÜERO 122
EMILE HESKEY 110
DIDIER DROGBA 104
YAKUBU 95
KEVIN PHILLIPS 92
DENNIS BERGKAMP 87
CARLOS TEVEZ 84
CRAIG BELLAMY 81
GABRIEL AGBONLAHOR 74

Source: Opta (May 2017)
Color relates to the team the player scored the highest number of goals for.

STOKE CITY 363
CHARLTON ATHLETIC 342
QUEENS PARK RANGERS 339
WIGAN ATHLETIC 316
PORTSMOUTH 292
BIRMINGHAM CITY 273
DERBY COUNTY 271
NOTTINGHAM FOREST 229
IPSWICH TOWN 219
HULL CITY 181
WOLVERHAMPTON WANDERERS 156
WATFORD 144
READING 136
SHEFFIELD UNITED 128
BURNLEY 109
OLDHAM ATHLETIC 105
BOURNEMOUTH 100
BRADFORD CITY 68
BLACKPOOL 55
SWINDON TOWN 47
BARNSLEY 37
CARDIFF CITY 32

111

PREMIER LEAGUE PLAYER APPEARANCES

With only 38 Premier League games played a season, a player needs a long career at the highest level to get anywhere near this list. It helps, of course, to start young (you'll need at least 12 seasons in the first team), stay injury-free and play into your 30s. Even then, it's tough. The youngest to play was Fulham's Matthew Brigg, 16, and 65 days when he made his debut in 2007, he amassed a total of 30 appearances. No wonder only around 100 players have notched up over 300 appearances.

KEY:

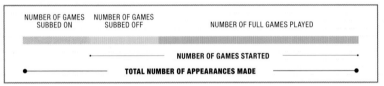

NUMBER OF GAMES SUBBED ON | NUMBER OF GAMES SUBBED OFF | NUMBER OF FULL GAMES PLAYED

NUMBER OF GAMES STARTED

TOTAL NUMBER OF APPEARANCES MADE

* Active up to and including season 2016–17

Source: Opta (May 2017)

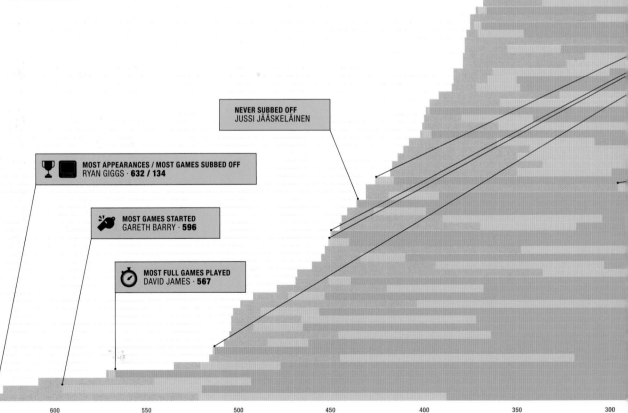

NEVER SUBBED OFF
JUSSI JÄÄSKELÄINEN

MOST APPEARANCES / MOST GAMES SUBBED OFF
RYAN GIGGS · 632 / 134

MOST GAMES STARTED
GARETH BARRY · 596

MOST FULL GAMES PLAYED
DAVID JAMES · 567

600   550   500   450   400   350   300

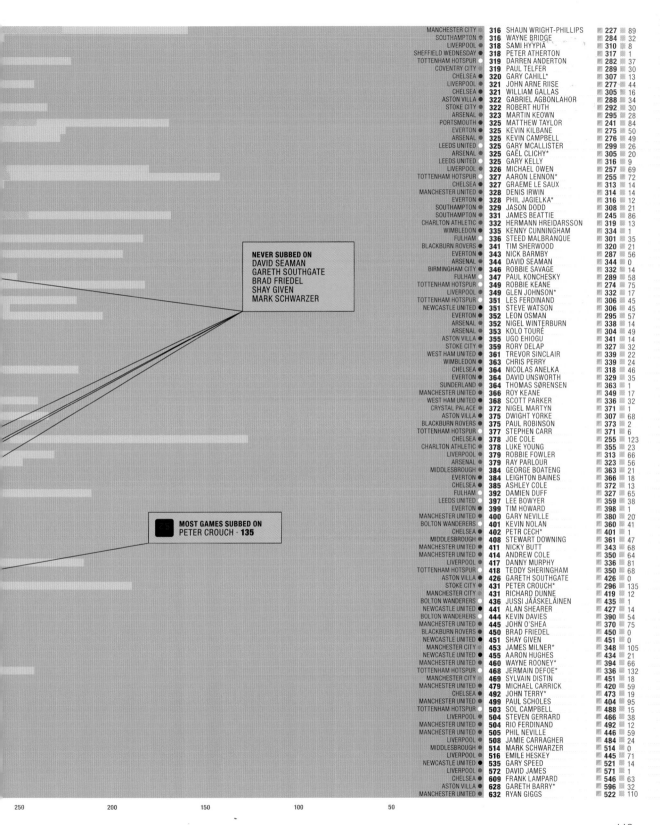

Club	Games	Player	Started	Subbed
MANCHESTER CITY	316	SHAUN WRIGHT-PHILLIPS	227	89
SOUTHAMPTON	316	WAYNE BRIDGE	284	32
LIVERPOOL	318	SAMI HYYPIÄ	310	8
SHEFFIELD WEDNESDAY	318	PETER ATHERTON	317	1
TOTTENHAM HOTSPUR	319	DARREN ANDERTON	282	37
COVENTRY CITY	319	PAUL TELFER	289	30
CHELSEA	320	GARY CAHILL*	307	13
LIVERPOOL	321	JOHN ARNE RIISE	277	44
CHELSEA	321	WILLIAM GALLAS	305	16
ASTON VILLA	322	GABRIEL AGBONLAHOR	288	34
STOKE CITY	322	ROBERT HUTH	292	30
ARSENAL	323	MARTIN KEOWN	295	28
PORTSMOUTH	325	MATTHEW TAYLOR	241	84
EVERTON	325	KEVIN KILBANE	275	50
ARSENAL	325	KEVIN CAMPBELL	276	49
LEEDS UNITED	325	GARY MCALLISTER	299	26
ARSENAL	325	GAËL CLICHY*	305	20
LEEDS UNITED	325	GARY KELLY	316	9
LIVERPOOL	326	MICHAEL OWEN	257	69
CHELSEA	327	GRAEME LE SAUX	313	14
TOTTENHAM HOTSPUR	327	AARON LENNON*	255	72
MANCHESTER UNITED	328	DENIS IRWIN	314	14
EVERTON	328	PHIL JAGIELKA*	316	12
SOUTHAMPTON	329	JASON DODD	308	21
SOUTHAMPTON	331	JAMES BEATTIE	245	86
CHARLTON ATHLETIC	332	HERMANN HREIDARSSON	319	13
WIMBLEDON	335	KENNY CUNNINGHAM	334	1
FULHAM	336	STEED MALBRANQUE	301	35
BLACKBURN ROVERS	341	TIM SHERWOOD	320	21
EVERTON	343	NICK BARMBY	287	56
ARSENAL	344	DAVID SEAMAN	344	0
BIRMINGHAM CITY	346	ROBBIE SAVAGE	332	14
FULHAM	347	PAUL KONCHESKY	289	58
TOTTENHAM HOTSPUR	349	ROBBIE KEANE	274	75
LIVERPOOL	349	GLEN JOHNSON*	332	17
TOTTENHAM HOTSPUR	351	LES FERDINAND	306	45
NEWCASTLE UNITED	351	STEVE WATSON	306	45
EVERTON	352	LEON OSMAN	295	57
ARSENAL	352	NIGEL WINTERBURN	338	14
ARSENAL	353	KOLO TOURÉ	304	49
ASTON VILLA	355	UGO EHIOGU	341	14
STOKE CITY	359	RORY DELAP	327	32
WEST HAM UNITED	361	TREVOR SINCLAIR	339	22
WIMBLEDON	363	CHRIS PERRY	339	24
CHELSEA	364	NICOLAS ANELKA	318	46
EVERTON	364	DAVID UNSWORTH	329	35
SUNDERLAND	364	THOMAS SØRENSEN	363	1
MANCHESTER UNITED	366	ROY KEANE	349	17
WEST HAM UNITED	368	SCOTT PARKER	336	32
CRYSTAL PALACE	372	NIGEL MARTYN	371	1
ASTON VILLA	375	DWIGHT YORKE	307	68
BLACKBURN ROVERS	375	PAUL ROBINSON	373	2
TOTTENHAM HOTSPUR	377	STEPHEN CARR	371	6
CHELSEA	378	JOE COLE	255	123
CHARLTON ATHLETIC	378	LUKE YOUNG	355	23
LIVERPOOL	379	ROBBIE FOWLER	313	66
ARSENAL	379	RAY PARLOUR	323	56
MIDDLESBROUGH	384	GEORGE BOATENG	363	21
EVERTON	384	LEIGHTON BAINES	366	18
CHELSEA	385	ASHLEY COLE	372	13
FULHAM	392	DAMIEN DUFF	327	65
LEEDS UNITED	397	LEE BOWYER	359	38
EVERTON	399	TIM HOWARD	398	1
MANCHESTER UNITED	400	GARY NEVILLE	380	20
BOLTON WANDERERS	401	KEVIN NOLAN	360	41
CHELSEA	402	PETR CECH*	401	1
MIDDLESBROUGH	408	STEWART DOWNING	361	47
MANCHESTER UNITED	411	NICKY BUTT	343	68
MANCHESTER UNITED	414	ANDREW COLE	350	64
LIVERPOOL	417	DANNY MURPHY	336	81
TOTTENHAM HOTSPUR	418	TEDDY SHERINGHAM	350	68
ASTON VILLA	426	GARETH SOUTHGATE	426	0
STOKE CITY	431	PETER CROUCH*	296	135
MANCHESTER CITY	431	RICHARD DUNNE	419	12
BOLTON WANDERERS	436	JUSSI JÄÄSKELÄINEN	435	1
NEWCASTLE UNITED	441	ALAN SHEARER	427	14
BOLTON WANDERERS	444	KEVIN DAVIES	390	54
MANCHESTER UNITED	445	JOHN O'SHEA	370	75
BLACKBURN ROVERS	450	BRAD FRIEDEL	450	0
NEWCASTLE UNITED	451	SHAY GIVEN	451	0
MANCHESTER CITY	453	JAMES MILNER*	348	105
NEWCASTLE UNITED	455	AARON HUGHES	434	21
MANCHESTER UNITED	460	WAYNE ROONEY*	394	66
TOTTENHAM HOTSPUR	468	JERMAIN DEFOE*	336	132
MANCHESTER CITY	469	SYLVAIN DISTIN	451	18
MANCHESTER UNITED	479	MICHAEL CARRICK	420	59
CHELSEA	492	JOHN TERRY*	473	19
MANCHESTER UNITED	499	PAUL SCHOLES	404	95
TOTTENHAM HOTSPUR	503	SOL CAMPBELL	488	15
LIVERPOOL	504	STEVEN GERRARD	466	38
MANCHESTER UNITED	504	RIO FERDINAND	492	12
MANCHESTER UNITED	505	PHIL NEVILLE	446	59
LIVERPOOL	508	JAMIE CARRAGHER	484	24
MIDDLESBROUGH	514	MARK SCHWARZER	514	0
LIVERPOOL	516	EMILE HESKEY	445	71
NEWCASTLE UNITED	535	GARY SPEED	521	14
LIVERPOOL	572	DAVID JAMES	571	1
CHELSEA	609	FRANK LAMPARD	546	63
ASTON VILLA	628	GARETH BARRY*	596	32
MANCHESTER UNITED	632	RYAN GIGGS	522	110

NEVER SUBBED ON
DAVID SEAMAN
GARETH SOUTHGATE
BRAD FRIEDEL
SHAY GIVEN
MARK SCHWARZER

MOST GAMES SUBBED ON
PETER CROUCH · 135

250   200   150   100   50

PREMIER LEAGUE FOULS AND CARDS

The number of bookings and dismissals has been gradually increasing since the Premier League began in 1992. Although referee clampdowns and new rules to protect players from reckless challenges have increased the tally, statistics reveal a large number of indiscretions are due to rash decisions and second offenses. It appears that as the game gets quicker, and more skillful, tackling becomes a much riskier business. So, hats off to Ryan Giggs. He managed 632 Premier League appearances without seeing red once.

CHELSEA 1,536	EVERTON 1,465	ARSENAL 1,417	TOTTENHAM HOTSPUR 1,397	ASTON VILLA 1,362
MANCHESTER UNITED 1,336	WEST HAM UNITED 1,321	LIVERPOOL 1,220	NEWCASTLE UNITED 1,220	MANCHESTER CITY 1,158
BLACKBURN ROVERS 1,111	SUNDERLAND 1,095	SOUTHAMPTON 996	MIDDLESBROUGH 973	BOLTON WANDERERS 845
LEEDS UNITED 790	FULHAM 708	WEST BROMWICH ALBION 645	LEICESTER CITY 619	STOKE CITY 617
DERBY COUNTY 538	WIGAN ATHLETIC 513	COVENTRY CITY 481	CRYSTAL PALACE 477	BIRMINGHAM CITY 428
CHARLTON ATHLETIC 408	WIMBLEDON 407	PORTSMOUTH 398	NORWICH CITY 394	QUEENS PARK RANGERS 364
SHEFFIELD WEDNESDAY 341	HULL CITY 328	SWANSEA CITY 318	NOTTINGHAM FOREST 287	WATFORD 272
WOLVERHAMPTON WANDERERS 255	BURNLEY 186	IPSWICH TOWN 183	SHEFFIELD UNITED 170	READING 142
BRADFORD CITY 113	BOURNEMOUTH 105	OLDHAM ATHLETIC 70	BARNSLEY 66	CARDIFF CITY 50

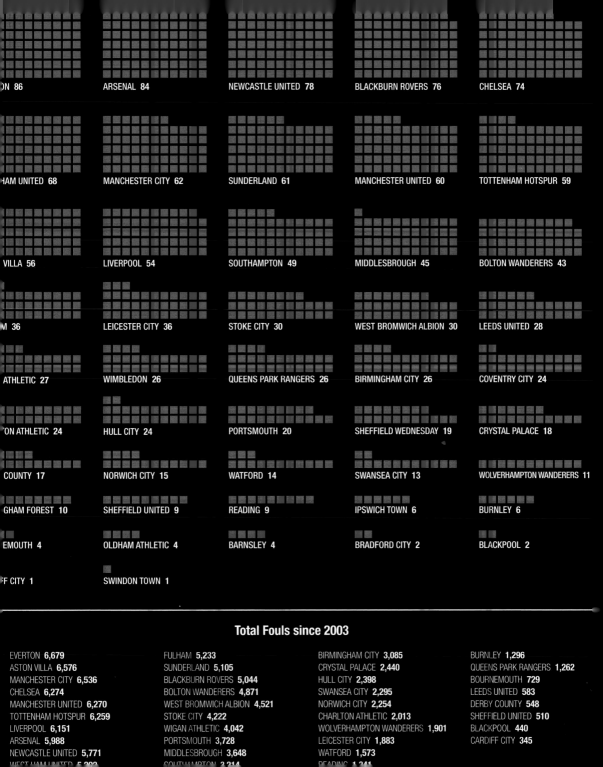

ON 86   ARSENAL 84   NEWCASTLE UNITED 78   BLACKBURN ROVERS 76   CHELSEA 74

HAM UNITED 68   MANCHESTER CITY 62   SUNDERLAND 61   MANCHESTER UNITED 60   TOTTENHAM HOTSPUR 59

VILLA 56   LIVERPOOL 54   SOUTHAMPTON 49   MIDDLESBROUGH 45   BOLTON WANDERERS 43

M 36   LEICESTER CITY 36   STOKE CITY 30   WEST BROMWICH ALBION 30   LEEDS UNITED 28

ATHLETIC 27   WIMBLEDON 26   QUEENS PARK RANGERS 26   BIRMINGHAM CITY 26   COVENTRY CITY 24

ON ATHLETIC 24   HULL CITY 24   PORTSMOUTH 20   SHEFFIELD WEDNESDAY 19   CRYSTAL PALACE 18

COUNTY 17   NORWICH CITY 15   WATFORD 14   SWANSEA CITY 13   WOLVERHAMPTON WANDERERS 11

GHAM FOREST 10   SHEFFIELD UNITED 9   READING 9   IPSWICH TOWN 6   BURNLEY 6

EMOUTH 4   OLDHAM ATHLETIC 4   BARNSLEY 4   BRADFORD CITY 2   BLACKPOOL 2

F CITY 1   SWINDON TOWN 1

Total Fouls since 2003

EVERTON **6,679**	FULHAM **5,233**	BIRMINGHAM CITY **3,085**	BURNLEY **1,296**
ASTON VILLA **6,576**	SUNDERLAND **5,105**	CRYSTAL PALACE **2,440**	QUEENS PARK RANGERS **1,262**
MANCHESTER CITY **6,536**	BLACKBURN ROVERS **5,044**	HULL CITY **2,398**	BOURNEMOUTH **729**
CHELSEA **6,274**	BOLTON WANDERERS **4,871**	SWANSEA CITY **2,295**	LEEDS UNITED **583**
MANCHESTER UNITED **6,270**	WEST BROMWICH ALBION **4,521**	NORWICH CITY **2,254**	DERBY COUNTY **548**
TOTTENHAM HOTSPUR **6,259**	STOKE CITY **4,222**	CHARLTON ATHLETIC **2,013**	SHEFFIELD UNITED **510**
LIVERPOOL **6,151**	WIGAN ATHLETIC **4,042**	WOLVERHAMPTON WANDERERS **1,901**	BLACKPOOL **440**
ARSENAL **5,988**	PORTSMOUTH **3,728**	LEICESTER CITY **1,883**	CARDIFF CITY **345**
NEWCASTLE UNITED **5,771**	MIDDLESBROUGH **3,648**	WATFORD **1,573**	
WEST HAM UNITED **5,393**	SOUTHAMPTON **3,214**	READING **1,341**	

GAMES TO REACH 100 GOALS

t's true that you need more than star power in order to score goals consistently.
You need a little luck, talented teammates, and a crumbling opposition too.
But when it comes to scoring a century (and more) for their club, the Premier
League players below have shown they've got what it takes to become truly
magical and, as a result, have joined an elite squad of top-scoring centurions.
For all strikers, this is the benchmark worth getting out of bed for.

Source: Opta (May 201

The players' colors below represents the tea
color for which the player scored their 100th goa

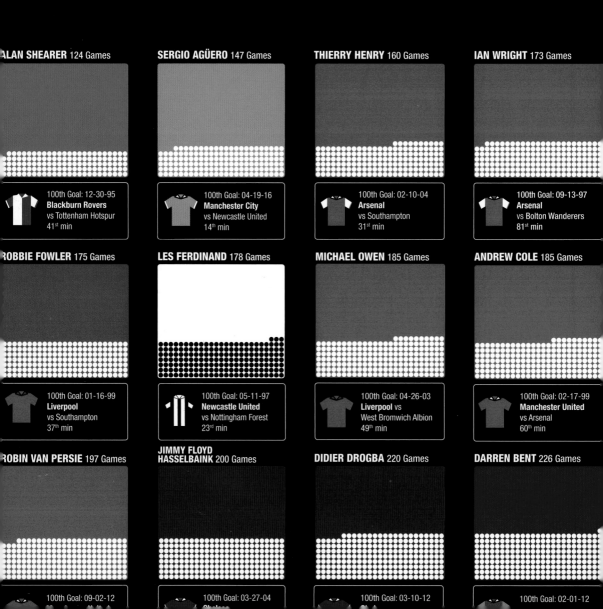

ALAN SHEARER 124 Games

100th Goal: 12-30-95
Blackburn Rovers
vs Tottenham Hotspur
41st min

SERGIO AGÜERO 147 Games

100th Goal: 04-19-16
Manchester City
vs Newcastle United
14th min

THIERRY HENRY 160 Games

100th Goal: 02-10-04
Arsenal
vs Southampton
31st min

IAN WRIGHT 173 Games

100th Goal: 09-13-97
Arsenal
vs Bolton Wanderers
81st min

ROBBIE FOWLER 175 Games

100th Goal: 01-16-99
Liverpool
vs Southampton
37th min

LES FERDINAND 178 Games

100th Goal: 05-11-97
Newcastle United
vs Nottingham Forest
23rd min

MICHAEL OWEN 185 Games

100th Goal: 04-26-03
Liverpool vs
West Bromwich Albion
49th min

ANDREW COLE 185 Games

100th Goal: 02-17-99
Manchester United
vs Arsenal
60th min

ROBIN VAN PERSIE 197 Games

100th Goal: 09-02-12

JIMMY FLOYD HASSELBAINK 200 Games

100th Goal: 03-27-04

DIDIER DROGBA 220 Games

100th Goal: 03-10-12

DARREN BENT 226 Games

100th Goal: 02-01-12

WAYNE ROONEY 247 Games

DWIGHT YORKE 254 Games

Alan Shearer's record may never be beaten, but he is not the record-holder for English top-flight soccer. That honor goes to a Scotsman, Dave Halliday, who signed for Sunderland from Dundee in 1925. In the old Division One, Halliday hit 100 goals in just 101 games. To this day he is still the only player in top-flight soccer in England to score more than 30 goals in four consecutive seasons.

100th Goal: 01-31-10
Manchester United
vs Arsenal
37th min

100th Goal: 11-25-00
Manchester United
vs Derby County
76th min

TEDDY SHERINGHAM 254 Games

ROBBIE KEANE 255 Games

NICOLAS ANELKA 258 Games

MATT LE TISSIER 266 Games

100th Goal: 10-28-00
Manchester United
vs Southampton
51st min

100th Goal: 12-26-07
Tottenham Hotspur
vs Fulham
62nd min

100th Goal: 12-14-08
Chelsea
vs West Ham United
51st min

100th Goal: 04-02-01
Southampton
vs Arsenal
89th min

DION DUBLIN 271 Games

JERMAIN DEFOE 303 Games

FRANK LAMPARD 406 Games

EMILE HESKEY 414 Games

100th Goal: 11-23-02
Aston Villa
vs West Ham United
71st min

100th Goal: 04-23-11
Tottenham Hotspur vs
West Bromwich Albion
66th min

100th Goal: 11-01-08
Chelsea
vs Sunderland
51st min

100th Goal: 11-01-08
Wigan Athletic
vs Portsmouth
90th min

PETER CROUCH 419 Games

PAUL SCHOLES 436 Games

STEVEN GERRARD 449 Games

RYAN GIGGS 534 Games

100th Goal: 02-01-17
Stoke City
vs Everton
7th min

100th Goal: 03-06-10
Manchester United
vs Wolverhampton
Wanderers, 72nd min

100th Goal: 10-19-13
Liverpool
vs Newcastle United
42nd min

100th Goal 11-28-2009
Manchester United
vs Portsmouth
87th min

FA CUP WINNERS AND RUNNERS-UP

Although overshadowed in recent times by the Premier League, the FA Cup remains the showpiece of English football. First played in the 1871–72 season, the English FA Cup is the oldest soccer competition in the world. Open to the top 10 levels of English football, the tournament includes hundreds of non-league teams (in 1901, Tottenham Hotspur became the only non-league team ever to win the trophy). Since 1923, the final has been played at Wembley (old and new) apart from the period between 2001 and 2006, when it was hosted at the Millennium Stadium in Cardiff.

Source: Opta (May 2017)

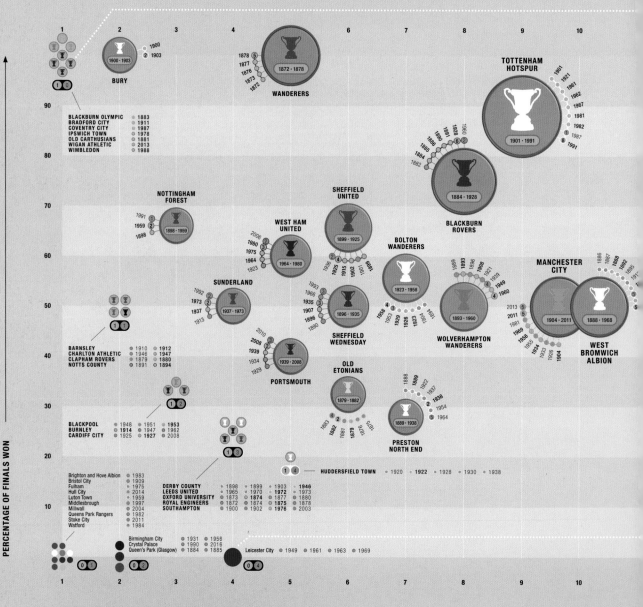

PERCENTAGE OF FINALS WON

NUMBER OF APPEARANCES IN THE FA CUP FINAL

Among the many gems of FA Cup trivia are that Wigan Athletic are the only club to win the FA Cup and be relegated from the Premier League in the same season (2013); Leicester City have reached the final four times but have never won the cup; and Ashley Cole holds a record seven FA Cup winner's medals through his victories with Arsenal and Chelsea.

WIGAN ATHLETIC — 2013 ↓

LEICESTER CITY — 0 4

ASHLEY COLE — 🏆🏆🏆🏆🏆🏆🏆

KEY:

TEAM NAME

Year of first win
Year of last win
XXXX · XXXX
Total number of final wins
Final appearances
Total number of final runners-up finishes

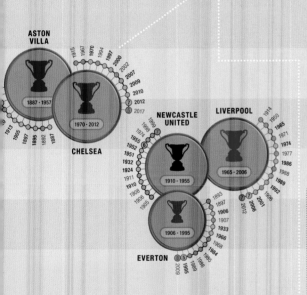

ASTON VILLA — 1887 · 1957
CHELSEA — 1970 · 2012
NEWCASTLE UNITED — 1910 · 1955
LIVERPOOL — 1965 · 2006
EVERTON — 1906 · 1995
MANCHESTER UNITED — 1909 · 2016
ARSENAL — 1930 · 2017

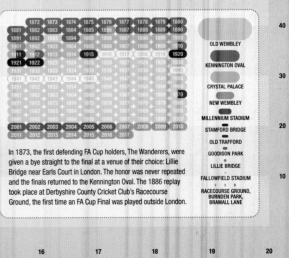

In 1873, the first defending FA Cup holders, The Wanderers, were given a bye straight to the final at a venue of their choice: Lillie Bridge near Earls Court in London. The honor was never repeated and the finals returned to the Kennington Oval. The 1886 replay took place at Derbyshire County Cricket Club's Racecourse Ground, the first time an FA Cup Final was played outside London.

OLD WEMBLEY
KENNINGTON OVAL
CRYSTAL PALACE
NEW WEMBLEY
MILLENNIUM STADIUM
STAMFORD BRIDGE
OLD TRAFFORD
GOODISON PARK
LILLIE BRIDGE
FALLOWFIELD STADIUM
RACECOURSE GROUND, BURNDEN PARK, BRAMALL LANE

LA LIGA TITLE WINNERS

La Liga, the elite league of Spanish soccer, was born in 1929 from a core group of teams playing for the national knockout competition, the Copa del Rey. Sixty different teams have since competed in the league and nine different teams have lifted the trophy. The league has been dominated by Barcelona and Real Madrid, the giants of Spanish football, while Athletic Bilbao, Atlético Madrid, and Valencia deserve honorable mentions too. With its teams faring well in European competition, La Liga is currently rated the best league in Europe.

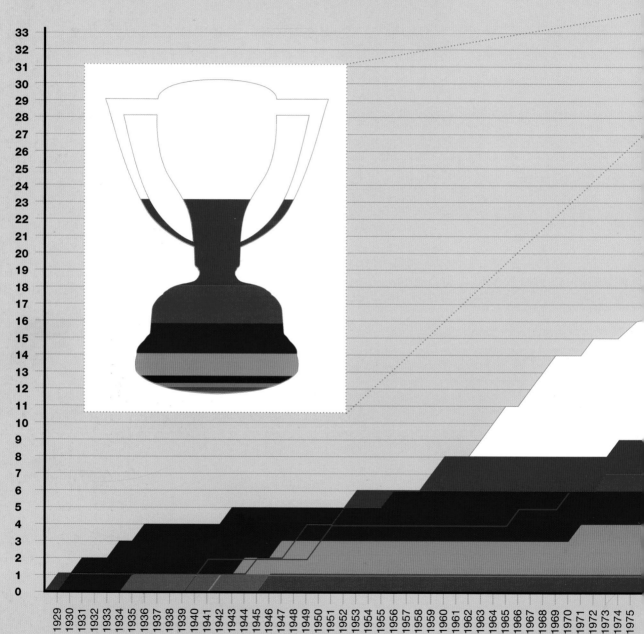

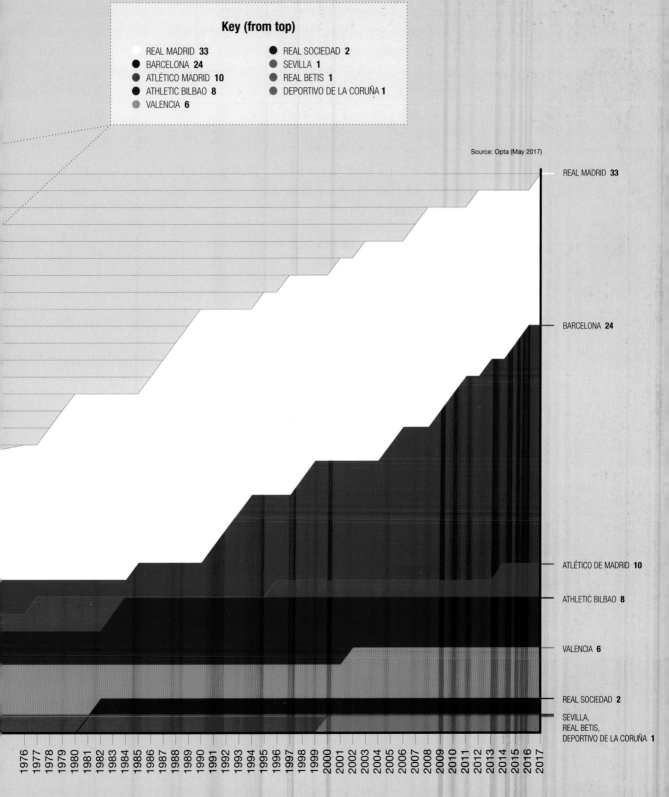

Key (from top)

- REAL MADRID **33**
- BARCELONA **24**
- ATLÉTICO MADRID **10**
- ATHLETIC BILBAO **8**
- VALENCIA **6**
- REAL SOCIEDAD **2**
- SEVILLA **1**
- REAL BETIS **1**
- DEPORTIVO DE LA CORUÑA **1**

Source: Opta (May 2017)

REAL MADRID **33**

BARCELONA **24**

ATLÉTICO DE MADRID **10**

ATHLETIC BILBAO **8**

VALENCIA **6**

REAL SOCIEDAD **2**

SEVILLA,
REAL BETIS,
DEPORTIVO DE LA CORUÑA **1**

1976 1977 1978 1979 1980 1981 1982 1983 1984 1985 1986 1987 1988 1989 1990 1991 1992 1993 1994 1995 1996 1997 1998 1999 2000 2001 2002 2003 2004 2005 2006 2007 2008 2009 2010 2011 2012 2013 2014 2015 2016 2017

LA LIGA GAME WINS PER CLUB

According to UEFA, La Liga has been the top league in Europe since 2012, and it has produced the continent's top-rated club twice as often as any other league. Few will be surprised to find the La Liga giants Real Madrid and Barcelona dominating this most-wins chart, but may be astounded by just how evenly matched they are. Even Real Madrid's 2011–12 record of 32 wins in a season was matched by Barcelona the following season and, although it took them until 2016, Real Madrid eventually equalled Barcelona's 2010–11 record of 16 consecutive victories.

Club	Wins
ELCHE	20
TENERIFE	26
REAL OVIEDO	33
EIBAR	35
NUMANCIA	37
RECREATIVO	42
LAS PALMAS	44
GRANADA CF	56
SPORTING DE GIJÓN	61
ALMERÍA	62
ALAVÉS	90
LEVANTE	95
RAYO VALLECANO	111
REAL VALLADOLID	120
RACING DE SANTANDER	141
GETAFE	147
REAL ZARAGOZA	156
OSASUNA	172
REAL BETIS	178
CELTA DE VIGO	187
MÁLAGA	204
MALLORCA	210
REAL SOCIEDAD	217
ESPANYOL	242

"You want to win games, break records, but I don't do it just for the records. I do it because I want to improve and see my players improve."

Zinedine Zidane, Real Madrid coach

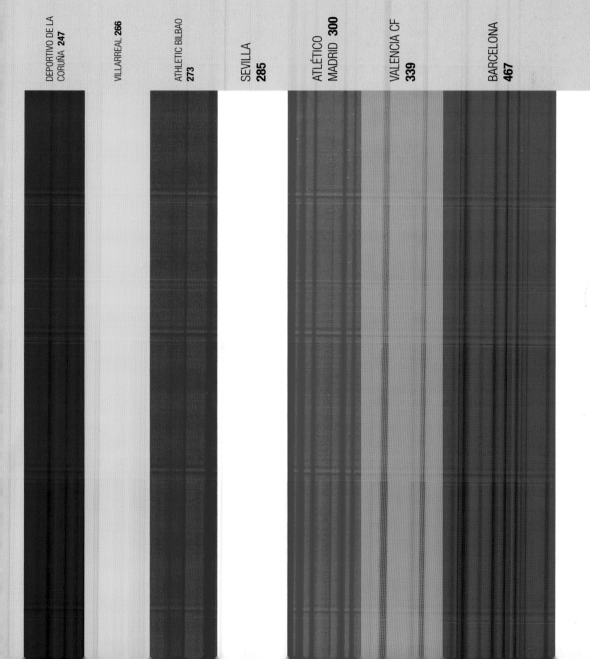

DEPORTIVO DE LA CORUÑA **247**

VILLARREAL **266**

ATHLETIC BILBAO **273**

SEVILLA **285**

ATLÉTICO MADRID **300**

VALENCIA CF **339**

BARCELONA **467**

REAL MADRID **475**

LA LIGA GOALS PER CLUB

The history of La Liga is filled with great coaches whose dynamic team engineering has helped squads amass huge goalscoring tallies—from the bowler-hatted Englishman Fred Pentland, whose 1930s' Athletic Bilbao conquered any team that stood before them, to the star-studded era of Miguel Muñoz at Real Madrid in the 1960s and 1970s. Johan Cruyff, and his successor Louis van Gaal, brought success back to Barcelona in the '90s. Leo Beenhakker, Vicente del Bosque, and Carlo Ancelotti have brought glory to Real Madrid in recent years, while Frank Rijkaard and Pep Guardiola made Barcelona the most feared team in Europe—though judging by the goal totals between those two teams now, there's still everything to play for...

In the 2011–12 season, *La Liga de los Récords* (The League of the Records), a rampant Real Madrid ripped up the record books. Among their notable achievements was the most league goals in a season, as they racked up an astonishing 121. Real boasted 13 different scorers, with Cristiano Ronaldo leading the list on 46, not so closely followed by Gonzalo Higuaín (22) and Karim Benzema (21).

After scoring in 64 consecutive matches, a 0-0 draw at Osasuna on October 19, 2013, brought to an end Real Madrid's record. Then, in February 2016, Barcelona began a run of their own; at the end of the 2016–17 season they had netted in 50 consecutive games … and counting.

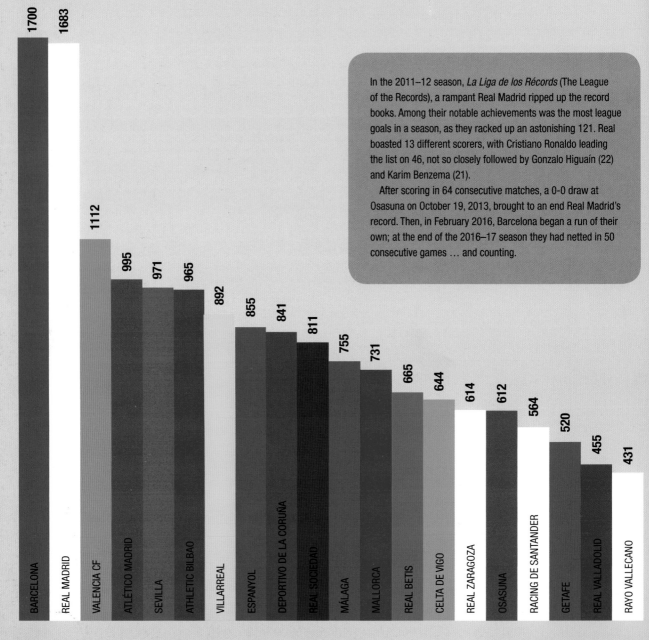

Club	Goals
BARCELONA	1700
REAL MADRID	1683
VALENCIA CF	1112
ATLÉTICO MADRID	995
SEVILLA	971
ATHLETIC BILBAO	965
VILLARREAL	892
ESPANYOL	855
DEPORTIVO DE LA CORUÑA	841
REAL SOCIEDAD	811
MÁLAGA	755
MALLORCA	731
REAL BETIS	665
CELTA DE VIGO	644
REAL ZARAGOZA	614
OSASUNA	612
RACING DE SANTANDER	564
GETAFE	520
REAL VALLADOLID	455
RAYO VALLECANO	431

"MSN", the fearsome Barcelona forward line of Messi, Suárez, and Neymar (before Neymar left for Paris Saint-Germain in summer 2017), amassed 79 goals between them in the 2016–17 season.

Source: Opta (May 2017)

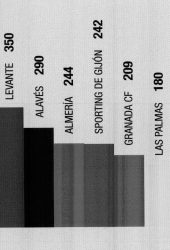

LEVANTE **350**
ALAVÉS **290**
ALMERÍA **244**
SPORTING DE GIJÓN **242**
GRANADA CF **209**
LAS PALMAS **180**
RECREATIVO **163**
NUMANCIA **155**
EIBAR **139**
REAL OVIEDO **136**
TENERIFE **113**
ALBACETE **73**
REAL MURCIA **65**
ELCHE **65**
XEREZ **38**
CÁDIZ **36**
HÉRCULES **36**
LEGANÉS **36**
GIMNÀSTIC DE TARRAGONA **34**
SALAMANCA **29**
CF EXTREMADURA **27**
CÓRDOBA **22**

RONALDO vs MESSI

Future generations might well consider us blessed to have seen the two greatest players in the history of the game. Between them they have been named as FIFA's best two players in the world every year since 2008 (except 2010 when Iniesta was runner-up to Messi). Both players have scored in two UEFA Champions League finals, have regularly scored more than 50 goals in a single season, and struck their 500th goals for their club in 2017. But who wouldn't doubt the Argentinian would trade a fair few of them to match the South American equivalent of the European Championship winner's medal, won by Ronaldo in 2016?

CRISTIANO RONALDO

Club Record

Matches won	**469**
Goals scored	**529**
Games played	**717**

0   800

International Record

Matches won	**84**
Goals scored	**75**
Games played	**142**

0   800

League Championships	🏆🏆🏆🏆🏆
National Cups	🏆🏆🏆
National League Cups	🏆🏆
Comm Shield/Super Cup	🏆🏆🏆
Champions League	🏆🏆🏆🏆
UEFA Super Cup	🏆
Club World Cup	🏆🏆🏆
European Championship	🏆
Total	**21**

> " Messi is outstanding in certain attributes but Ronaldo is such an all-round player."
>
> England international Michael Owen

Comm Shield = FA Community Shield / Super Cup = Spanish Super Cup

"Messi or Ronaldo best player in the world? In the world, I would say Ronaldo. Messi is from another planet."

Turkey international Arda Turan

Source: Opta (June 2017)

LIONEL MESSI

Club Record

413	Matches won
507	Goals scored
583	Games played

800   0

International Record

73	Matches won
58	Goals scored
118	Games played

800   0

🏆🏆🏆🏆🏆🏆🏆🏆   League Championships
🏆🏆🏆🏆🏆   National Cups
National League Cups
🏆🏆🏆🏆🏆🏆   Comm Shield/Super Cup

🏆🏆🏆🏆   Champions League
🏆🏆🏆   UEFA Super Cup
🏆🏆🏆   Club World Cup

🏆   Olympic Gold Medal

30   **Total**

LA LIGA TOP GOALSCORERS 1998–2017

ROBERTO SOLDADO 110
GONZALO HIGUAÍN 107
ANTOINE GRIEZMANN 100
FERNANDO TORRES 97
DIEGO TRISTÁN 95
ROY MAKAAY 93
RUBÉN CASTRO 92
ISMAEL URZAIZ 91
SAVO MILOŠEVIĆ 91
PATRICK KLUIVERT 90
FRÉDÉRIC KANOUTÉ 89
LUIS SUÁREZ 85
RONALDO 83
WALTER PANDIANI 82
FERNANDO MORIENTES 79
NIHAT KAHVECI 76
SALVA BALLESTA 75
SERGIO AGÜERO 74
LUIS GARCÍA 73
LUÍS FABIANO 72
VICTOR 71
SERGIO GARCÍA 71
JAVIER SAVIOLA 70
RONALDINHO 69
CARLOS VELA 68
DELY VALDÉS 68
NEYMAR 68
DARKO KOVAČEVIĆ 67
RIVALDO 67
GUISEPPE ROSSI 64
ETXEBERRIA 63

Lionel Messi, all-time top goalscorer. In November 2012, the prodigious striker began a run of scoring in 21 consecutive games, including a goal against every other La Liga team.

Lionel Messi and Cristiano Ronaldo tower over La Liga goalscoring records. Their lead is considerable, but they also score around a goal a game—almost twice the rate of others in the chart. The only player in the league's history whose record stands the equal of these modern superstars is the great Telma Zarra. He played at Athletic Bilbao for 15 seasons, scoring at nearly a goal a game and helping Bilbao to a league title in 1943. His name now lives on in the award given to La Liga's top goalscorer each season.

In the 2010–11 season Cristiano Ronaldo became the first La Liga player in 20 years to score at a ratio of over a goal per game. Since then the feat has been achieved every season, Lionel Messi achieving the best ratio of 1.44 in 2012–13.

Source: Opta (May 2017)
Stats from La Liga 1998–99 to 2016–17

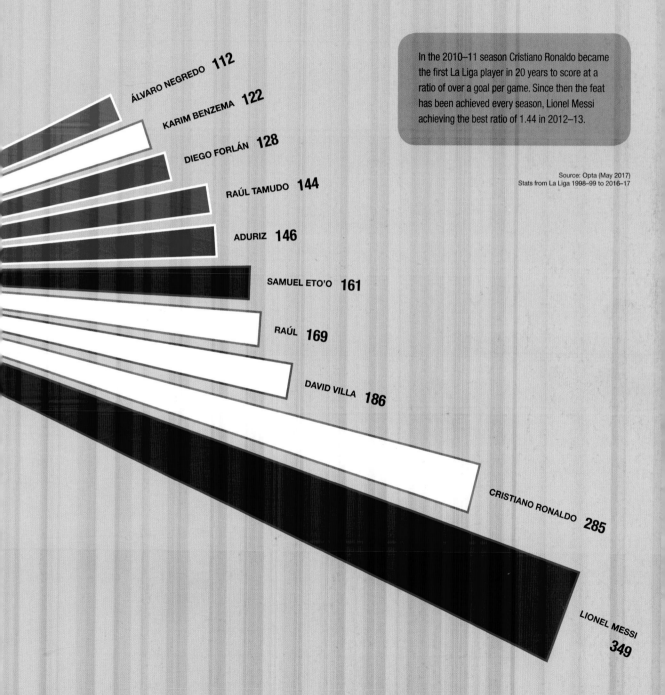

ÁLVARO NEGREDO **112**

KARIM BENZEMA **122**

DIEGO FORLÁN **128**

RAÚL TAMUDO **144**

ADURIZ **146**

SAMUEL ETO'O **161**

RAÚL **169**

DAVID VILLA **186**

CRISTIANO RONALDO **285**

LIONEL MESSI **349**

SERIE A TITLE WINNERS

Serie A has been the top-flight tournament in Italian soccer since the 1929–30 season. Rated as one of the most entertaining and thrilling leagues in the world, Serie A has a reputation for highly tactical performances and players with virtuoso and prodigious technical ability. However, the league has also been rocked by controversy and scandal, including the 2006 *Calciopoli*, as it became known, where some top teams were accused of rigging games by selecting biased referees. The winner of the league is awarded the *Scudetto*, a badge with the colors of the Italian flag, to be worn on the champions' shirts the following season.

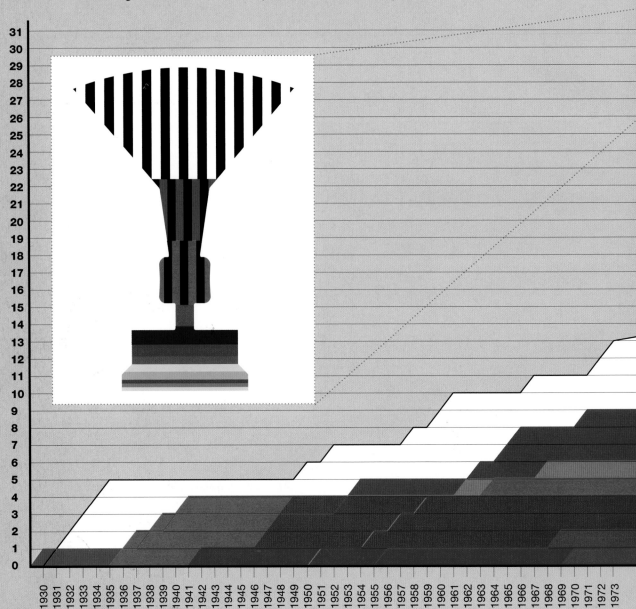

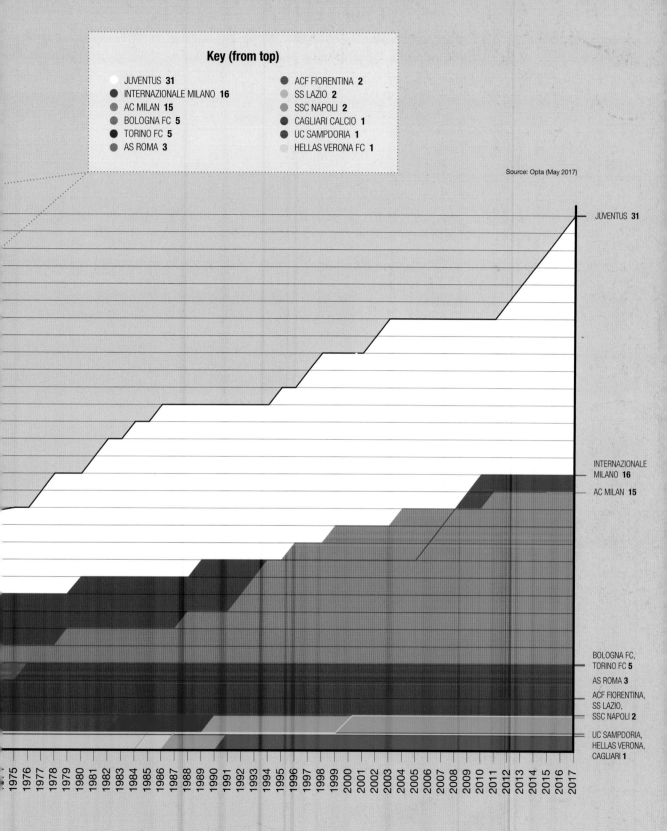

Key (from top)

- JUVENTUS **31**
- INTERNAZIONALE MILANO **16**
- AC MILAN **15**
- BOLOGNA FC **5**
- TORINO FC **5**
- AS ROMA **3**
- ACF FIORENTINA **2**
- SS LAZIO **2**
- SSC NAPOLI **2**
- CAGLIARI CALCIO **1**
- UC SAMPDORIA **1**
- HELLAS VERONA FC **1**

Source: Opta (May 2017)

JUVENTUS **31**

INTERNAZIONALE MILANO **16**

AC MILAN **15**

BOLOGNA FC, TORINO FC **5**

AS ROMA **3**

ACF FIORENTINA, SS LAZIO, SSC NAPOLI **2**

UC SAMPDORIA, HELLAS VERONA, CAGLIARI **1**

1975 1976 1977 1978 1979 1980 1981 1982 1983 1984 1985 1986 1987 1988 1989 1990 1991 1992 1993 1994 1995 1996 1997 1998 1999 2000 2001 2002 2003 2004 2005 2006 2007 2008 2009 2010 2011 2012 2013 2014 2015 2016 2017

SERIE A GAME WINS PER CLUB

There are 65 teams who have participated in the 84 Serie A championships to have taken place to date, with only Internazionale having competed in every season. Apart from the largely pre-war success of Torino and Bologna, Serie A has been dominated by *Le Sette Sorelle* (The Seven Sisters): Juventus, Roma, Milan, Inter, Fiorentina, Lazio—and Parma, who have more recently been replaced by Napoli. The Italian league is usually secured by a team amassing a total of around 25 victories in the season, although Juventus won 33 and 29 out of 38, respectively, in their title-winning seasons of 2013–14 and 2015–16.

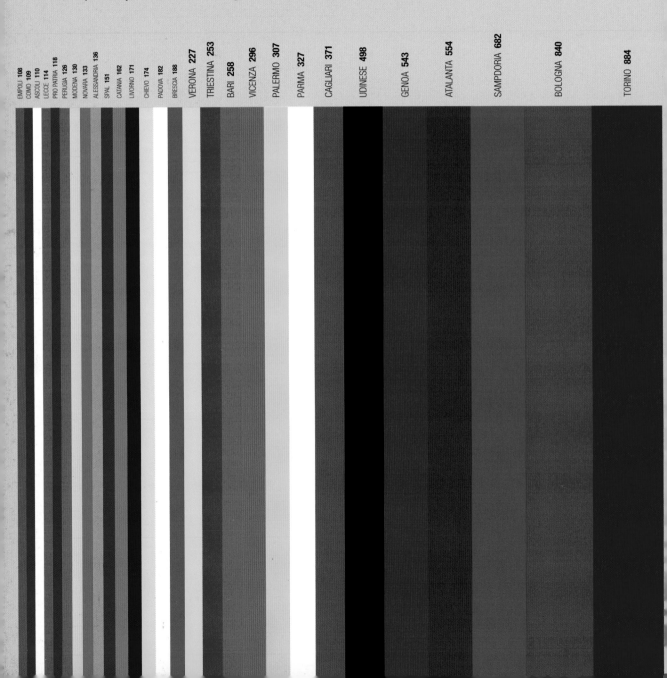

EMPOLI 108
COMO 109
ASCOLI 110
LECCE 114
PRO PATRIA 118
PERUGIA 126
MODENA 130
NOVARA 133
ALESSANDRIA 136
SPAL 151
CATANIA 162
LIVORNO 171
CHIEVO 174
PADOVA 182
BRESCIA 188
VERONA 227
TRIESTINA 253
BARI 258
VICENZA 296
PALERMO 307
PARMA 327
CAGLIARI 371
UDINESE 498
GENOA 543
ATALANTA 554
SAMPDORIA 682
BOLOGNA 840
TORINO 884

Under 100 Wins

FOGGIA **95**	PRO VERCELLI **65**	PESCARA **36**	CARPI **9**
VENEZIA **94**	SASSUOLO **50**	VARESE **36**	CROTONE **9**
REGGINA **83**	MANTOVA **48**	CASALE **33**	ANCONA **8**
SIENA **83**	LIGURIA **44**	SAMPIERDARENESE **24**	FROSINONE **8**
CESENA **80**	CREMONESE **43**	SALERNITANA **23**	TERNANA **7**
LUCCHESE **80**	PISA **42**	LECCO **19**	PISTOIESE **6**
AVELLINO **79**	MESSINA **39**	LEGNANO **16**	TREVISO **3**
PIACENZA **65**	CATANZARO **38**	REGGIANA **16**	

NAPOLI **911**

LAZIO **935**

FIORENTINA **1054**

ROMA **1170**

AC MILAN **1340**

INTERNAZIONALE MILANO **1404**

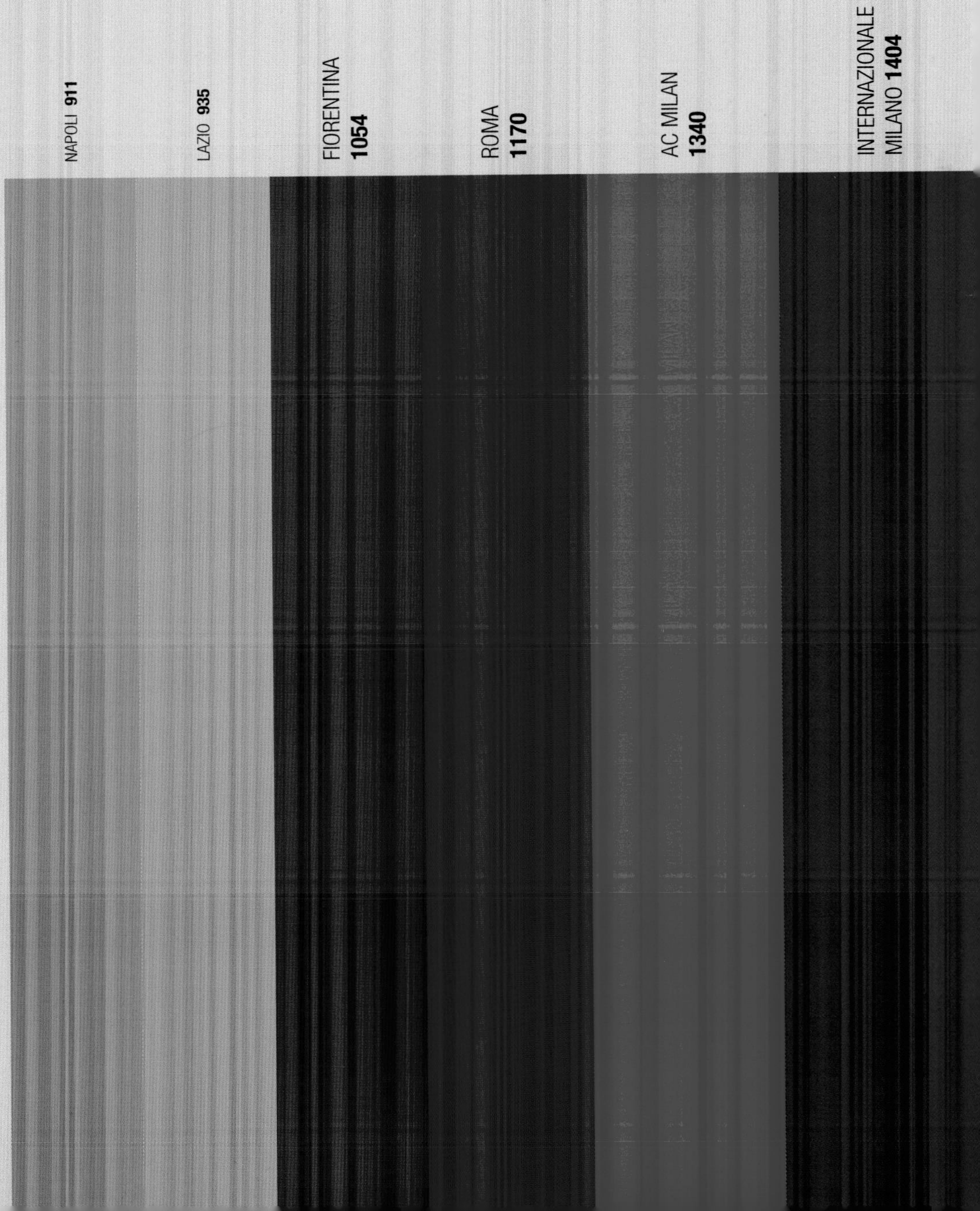

SERIE A GOALS PER CLUB

Goals are said to be hard to come by in an often defensively minded Serie A, but if you are good enough… It certainly wasn't a problem for 1930s star Silvio Piola, whose record of 274 goals in 537 games—set with Novarro, Lazio, Juventus, and others—looks unassailable. Even the great Francesco Totti had eventually to concede that the target was out of sight. Among the young guns in the league, only Inter's Mauro Icardi (82 goals), Torino's Andrea Belotti (67), and Lazio's Keita (25) look capable of inclusion in future charts.

"When Totti plays—but it's the same in training and even when he's playing with his boy—he's the Muhammad Ali of football, always looking to land that knockout blow: to swing the punch no one else can see."

Roma coach Luciano Spalletti

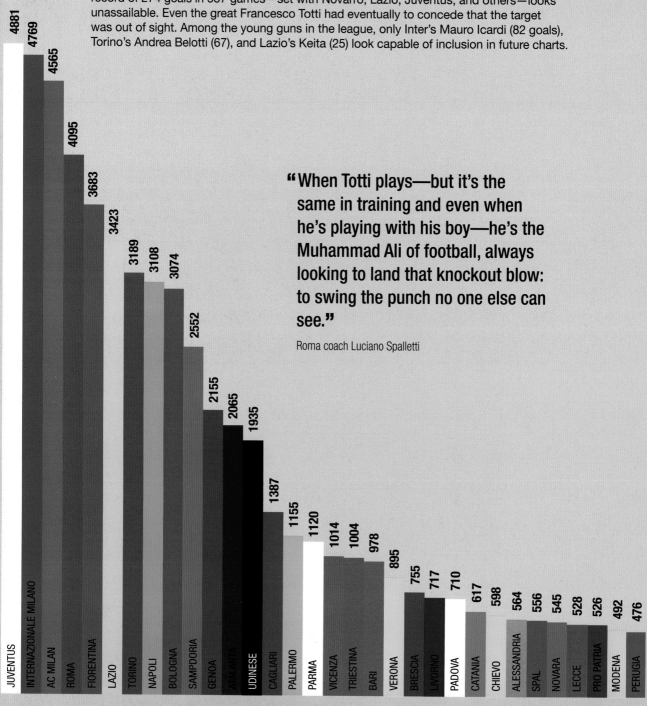

Club	Goals
JUVENTUS	4881
INTERNAZIONALE MILANO	4769
AC MILAN	4565
ROMA	4095
FIORENTINA	3683
LAZIO	3423
TORINO	3189
NAPOLI	3108
BOLOGNA	3074
SAMPDORIA	2552
GENOA	2155
ATALANTA	2065
UDINESE	1935
CAGLIARI	1387
PALERMO	1155
PARMA	1120
VICENZA	1014
TRIESTINA	1004
BARI	978
VERONA	895
BRESCIA	755
LIVORNO	717
PADOVA	710
CATANIA	617
CHIEVO	598
ALESSANDRIA	564
SPAL	556
NOVARA	545
LECCE	528
PRO PATRIA	526
MODENA	492
PERUGIA	476

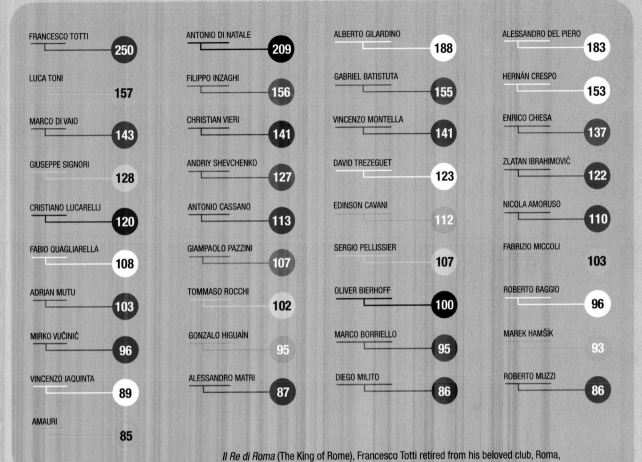

FRANCESCO TOTTI **250**	ANTONIO DI NATALE **209**	ALBERTO GILARDINO **188**	ALESSANDRO DEL PIERO **183**
LUCA TONI **157**	FILIPPO INZAGHI **156**	GABRIEL BATISTUTA **155**	HERNÁN CRESPO **153**
MARCO DI VAIO **143**	CHRISTIAN VIERI **141**	VINCENZO MONTELLA **141**	ENRICO CHIESA **137**
GIUSEPPE SIGNORI **128**	ANDRIY SHEVCHENKO **127**	DAVID TREZEGUET **123**	ZLATAN IBRAHIMOVIĆ **122**
CRISTIANO LUCARELLI **120**	ANTONIO CASSANO **113**	EDINSON CAVANI **112**	NICOLA AMORUSO **110**
FABIO QUAGLIARELLA **108**	GIAMPAOLO PAZZINI **107**	SERGIO PELLISSIER **107**	FABRIZIO MICCOLI **103**
ADRIAN MUTU **103**	TOMMASO ROCCHI **102**	OLIVER BIERHOFF **100**	ROBERTO BAGGIO **96**
MIRKO VUČINIĆ **96**	GONZALO HIGUAÍN **95**	MARCO BORRIELLO **95**	MAREK HAMŠÍK **93**
VINCENZO IAQUINTA **89**	ALESSANDRO MATRI **87**	DIEGO MILITO **86**	ROBERTO MUZZI **86**
AMAURI **85**			

Il Re di Roma (The King of Rome), Francesco Totti retired from his beloved club, Roma, at the end of the 2016–17 season. The five-time Italian footballer of the year, European Golden Boot holder (2007), and World Cup winner (2006) scored his first goal for the Giallorossi on the opening day of the 1994–95 season. His 250th and final league goal came in September 2016 at the age of 40. His loyalty to Roma has meant he has never achieved Champions League success, but there is no doubt of his status in the game. When Roma met Barcelona in a pre-season friendly, Lionel Messi uploaded a shot of him in Totti's shirt with the caption: "A great! What a phenomenon!!" It got 1.8 million likes.

Source: Opta (May 2017)
Player data: 1994–95 to 2016–17
Color relates to the team for which the player scored the highest number of goals.

ASCOLI 425 · VENEZIA 413 · COMO 411 · EMPOLI 404 · CESENA 364 · FOGGIA 360 · SIENA 356 · LUCCHESE 347 · REGGINA 324 · PIACENZA 281 · AVELLINO 268 · PRO VERCELLI 251 · CREMONESE 222 · PESCARA 205 · SASSUOLO 199 · MANTOVA 182 · PISA 174 · LIGURIA 168 · MESSINA 165 · VARESE 164 · CATANZARO 156 · CASALE 149 · LEGNANO 111 · SAMPIERDARENESE 93 · LECCO 84 · SALERNITANA 83 · REGGIANA 81 · ANCONA 60 · CARPI 37 · FROSINONE 35 · CROTONE 34 · TERNANA 33 · TREVISO 24 · PISTOIESE 19

BUNDESLIGA TITLE WINNERS

The Bundesliga was formed in 1963 to bring professionalism to the German game. The early years saw five different champions in five seasons before two promoted teams, Bayern München and Borussia Mönchengladbach, went on to dominate the league, both winning three successive titles. Bayern would continue to lead even after the league was revolutionized after 1989 at the unification of Germany. Various clubs—the latest being Borussia Dortmund—have risen to challenge Bayern's supremacy, but "FC Hollywood", as other teams' fans have continued to call them, remain the undisputed giants of the Bundesliga.

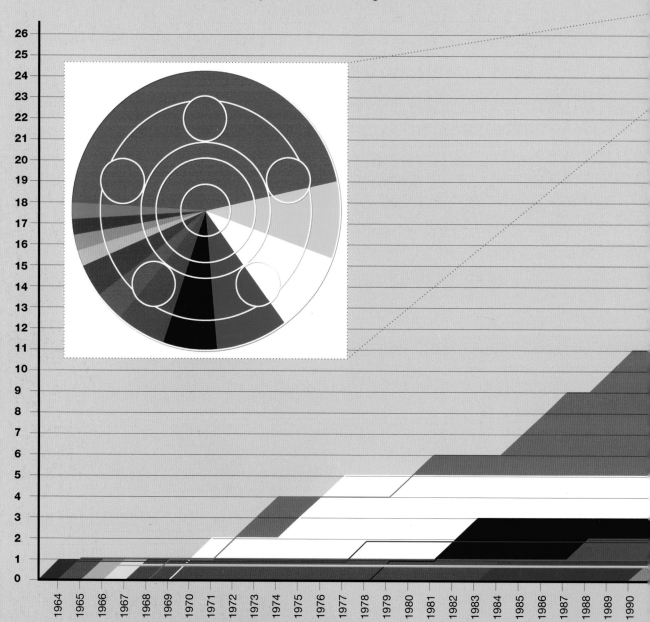

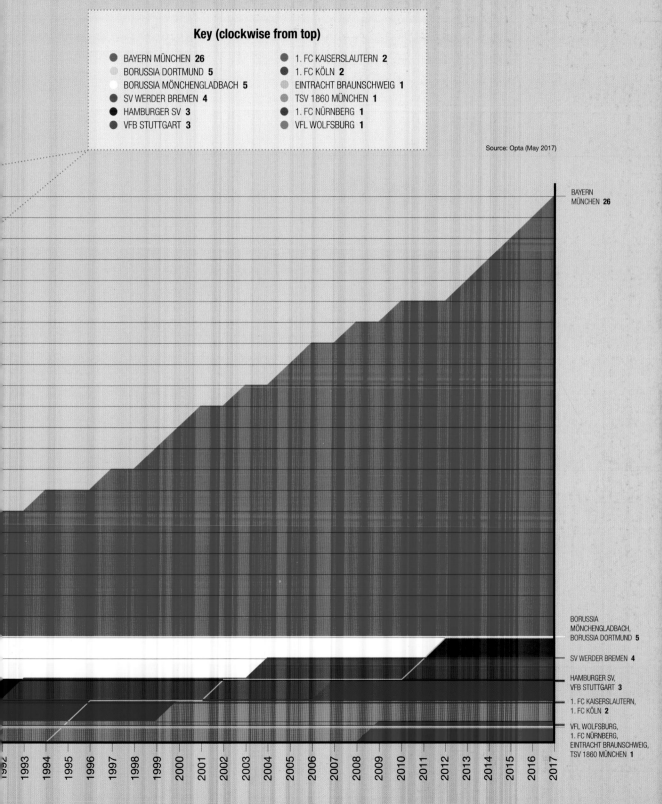

Key (clockwise from top)

- BAYERN MÜNCHEN **26**
- BORUSSIA DORTMUND **5**
- BORUSSIA MÖNCHENGLADBACH **5**
- SV WERDER BREMEN **4**
- HAMBURGER SV **3**
- VFB STUTTGART **3**
- 1. FC KAISERSLAUTERN **2**
- 1. FC KÖLN **2**
- EINTRACHT BRAUNSCHWEIG **1**
- TSV 1860 MÜNCHEN **1**
- 1. FC NÜRNBERG **1**
- VFL WOLFSBURG **1**

Source: Opta (May 2017)

BAYERN MÜNCHEN **26**

BORUSSIA MÖNCHENGLADBACH, BORUSSIA DORTMUND **5**

SV WERDER BREMEN **4**

HAMBURGER SV, VFB STUTTGART **3**

1. FC KAISERSLAUTERN, 1. FC KÖLN **2**

VFL WOLFSBURG, 1. FC NÜRNBERG, EINTRACHT BRAUNSCHWEIG, TSV 1860 MÜNCHEN **1**

1992 1993 1994 1995 1996 1997 1998 1999 2000 2001 2002 2003 2004 2005 2006 2007 2008 2009 2010 2011 2012 2013 2014 2015 2016 2017

BUNDESLIGA GAME WINS PER CLUB

Although there is no doubting the dominance of Bayern München over their Bundesliga rivals, this infographic illustrates the competitive nature of the league. A total of 53 clubs have competed in the Bundesliga over the 30 plus years, with more than 10 teams earning a win ratio of over 40%. Bayern hold the record for the most wins in a season, reaching 29 in both 2012–13 and 2013–14, clocking up a run of 19 games in the latter season. The last two seasons have seen Bayern extend their lead in this category with two emphatic Bundesliga titles, while only Borussia Dortmund, Lokomotive Leipzig, and Bayer Leverkusen have recorded better than a 50% win ratio.

Club	Wins
ROT-WEISS ESSEN	61
FC AUGSBURG	64
SV WALDHOF MANNHEIM	71
OFC KICKERS 1901	77
TSG 1899 HOFFENHEIM	103
FC HANSA ROSTOCK	124
1. FSV MAINZ 05	127
KFC UERDINGEN 05	138
DSC ARMINIA BIELEFELD	159
SC FREIBURG	180
TSV 1860 MÜNCHEN	238
KARLSRUHER SC	241
EINTRACHT BRAUNSCHWEIG	242
FORTUNA DÜSSELDORF	245
VFL WOLFSBURG	261
HANNOVER 96	293
MSV DUISBERG	296
1. FC NÜRNBERG	341
VFL BOCHUM 1848	356
HERTHA BSC	421
BAYER 04 LEVERKUSEN	550
1. FC KAISERSLAUTERN	575
EINTRACHT FRANKFURT	592

Source: Opta (May 2017)

Under 60 Wins

FC ST PAULI **58**	1. FC SAARBRÜCKEN **32**	STUTTGARTER KICKERS **20**	SC PADERBORN 07 **7**
FC ENERGIE COTTBUS **56**	SV DARMSTADT 98 **28**	RB LEIPZIG **20**	SC PREUSSEN MÜNSTER **7**
ALEMANNIA AACHEN **43**	SC BORUSSIA NEUNKIRCHEN **25**	FC INGOLSTADT **18**	SPVGG GREUTHER FÜRTH **4**
ROT-WEISS OBERHAUSEN **36**	WUPPERTALER SV **25**	TENNIS BORUSSIA BERLIN **11**	BLAU-WEISS 1890 BERLIN **3**
SG WATTENSCHEID 09 **34**	FC 08 HOMBURG **21**	SSV ULM 1846 **9**	VFB LEIPZIG **3**
SG DYNAMO DRESDEN **33**	SPVGG UNTERHACHING **20**	SC FORTUNA KÖLN **8**	TASMANIA 1900 BERLIN **2**

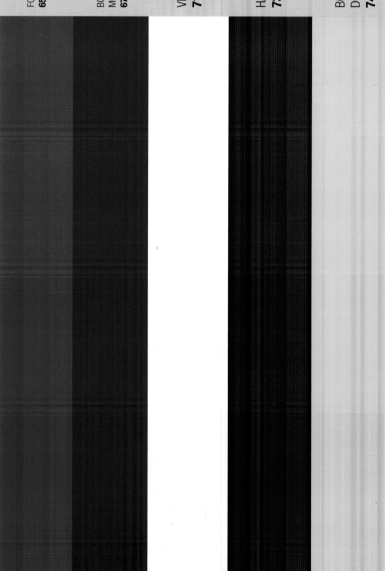

1. FC KÖLN **624**

FC SCHALKE 04 **655**

BORUSSIA MÖNCHENGLADBACH **672**

VFB STUTTGART **718**

HAMBURGER SV **738**

BORUSSIA DORTMUND **746**

SV WERDER BREMEN **761**

BAYERN MÜNCHEN **1043**

BUNDESLIGA GOALS PER CLUB

The German Bundesliga is the go-to league for goals with the highest goals per game ratio in Europe at 2.94 a game. As in all Bundesliga records, it's hard to ignore Bayern München. They are the only team to net 100 goals in a season (101 in 1971–72) and in Gerd Müller, seven-time leading goalscorer, they have arguably the game's greatest ever goal poacher. Among recent heroes stand Robert Lewandowski with his incredible five goals in nine minutes against VfL Wolfsburg in September 2015, and Borussia Dortmund's Pierre-Emerick Aubameyang whose 31 strikes in 2016–17 made him the first player to score over 30 goals in a season for 40 years.

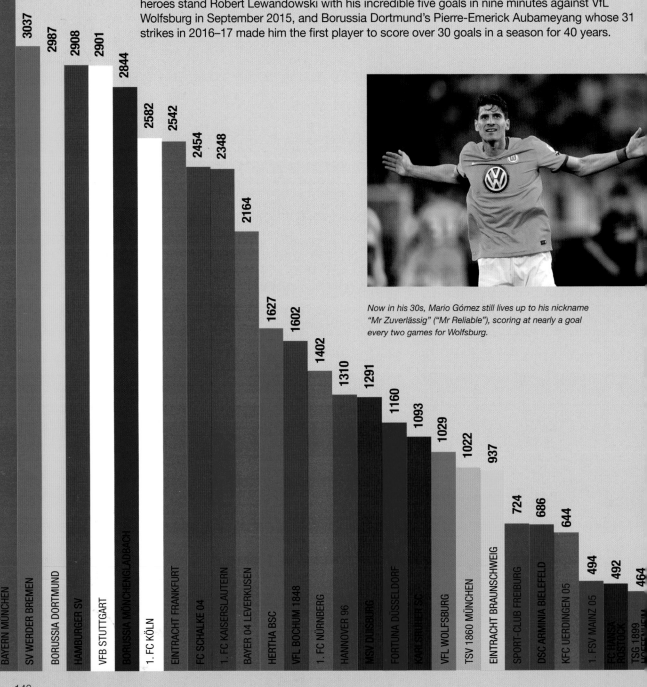

Now in his 30s, Mario Gómez still lives up to his nickname "Mr Zuverlässig" ("Mr Reliable"), scoring at nearly a goal every two games for Wolfsburg.

Club	Goals
BAYERN MÜNCHEN	3853
SV WERDER BREMEN	3037
BORUSSIA DORTMUND	2987
HAMBURGER SV	2908
VFB STUTTGART	2901
BORUSSIA MÖNCHENGLADBACH	2844
1. FC KÖLN	2582
EINTRACHT FRANKFURT	2542
FC SCHALKE 04	2454
1. FC KAISERSLAUTERN	2348
BAYER 04 LEVERKUSEN	2164
HERTHA BSC	1627
VFL BOCHUM 1848	1602
1. FC NÜRNBERG	1402
HANNOVER 96	1310
MSV DUISBURG	1291
FORTUNA DÜSSELDORF	1160
KARLSRUHER SC	1093
VFL WOLFSBURG	1029
TSV 1860 MÜNCHEN	1022
EINTRACHT BRAUNSCHWEIG	937
SPORT-CLUB FREIBURG	724
DSC ARMINIA BIELEFELD	686
KFC UERDINGEN 05	644
1. FSV MAINZ 05	494
FC HANSA ROSTOCK	492
TSG 1899	464

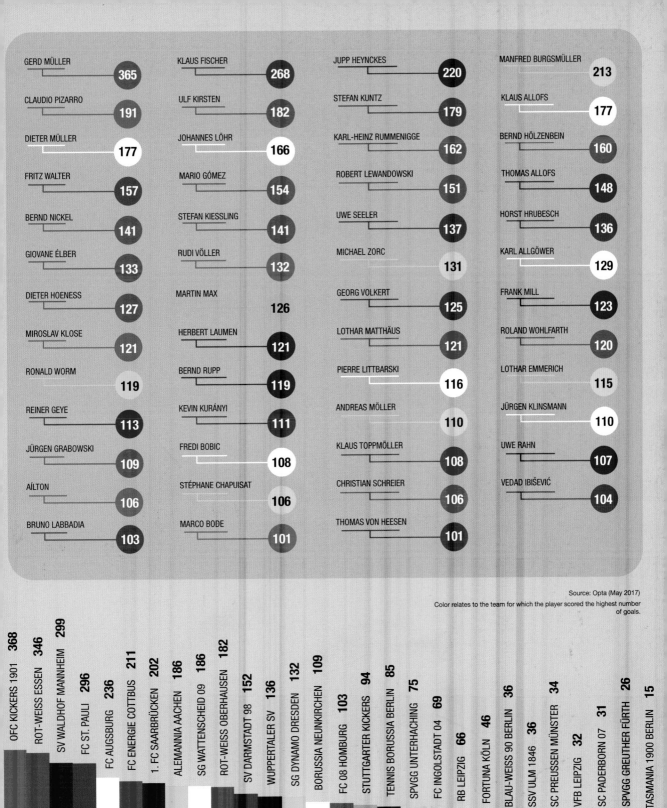

GERD MÜLLER	365
CLAUDIO PIZARRO	191
DIETER MÜLLER	177
FRITZ WALTER	157
BERND NICKEL	141
GIOVANE ÉLBER	133
DIETER HOENESS	127
MIROSLAV KLOSE	121
RONALD WORM	119
REINER GEYE	113
JÜRGEN GRABOWSKI	109
AÍLTON	106
BRUNO LABBADIA	103

KLAUS FISCHER	268
ULF KIRSTEN	182
JOHANNES LÖHR	166
MARIO GÓMEZ	154
STEFAN KIESSLING	141
RUDI VÖLLER	132
MARTIN MAX	126
HERBERT LAUMEN	121
BERND RUPP	119
KEVIN KURÁNYI	111
FREDI BOBIC	108
STÉPHANE CHAPUISAT	106
MARCO BODE	101

JUPP HEYNCKES	220
STEFAN KUNTZ	179
KARL-HEINZ RUMMENIGGE	162
ROBERT LEWANDOWSKI	151
UWE SEELER	137
MICHAEL ZORC	131
GEORG VOLKERT	125
LOTHAR MATTHÄUS	121
PIERRE LITTBARSKI	116
ANDREAS MÖLLER	110
KLAUS TOPPMÖLLER	108
CHRISTIAN SCHREIER	106
THOMAS VON HEESEN	101

MANFRED BURGSMÜLLER	213
KLAUS ALLOFS	177
BERND HÖLZENBEIN	160
THOMAS ALLOFS	148
HORST HRUBESCH	136
KARL ALLGÖWER	129
FRANK MILL	123
ROLAND WOHLFARTH	120
LOTHAR EMMERICH	115
JÜRGEN KLINSMANN	110
UWE RAHN	107
VEDAD IBIŠEVIĆ	104

Source: Opta (May 2017)

Color relates to the team for which the player scored the highest number of goals.

Team	Goals
OFC KICKERS 1901	368
ROT-WEISS ESSEN	346
SV WALDHOF MANNHEIM	299
FC ST. PAULI	296
FC AUGSBURG	236
FC ENERGIE COTTBUS	211
1. FC SAARBRÜCKEN	202
ALEMANNIA AACHEN	186
SG WATTENSCHEID 09	186
ROT-WEISS OBERHAUSEN	182
SV DARMSTADT 98	152
WUPPERTALER SV	136
SG DYNAMO DRESDEN	132
BORUSSIA NEUNKIRCHEN	109
FC 08 HOMBURG	103
STUTTGARTER KICKERS	94
TENNIS BORUSSIA BERLIN	85
SPVGG UNTERHACHING	75
FC INGOLSTADT 04	69
RB LEIPZIG	66
FORTUNA KÖLN	46
BLAU-WEISS 90 BERLIN	36
SSV ULM 1846	36
SC PREUSSEN MÜNSTER	34
VFB LEIPZIG	32
SC PADERBORN 07	31
SPVGG GREUTHER FÜRTH	26
TASMANIA 1900 BERLIN	15

LIGUE 1 TITLE WINNERS

Ligue 1 has been graced by 69 teams in its history, with a third of them making a serious impression on league records. The sixth-ranked league in Europe, it has seen one of the most evident shifts between traditional clubs and those benefitting from wealthy benefactors and investors. Those familiar with the recent success of PSG might find it surprising to view their win record still lagging some way behind the league's long-standing clubs, including Sochaux, now a Ligue 2 side and still living off their glories of the 1930s and 1960s.

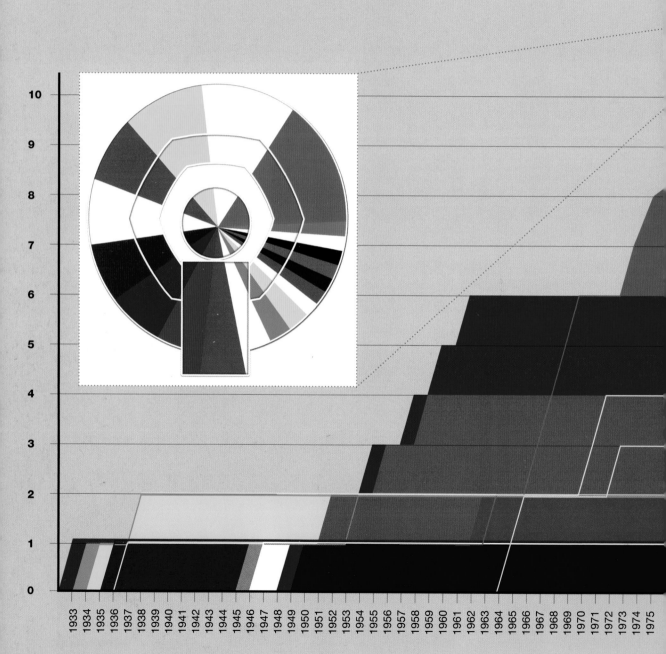

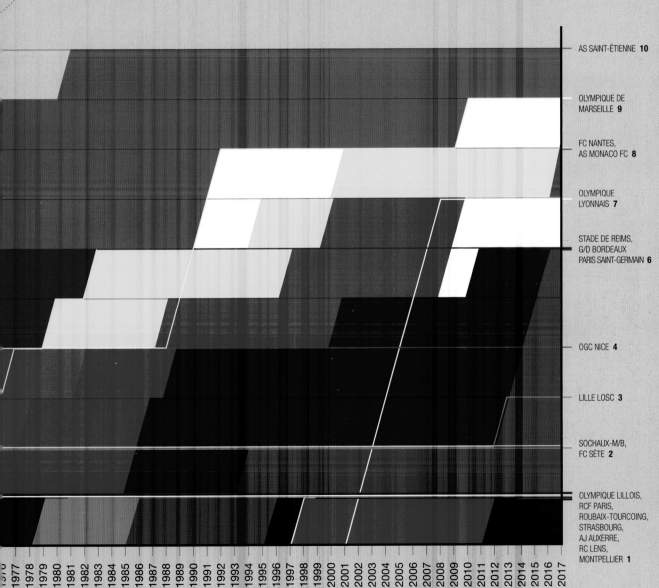

Key (anticlockwise from top-right)

- AS SAINT-ÉTIENNE **10**
- OLYMPIQUE DE MARSEILLE **9**
- FC NANTES **8**
- AS MONACO FC **8**
- OLYMPIQUE LYONNAIS **7**
- GIRONDINS DE BORDEAUX **6**
- STADE DE REIMS **6**

- PARIS SAINT-GERMAIN **6**
- OGC NICE **4**
- LILLE LOSC **3**
- FC SÈTE 34 **2**
- FC SOCHAUX-MONTBÉLIARD **2**
- AJ AUXERRE **1**

- OLYMPIQUE LILLOIS **1**
- MONTPELLIER HÉRRAULT SC **1**
- RC LENS **1**
- RCF PARIS **1**
- CO ROUBAIX-TOURCOING **1**
- RC STRASBOURG ALSACE **1**

Source: Opta (May 2017)

AS SAINT-ÉTIENNE **10**

OLYMPIQUE DE MARSEILLE **9**

FC NANTES, AS MONACO FC **8**

OLYMPIQUE LYONNAIS **7**

STADE DE REIMS, G/D BORDEAUX PARIS SAINT-GERMAIN **6**

OGC NICE **4**

LILLE LOSC **3**

SOCHAUX-M/B, FC SÈTE **2**

OLYMPIQUE LILLOIS, RCF PARIS, ROUBAIX-TOURCOING, STRASBOURG, AJ AUXERRE, RC LENS, MONTPELLIER **1**

1977 1978 1979 1980 1981 1982 1983 1984 1985 1986 1987 1988 1989 1990 1991 1992 1993 1994 1995 1996 1997 1998 1999 2000 2001 2002 2003 2004 2005 2006 2007 2008 2009 2010 2011 2012 2013 2014 2015 2016 2017

143

LIGUE 1 GAME WINS PER CLUB

Ligue 1 began in 1932, switching to its current name in 2002. Although many view it as one of the weaker of the major European leagues, it is one of the most evenly contested. Until Monaco's 2017 triumph, PSG have recently held sway, but in modern times AS Saint-Etienne (League 1's most successful club), Olympique Lyon (winner of a record seven consecutive titles between 2002 and 2008), and Olympique de Marseille (most seasons and wins in top flight) have all dominated the league.

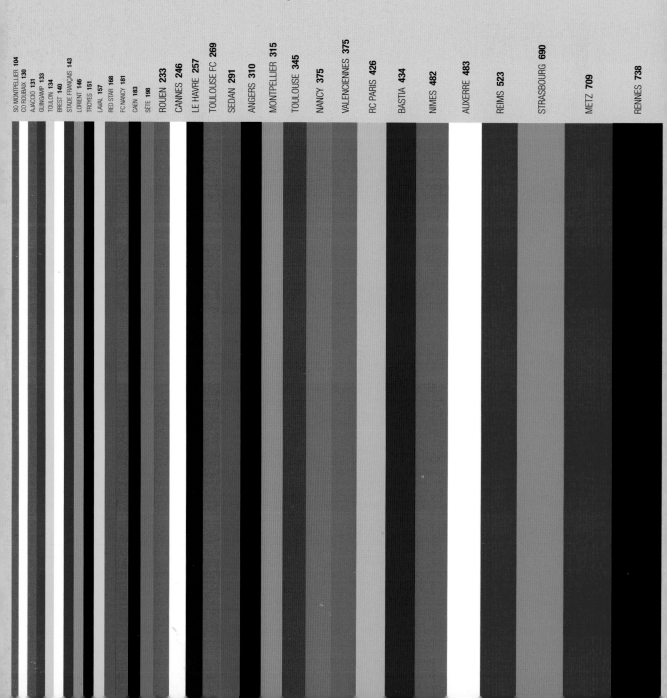

SO MONTPELLIER 104
CO ROUBAIX 130
AJACCIO 131
GUINGAMP 133
TOULON 134
BREST 140
STADE FRANÇAIS 143
LORIENT 146
TROYES 151
LAVAL 157
RED STAR 168
FC NANCY 181
CAEN 183
SETE 198
ROUEN 233
CANNES 246
LE HAVRE 257
TOULOUSE FC 269
SEDAN 291
ANGERS 310
MONTPELLIER 315
TOULOUSE 345
NANCY 375
VALENCIENNES 375
RC PARIS 426
BASTIA 434
NIMES 482
AUXERRE 483
REIMS 523
STRASBOURG 690
METZ 709
RENNES 738

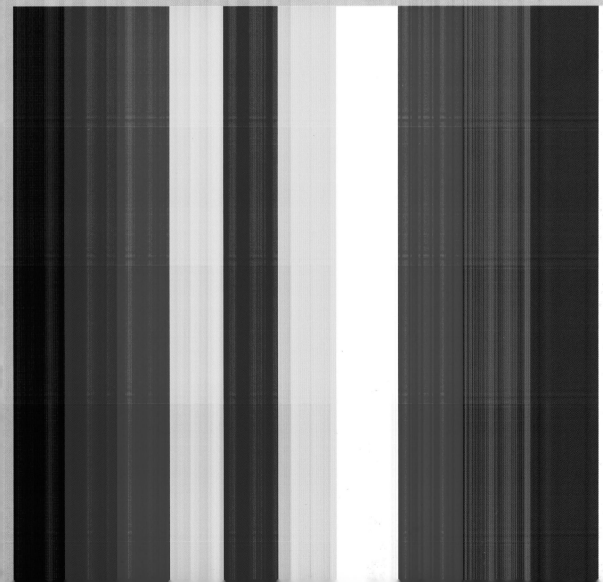

Source: Opta (May 2017)

Under 100 Wins

OLYMPIQUE LILLOIS **98**	ALÈS **42**	CA PARIS **13**	AVIGNON **7**
FIVES **77**	LIMOGES **37**	COLMAR **12**	BOULOGNE-SUR-MER **7**
EXCELSIOR **75**	PARIS FC **31**	LYON OU **11**	AIX **6**
ANTIBES **65**	ANGOULÊME **30**	NIORT **11**	ISTRES **6**
LE MANS **65**	GRENOBLE **30**	BÉZIERS **9**	CLUB FRANCAIS **5**
MULHOUSE **51**	MARTIGUES **27**	CHÂTEAUROUX **8**	HYÈRES **4**
ÉVIAN TG **45**	RC ROUBAIX **26**	GUEUGNON **8**	ARLES-AVIGNON **3**
TOURS **44**	DIJON **17**	GFC AJACCIO **8**	

PARIS SAINT-GERMAIN **747**
RC LENS **770**
NICE **780**
NANTES **788**
LILLE **794**
SOCHAUX **859**
OLYMPIQUE LYONNAIS **908**
MONACO **955**
SAINT-ÉTIENNE **1001**
BORDEAUX **1021**
MARSEILLE **1058**

LIGUE 1 GOALS PER CLUB

Seen by many of the world's richest clubs as a nursery for emerging young players, Ligue 1 has given renowned forwards such as Thierry Henry, Didier Drogba, Karim Benzema, and Eden Hazard their first team breaks. Zlatan Ibrahimović, a rare star import to the league, hit 113 goals in just 122 Ligue 1 games, but left France long before catching record holder Delio Onnis (an Argentinian nicknamed "The Italian"!) who netted 299 goals in 449 appearances between 1972 and 1986.

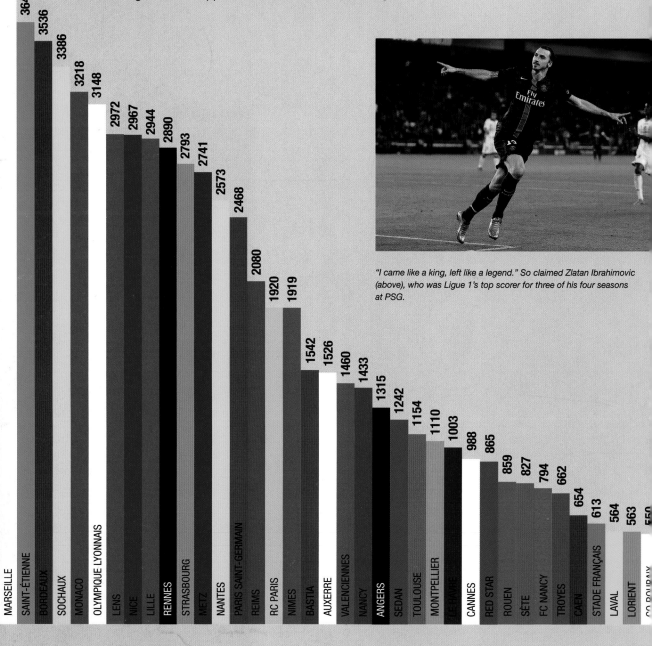

"I came like a king, left like a legend." So claimed Zlatan Ibrahimovic (above), who was Ligue 1's top scorer for three of his four seasons at PSG.

Club	Goals
MARSEILLE	3845
SAINT-ÉTIENNE	3641
BORDEAUX	3536
SOCHAUX	3386
MONACO	3218
OLYMPIQUE LYONNAIS	3148
LENS	2972
NICE	2967
LILLE	2944
RENNES	2890
STRASBOURG	2793
METZ	2741
NANTES	2573
PARIS SAINT-GERMAIN	2468
REIMS	2080
RC PARIS	1920
NIMES	1919
BASTIA	1542
AUXERRE	1526
VALENCIENNES	1460
NANCY	1433
ANGERS	1315
SEDAN	1242
TOULOUSE	1154
MONTPELLIER	1110
LE HAVRE	1003
CANNES	988
RED STAR	865
ROUEN	859
SÈTE	827
FC NANCY	794
TROYES	662
CAEN	654
STADE FRANÇAIS	613
LAVAL	564
LORIENT	563

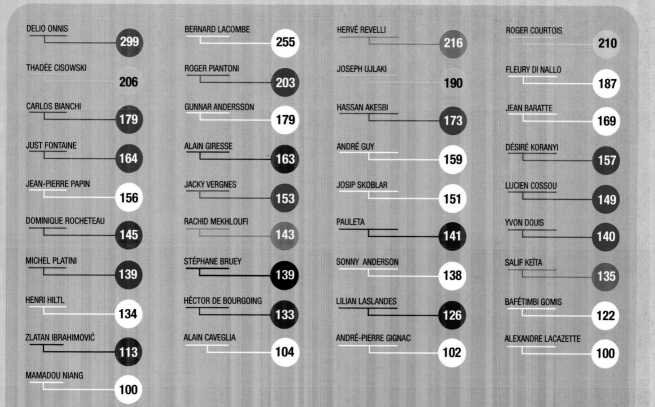

DELIO ONNIS **299**	BERNARD LACOMBE **255**	HERVÉ REVELLI **216**	ROGER COURTOIS **210**
THADÉE CISOWSKI **206**	ROGER PIANTONI **203**	JOSEPH UJLAKI **190**	FLEURY DI NALLO **187**
CARLOS BIANCHI **179**	GUNNAR ANDERSSON **179**	HASSAN AKESBI **173**	JEAN BARATTE **169**
JUST FONTAINE **164**	ALAIN GIRESSE **163**	ANDRÉ GUY **159**	DÉSIRÉ KORANYI **157**
JEAN-PIERRE PAPIN **156**	JACKY VERGNES **153**	JOSIP SKOBLAR **151**	LUCIEN COSSOU **149**
DOMINIQUE ROCHETEAU **145**	RACHID MEKHLOUFI **143**	PAULETA **141**	YVON DOUIS **140**
MICHEL PLATINI **139**	STÉPHANE BRUEY **139**	SONNY ANDERSON **138**	SALIF KEÏTA **135**
HENRI HILTL **134**	HÉCTOR DE BOURGOING **133**	LILIAN LASLANDES **126**	BAFÉTIMBI GOMIS **122**
ZLATAN IBRAHIMOVIĆ **113**	ALAIN CAVEGLIA **104**	ANDRÉ-PIERRE GIGNAC **102**	ALEXANDRE LACAZETTE **100**
MAMADOU NIANG **100**			

> **"I think that goalscoring is something that is born in a person—it's in the blood."**
>
> Jean-Pierre Papin

If ever there was a born goalscorer it was Papin. As Marseille's striker he was Ligue 1's top scorer in five consecutive seasons between 1988 and 1992. On returning to France from sojourns at Milan and Bayern, he carried on scoring at Bordeaux, taking his league tally to 156 goals in 270 appearances—the greatest goalscorer in modern French soccer.

Source: Opta (May 2017)
Seasons 1992–93 to 2016–17
Color relates to the team for which the player
scored the highest number of goals.

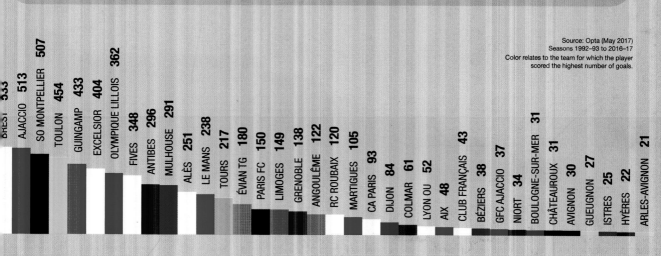

BREST 533 · AJACCIO 513 · SO MONTPELLIER 507 · TOULON 454 · GUINGAMP 433 · EXCELSIOR 404 · OLYMPIQUE LILLOIS 362 · FIVES 348 · ANTIBES 296 · MULHOUSE 291 · ALÈS 251 · LE MANS 238 · TOURS 217 · ÉVIAN TG 180 · PARIS FC 150 · LIMOGES 149 · GRENOBLE 138 · ANGOULÊME 122 · RC ROUBAIX 120 · MARTIGUES 105 · CA PARIS 93 · DIJON 84 · COLMAR 61 · LYON OU 52 · AIX 48 · CLUB FRANÇAIS 43 · BÉZIERS 38 · GFC AJACCIO 37 · NIORT 34 · BOULOGNE-SUR-MER 31 · CHÂTEAUROUX 31 · AVIGNON 30 · GUEUGNON 27 · ISTRES 25 · HYÈRES 22 · ARLES-AVIGNON 21

EREDIVISIE TITLE WINNERS

The Eredivisie, the top league of the Netherlands, was founded in 1956, two years after the start of professional soccer in the country. It is placed 13th in UEFA's ranking of European leagues. The Dutch league has been dominated by three teams, all ever-presents in the league: Ajax (24 titles), PSV Eindhoven (18), and Feyenoord (10), whose 2017 success was their first for 18 years. Only AZ Alkmaar and FC Twente have managed to break the grip of the "Big Three" this century.

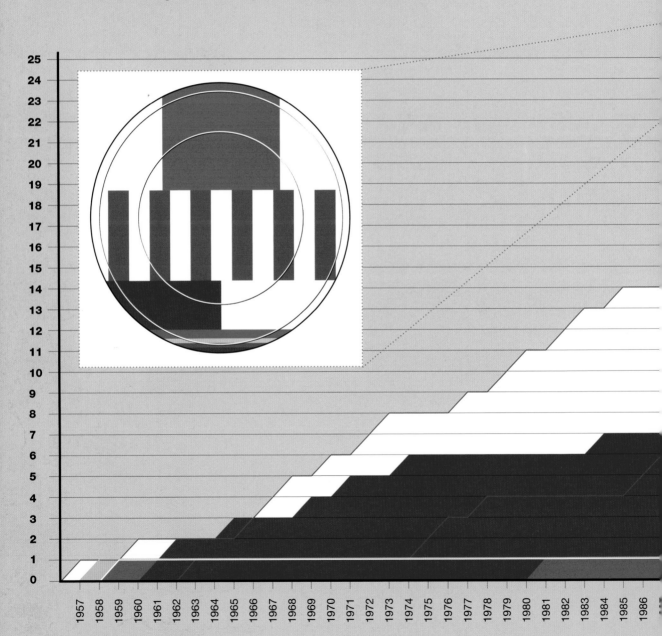

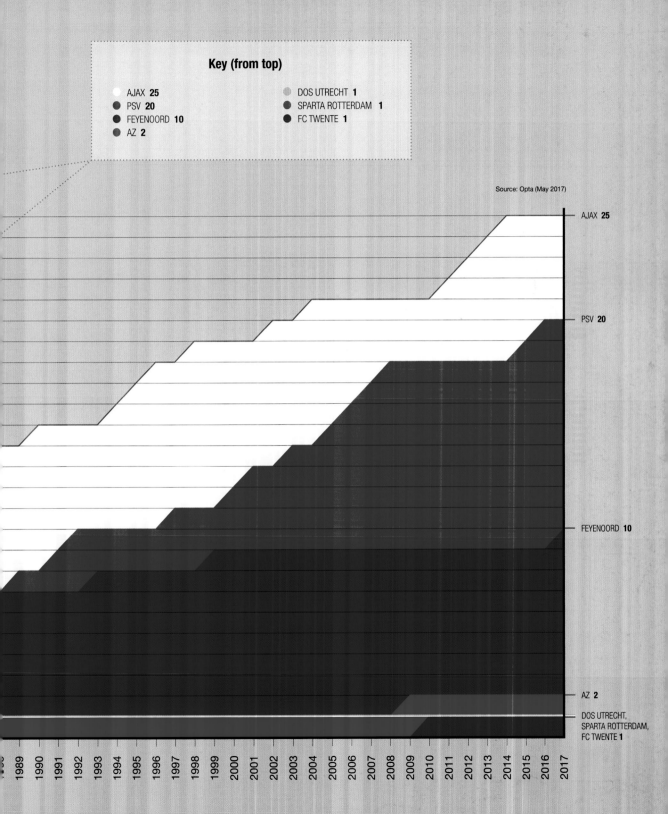

Key (from top)

- AJAX **25**
- PSV **20**
- FEYENOORD **10**
- AZ **2**
- DOS UTRECHT **1**
- SPARTA ROTTERDAM **1**
- FC TWENTE **1**

Source: Opta (May 2017)

AJAX **25**

PSV **20**

FEYENOORD **10**

AZ **2**

DOS UTRECHT,
SPARTA ROTTERDAM,
FC TWENTE **1**

1989 1990 1991 1992 1993 1994 1995 1996 1997 1998 1999 2000 2001 2002 2003 2004 2005 2006 2007 2008 2009 2010 2011 2012 2013 2014 2015 2016 2017

149

EREDIVISIE GAME WINS PER CLUB

Ajax, Feyenoord, and PSV have been the dominant Eredivisie clubs, with all three having many successful spells—often sharing the limelight with the others. PSV had the Romario-inspired team around 1990 and Gus Hiddink's all-conquering side in the early 2000s. Feyenoord's 1971 European Cup side boasted the talents of Willem van Hanegem and winger Coen Moulijn, and Ajax have consistently competed for the title, reaching almost unsurpassable heights with the 1970s team of Johan Neeskens and Johan Cruyff and the '90s line-ups including Dennis Bergkamp, Patrick Kluivert, Edgar Davids, and Clarence Seedorf.

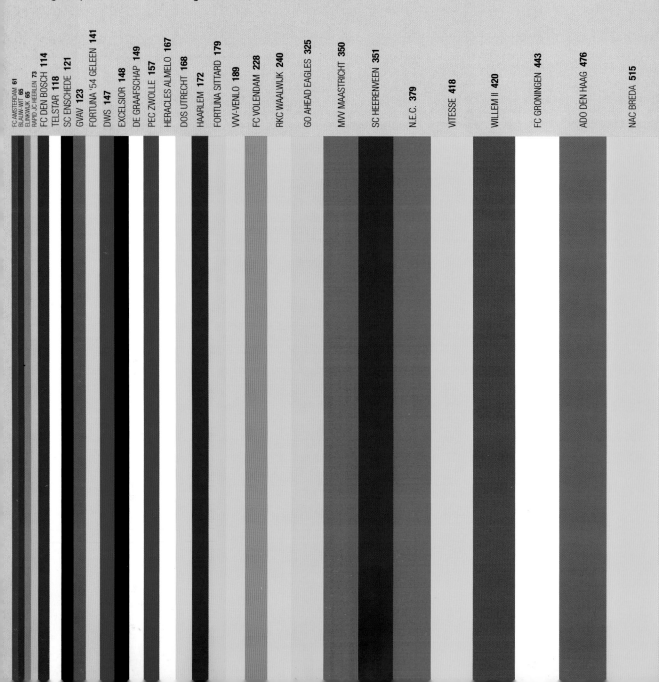

FC AMSTERDAM 61
BLAUW-WIT 65
RAPID JC HEERLEN 73
FC DEN BOSCH 114
TELSTAR 118
SC ENSCHEDE 121
GVAV 123
FORTUNA '54 GELEEN 141
DWS 147
EXCELSIOR 148
DE GRAAFSCHAP 149
PEC ZWOLLE 157
HERACLES ALMELO 167
DOS UTRECHT 168
HAARLEM 172
FORTUNA SITTARD 179
VVV-VENLO 189
FC VOLENDAM 228
RKC WAALWIJK 240
GO AHEAD EAGLES 325
MVV MAASTRICHT 350
SC HEERENVEEN 351
N.E.C. 379
VITESSE 418
WILLEM II 420
FC GRONINGEN 443
ADO DEN HAAG 476
NAC BREDA 515

Under 50 Wins

SC CAMBUUR **49**	XERXESDZB **26**	WAGENINGEN **13**
SHS **37**	FC EINDHOVEN **23**	HELMOND SPORT **12**
RBC ROOSENDAAL **35**	BVC AMSTERDAM **20**	VEENDAM **12**
NOAD **33**	BVV **18**	ALKMAAR **6**
SITTARDIA **32**	DE VOLEWIJCKERS **15**	
FC DORDRECHT **31**	SVV **13**	

RODA JC KERKRADE **555**

AZ **559**

FC UTRECHT **589**

SPARTA ROTTERDAM **612**

FC TWENTE **766**

FEYENOORD **1168**

PSV **1246**

AJAX **1360**

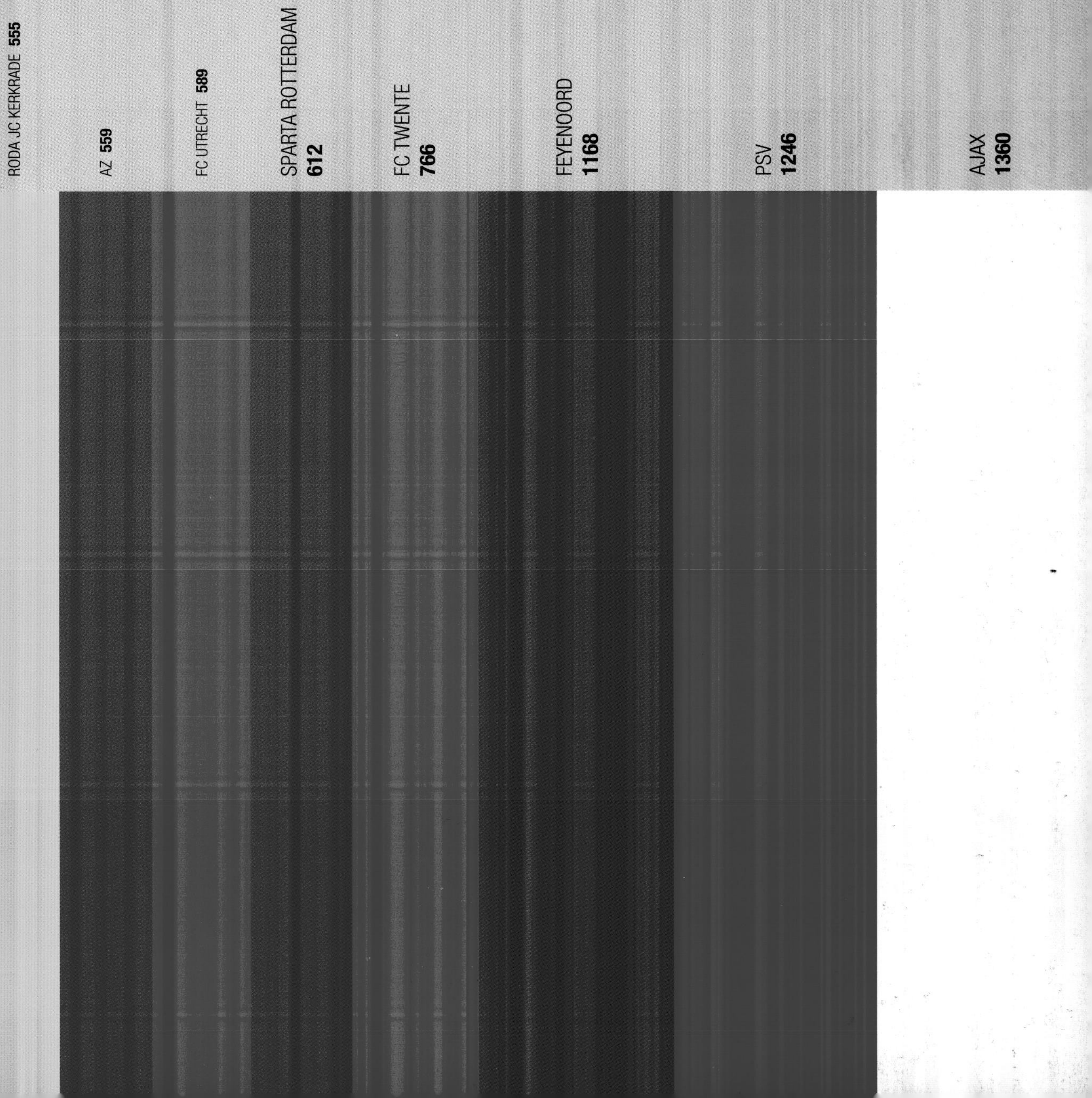

EREDIVISIE GOALS PER CLUB

Of course, the "big three" Netherlands teams dominate the goalscoring tables—Ajax even managed 122 in one season in 1966–67 and PSV's Coen Dillen, nicknamed "Het Kanon", struck 43 times in 1956–57. The modern Dutch goal masters—Cruyff, van Basten, Bergkamp, Van Nistelrooy—all figure as season's top scorers, but the lesser known Ruud Geels was the leading striker on five occasions (four times for Ajax, once for Sparta) between 1974 and 1981. More recently the minor teams strikers have topped the charts on several occasions, including Wilfrid Bony for Vitesse (2012–13), Alfreð Finnbogason of Heerenveen (2013–14), and AZ's Vincent Janssen (2015–16).

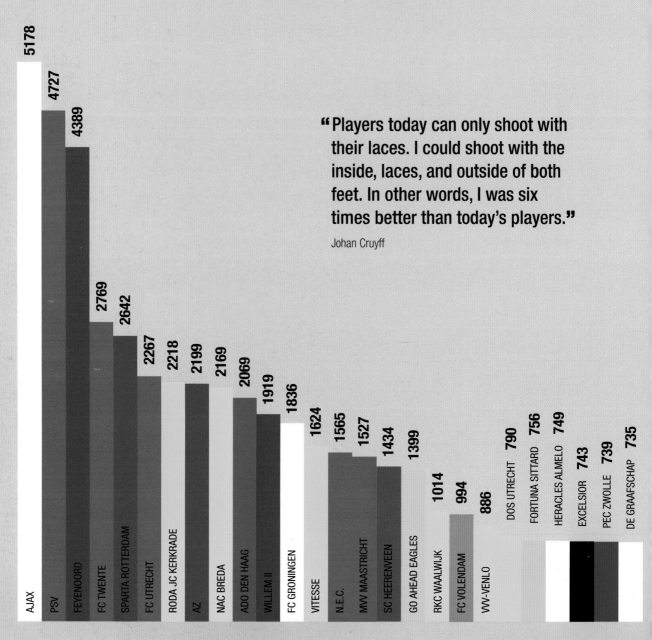

> " Players today can only shoot with their laces. I could shoot with the inside, laces, and outside of both feet. In other words, I was six times better than today's players. "
>
> Johan Cruyff

Club	Goals
AJAX	5178
PSV	4727
FEYENOORD	4389
FC TWENTE	2769
SPARTA ROTTERDAM	2642
FC UTRECHT	2267
RODA JC KERKRADE	2218
AZ	2199
NAC BREDA	2169
ADO DEN HAAG	2069
WILLEM II	1919
FC GRONINGEN	1836
VITESSE	1624
N.E.C.	1565
MVV MAASTRICHT	1527
SC HEERENVEEN	1434
GO AHEAD EAGLES	1399
RKC WAALWIJK	1014
FC VOLENDAM	994
VVV-VENLO	886
DOS UTRECHT	790
FORTUNA SITTARD	756
HERACLES ALMELO	749
EXCELSIOR	743
PEC ZWOLLE	739
DE GRAAFSCHAP	735

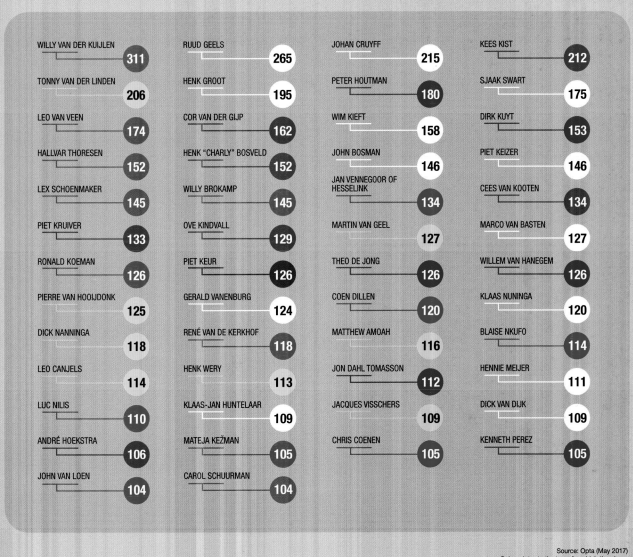

Player	Goals
WILLY VAN DER KUIJLEN	311
TONNY VAN DER LINDEN	206
LEO VAN VEEN	174
HALLVAR THORESEN	152
LEX SCHOENMAKER	145
PIET KRUIVER	133
RONALD KOEMAN	126
PIERRE VAN HOOIJDONK	125
DICK NANNINGA	118
LEO CANJELS	114
LUC NILIS	110
ANDRÉ HOEKSTRA	106
JOHN VAN LOEN	104

Player	Goals
RUUD GEELS	265
HENK GROOT	195
COR VAN DER GIJP	162
HENK "CHARLY" BOSVELD	152
WILLY BROKAMP	145
OVE KINDVALL	129
PIET KEUR	126
GERALD VANENBURG	124
RENÉ VAN DE KERKHOF	118
HENK WERY	113
KLAAS-JAN HUNTELAAR	109
MATEJA KEŽMAN	105
CAROL SCHUURMAN	104

Player	Goals
JOHAN CRUYFF	215
PETER HOUTMAN	180
WIM KIEFT	158
JOHN BOSMAN	146
JAN VENNEGOOR OF HESSELINK	134
MARTIN VAN GEEL	127
THEO DE JONG	126
COEN DILLEN	120
MATTHEW AMOAH	116
JON DAHL TOMASSON	112
JACQUES VISSCHERS	109
CHRIS COENEN	105

Player	Goals
KEES KIST	212
SJAAK SWART	175
DIRK KUYT	153
PIET KEIZER	146
CEES VAN KOOTEN	134
MARCO VAN BASTEN	127
WILLEM VAN HANEGEM	126
KLAAS NUNINGA	120
BLAISE NKUFO	114
HENNIE MEIJER	111
DICK VAN DIJK	109
KENNETH PEREZ	105

Source: Opta (May 2017)
Color relates to the team for which the player scored the highest number of goals.

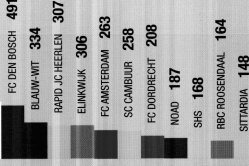
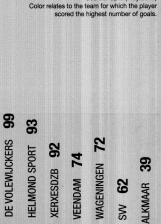

Team	Value
HAARLEM	695
FORTUNA '54 GELEEN	635
DWS	588
SC ENSCHEDE	565
GVAV	533
TELSTAR	530
FC DEN BOSCH	491
BLAUW-WIT	334
RAPID JC HEERLEN	307
ELINKWIJK	306
FC AMSTERDAM	263
SC CAMBUUR	258
FC DORDRECHT	208
NOAD	187
SHS	168
RBC ROOSENDAAL	164
SITTARDIA	148
BVV	126
FC EINDHOVEN	107
BVC AMSTERDAM	103
DE VOLEWIJCKERS	99
HELMOND SPORT	93
XERXESDZB	92
VEENDAM	74
WAGENINGEN	72
SVV	62
ALKMAAR	39

MLS TROPHY WINS PER CLUB

Major League Soccer (MLS), the top tier of soccer in the USA and Canada, was inspired by the success of the 1994 World Cup in the US. The league's first season took place in 1996 and consisted of 10 teams. In the following 20 years the number of teams has expanded to 22—including three teams from Canada—with further expansion planned for 2020. Organized into an Eastern and Western conference, clubs compete for a place in the national playoffs to represent their conference in a final to win the MLS—also known as the Philip F. Anschutz Trophy.

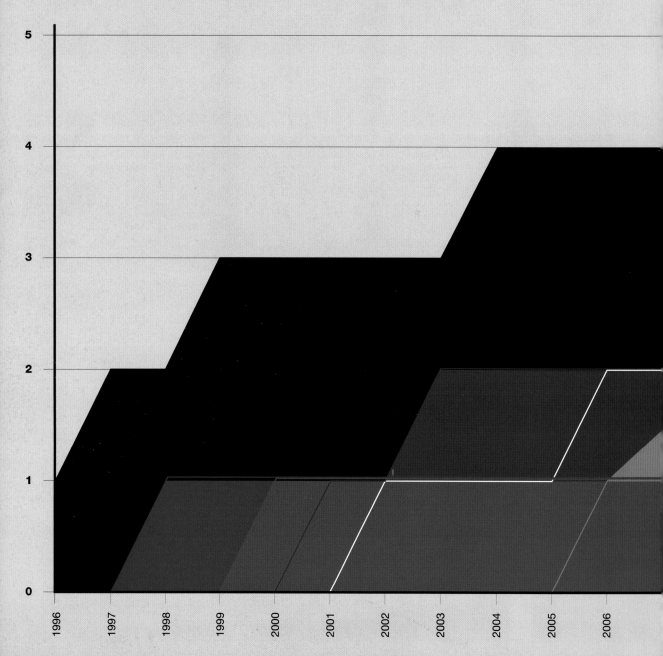

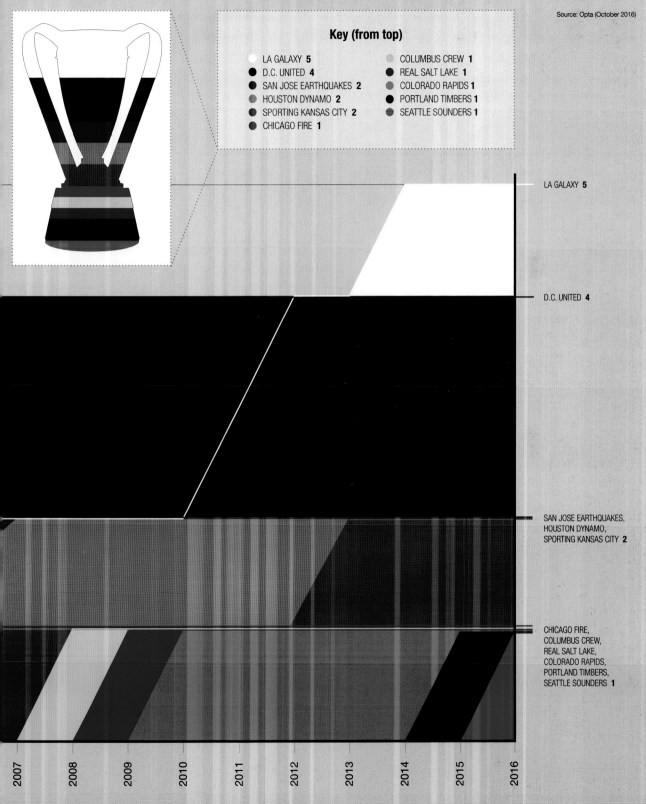

Source: Opta (October 2016)

Key (from top)

○ LA GALAXY **5**	● COLUMBUS CREW **1**
● D.C. UNITED **4**	● REAL SALT LAKE **1**
● SAN JOSE EARTHQUAKES **2**	● COLORADO RAPIDS **1**
● HOUSTON DYNAMO **2**	● PORTLAND TIMBERS **1**
● SPORTING KANSAS CITY **2**	● SEATTLE SOUNDERS **1**
● CHICAGO FIRE **1**	

LA GALAXY **5**

D.C. UNITED **4**

SAN JOSE EARTHQUAKES,
HOUSTON DYNAMO,
SPORTING KANSAS CITY **2**

CHICAGO FIRE,
COLUMBUS CREW,
REAL SALT LAKE,
COLORADO RAPIDS,
PORTLAND TIMBERS,
SEATTLE SOUNDERS **1**

2007 2008 2009 2010 2011 2012 2013 2014 2015 2016

MLS GAME WINS PER CLUB

The forerunner to the MLS was the ill-fated North American Soccer League (NASL), a division that relied too heavily on imported celebrity players such as Pelé and Franz Beckenbauer to have home success. The MLS too once enlisted the assistance of foreign stars to boost its appeal, including David Beckham, Cuauhtémoc Blanco, Andrea Pirlo, and David Villa, but in recent years it has established itself as a sustainable league, attracting an average of 18,600 fans a game and global TV interest, and is dedicated to nurturing home-grown talent. Today, the MLS is the world's fastest-growing sport.

Source: Opta (October 2016)

Club	Wins
ORLANDO CITY SC	21
NEW YORK CITY FC	25
MIAMI FUSION	49
MONTREAL IMPACT	64
VANCOUVER WHITECAPS	68
PHILADELPHIA UNION	72
TAMPA BAY MUTINY	75
PORTLAND TIMBERS	77
CHIVAS USA	93
SPORTING KANSAS CITY	94
TORONTO FC	95
SAN JOSE EARTHQUAKES	98
SAN JOSE	122
SEATTLE SOUNDERS FC	134
HOUSTON DYNAMO	142
REAL SALT LAKE	150
KANSAS CITY WIZARDS	175
COLORADO RAPIDS	248

ost recent major league in world soccer, the MLS is still
g. This table needs to be read in relation to the number of
he team has been playing in the MLS. Although some clubs have
their name, no teams have been relegated from the league.

e original 10 teams comprise: Colorado Rapids, Columbus
. United, Dallas Burn (later FC Dallas), Kansas City Wizards, LA
ew England Revolution, NY/NJ Metro Stars (later New York Red
n Jose Clash (later Earthquakes) and Tampa Bay Mutiny.
icago Fire, Miami Fusion

2005: Real Salt Lake, Chivas USA
2006: Houston Dynamo
2007: Toronto FC
2009: Seattle Sounders
2010: Philadelphia Union
2011: Portland Timbers, Vancouver Whitecaps
2012: Montreal Impact
2015: New York City FC, Orlando City
2017: Minnesota United, Atlanta United

CHICAGO FIRE **251**

NEW YORK RED BULLS **268**

COLUMBUS CREW SC **273**

FC DALLAS **275**

D.C. UNITED **279**

LA GALAXY **330**

MLS GOALS PER CLUB

Thierry Henry, Robbie Keane, and Didier Drogba have all scored freely in the States, but the record books are topped by home-grown heroes like Landon Donovan, Jeff Cunningham, and Chris Wondolowski. The goals recorded here include such gems as the 50-yard run by Metrostars' Clint Mathis to score the 2001 MLS Goal of the Year, the magnificent flick and volley from the Vancouver Whitecaps' Eric Hassli in 2011 and David Villa's exquisite chip from the halfway line for New York City FC in 2017.

Source: mlssoccer.com (October 2016)
Player data: Color relates to the team for which the player scored the highest number of goals.

Landon Donovan stands alone in MLS history. He is not only the clear all-time leading scorer but is also at the head of the all-time assists list. In 2009 he won the league's MVP award and in 2015 they named the award after him. Outside of short periods with Bayer Leverkusen, Bayern München, and Everton, Donovan has spent his whole career in the MLS; four seasons with San Jose Earthquakes (32 goals) and 11 seasons with LA Galaxy (113 goals). Donovan has won the MLS Cup a record six times—twice with the Earthquakes and four times with the Galaxy.

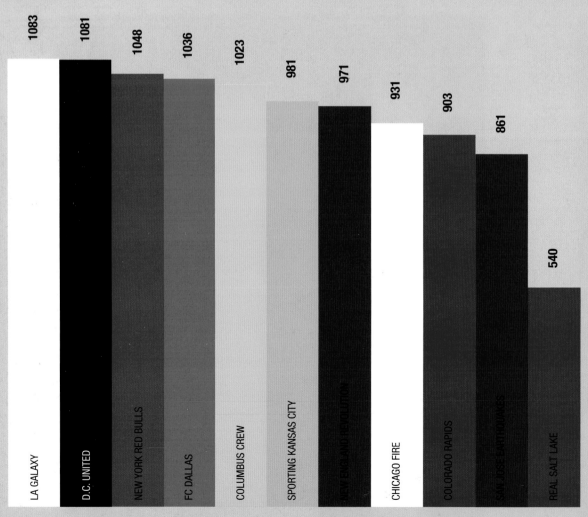

Club	Goals
LA GALAXY	1083
D.C. UNITED	1081
NEW YORK RED BULLS	1048
FC DALLAS	1036
COLUMBUS CREW	1023
SPORTING KANSAS CITY	981
NEW ENGLAND REVOLUTION	971
CHICAGO FIRE	931
COLORADO RAPIDS	903
SAN JOSE EARTHQUAKES	861
REAL SALT LAKE	540

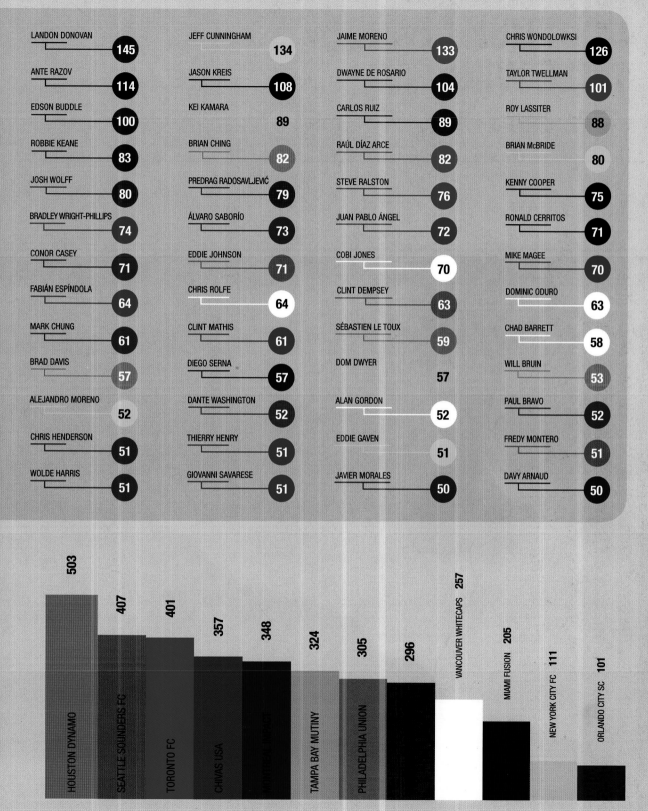

LANDON DONOVAN **145**

ANTE RAZOV **114**

EDSON BUDDLE **100**

ROBBIE KEANE **83**

JOSH WOLFF **80**

BRADLEY WRIGHT-PHILLIPS **74**

CONOR CASEY **71**

FABIÁN ESPÍNDOLA **64**

MARK CHUNG **61**

BRAD DAVIS **57**

ALEJANDRO MORENO **52**

CHRIS HENDERSON **51**

WOLDE HARRIS **51**

JEFF CUNNINGHAM **134**

JASON KREIS **108**

KEI KAMARA **89**

BRIAN CHING **82**

PREDRAG RADOSAVLJEVIĆ **79**

ÁLVARO SABORÍO **73**

EDDIE JOHNSON **71**

CHRIS ROLFE **64**

CLINT MATHIS **61**

DIEGO SERNA **57**

DANTE WASHINGTON **52**

THIERRY HENRY **51**

GIOVANNI SAVARESE **51**

JAIME MORENO **133**

DWAYNE DE ROSARIO **104**

CARLOS RUIZ **89**

RAÚL DÍAZ ARCE **82**

STEVE RALSTON **76**

JUAN PABLO ÁNGEL **72**

COBI JONES **70**

CLINT DEMPSEY **63**

SÉBASTIEN LE TOUX **59**

DOM DWYER **57**

ALAN GORDON **52**

EDDIE GAVEN **51**

JAVIER MORALES **50**

CHRIS WONDOLOWKSI **126**

TAYLOR TWELLMAN **101**

ROY LASSITER **88**

BRIAN McBRIDE **80**

KENNY COOPER **75**

RONALD CERRITOS **71**

MIKE MAGEE **70**

DOMINIC ODURO **63**

CHAD BARRETT **58**

WILL BRUIN **53**

PAUL BRAVO **52**

FREDY MONTERO **51**

DAVY ARNAUD **50**

HOUSTON DYNAMO **503**

SEATTLE SOUNDERS FC **407**

TORONTO FC **401**

CHIVAS USA **357**

MONTREAL IMPACT **348**

TAMPA BAY MUTINY **324**

PHILADELPHIA UNION **305**

296

VANCOUVER WHITECAPS **257**

MIAMI FUSION **205**

NEW YORK CITY FC **111**

ORLANDO CITY SC **101**

SCOTTISH LEAGUE TITLE WINNERS

The Scottish Football League was established in 1890 just two years after its English counterpart. Dumbarton captured the first two titles, but the domination of Glasgow's Old Firm—Celtic and Rangers—soon took hold. The top flight was reorganized into the Scottish Premier League (1998–2013) and the Scottish Premiership (since 2013)—comprising 12 clubs since the 2000–01 season. All clubs play each other three times before the league is split in half, with teams playing a further single match against each of their section.

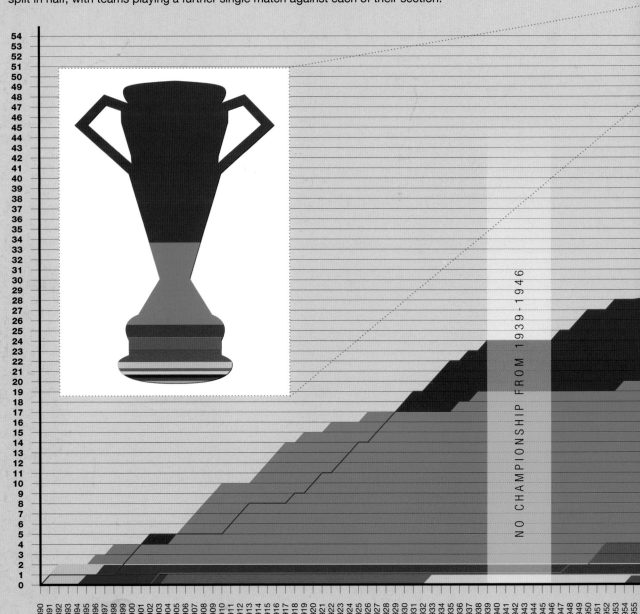

NO CHAMPIONSHIP FROM 1939-1946

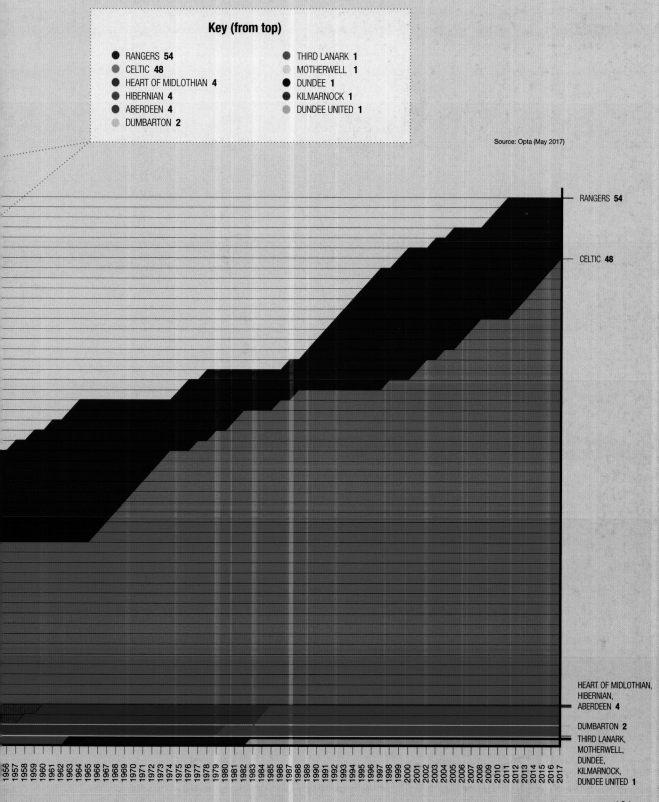

Key (from top)

- RANGERS **54**
- CELTIC **48**
- HEART OF MIDLOTHIAN **4**
- HIBERNIAN **4**
- ABERDEEN **4**
- DUMBARTON **2**
- THIRD LANARK **1**
- MOTHERWELL **1**
- DUNDEE **1**
- KILMARNOCK **1**
- DUNDEE UNITED **1**

Source: Opta (May 2017)

RANGERS **54**

CELTIC **48**

HEART OF MIDLOTHIAN,
HIBERNIAN,
ABERDEEN **4**

DUMBARTON **2**
THIRD LANARK,
MOTHERWELL,
DUNDEE,
KILMARNOCK,
DUNDEE UNITED **1**

1956 1957 1958 1959 1960 1961 1962 1963 1964 1965 1966 1967 1968 1969 1970 1971 1972 1973 1974 1975 1976 1977 1978 1979 1980 1981 1982 1983 1984 1985 1986 1987 1988 1989 1990 1991 1992 1993 1994 1995 1996 1997 1998 1999 2000 2001 2002 2003 2004 2005 2006 2007 2008 2009 2010 2011 2012 2013 2014 2015 2016 2017

EUROPEAN ATTENDANCES

Attendances in the top tiers of European soccer average around 30,000 per game, with the Bundesliga and the Premier League attracting the highest average crowds. Despite rising ticket prices and more televised games, the gates in England, Germany, and Spain continue to rise, while those in Italy and France remain static. Over the next few years major new stadia and expansions by clubs who already sell out many games, including Tottenham Hotspur, Atlético Madrid, Barcelona, Valencia, and Liverpool, could see further sharp rises in attendance.

Source: Opta (May 2017)

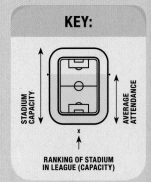

KEY:

STADIUM CAPACITY

AVERAGE ATTENDANCE

x

RANKING OF STADIUM IN LEAGUE (CAPACITY)

ENGLISH PREMIER LEAGUE

95%

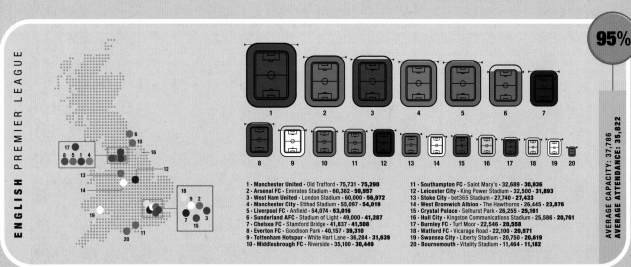

1 · **Manchester United** · Old Trafford · 75,731 · **75,290**
2 · **Arsenal FC** · Emirates Stadium · 60,362 · **59,957**
3 · **West Ham United** · London Stadium · 60,000 · **56,972**
4 · **Manchester City** · Etihad Stadium · 55,097 · **54,019**
5 · **Liverpool FC** · Anfield · 54,074 · **53,016**
6 · **Sunderland AFC** · Stadium of Light · 49,000 · **41,287**
7 · **Chelsea FC** · Stamford Bridge · 41,837 · **41,508**
8 · **Everton FC** · Goodison Park · 40,157 · **39,310**
9 · **Tottenham Hotspur** · White Hart Lane · 36,284 · **31,639**
10 · **Middlesbrough FC** · Riverside · 35,100 · **30,449**

11 · **Southampton FC** · Saint Mary's · 32,689 · **30,936**
12 · **Leicester City** · King Power Stadium · 32,500 · **31,893**
13 · **Stoke City** · bet365 Stadium · 27,740 · **27,433**
14 · **West Bromwich Albion** · The Hawthorns · 26,445 · **23,876**
15 · **Crystal Palace** · Selhurst Park · 26,255 · **25,161**
16 · **Hull City** · Kingston Communications Stadium · 25,586 · **20,761**
17 · **Burnley FC** · Turf Moor · 22,546 · **20,558**
18 · **Watford FC** · Vicarage Road · 22,100 · **20,571**
19 · **Swansea City** · Liberty Stadium · 20,750 · **20,619**
20 · **Bournemouth** · Vitality Stadium · 11,464 · **11,182**

AVERAGE CAPACITY: 37,786
AVERAGE ATTENDANCE: 35,822

GERMAN BUNDESLIGA

93%

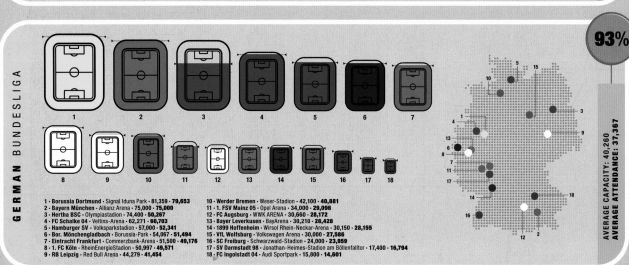

1 · **Borussia Dortmund** · Signal Iduna Park · 81,359 · **79,653**
2 · **Bayern München** · Allianz Arena · 75,000 · **75,000**
3 · **Hertha BSC** · Olympiastadion · 74,400 · **50,267**
4 · **FC Schalke 04** · Veltins-Arena · 62,271 · **60,703**
5 · **Hamburger SV** · Volksparkstadion · 57,000 · **52,341**
6 · **Bor. Mönchengladbach** · Borussia-Park · 54,067 · **51,494**
7 · **Eintracht Frankfurt** · Commerzbank-Arena · 51,500 · **49,176**
8 · **1. FC Köln** · RheinEnergieStadion · 50,997 · **49,571**
9 · **RB Leipzig** · Red Bull Arena · 44,279 · **41,454**

10 · **Werder Bremen** · Weser-Stadion · 42,100 · **40,881**
11 · **1. FSV Mainz 05** · Opel Arena · 34,000 · **29,096**
12 · **FC Augsburg** · WWK ARENA · 30,660 · **28,172**
13 · **Bayer Leverkusen** · BayArena · 30,210 · **28,428**
14 · **1899 Hoffenheim** · Wirsol Rhein-Neckar-Arena · 30,150 · **28,155**
15 · **VfL Wolfsburg** · Volkswagen Arena · 30,000 · **27,586**
16 · **SC Freiburg** · Schwarzwald-Stadion · 24,000 · **23,959**
17 · **SV Darmstadt 98** · Jonathan-Heimes-Stadion am Böllenfalltor · 17,400 · **16,794**
18 · **FC Ingolstadt 04** · Audi Sportpark · 15,800 · **14,601**

AVERAGE CAPACITY: 40,260
AVERAGE ATTENDANCE: 37,367

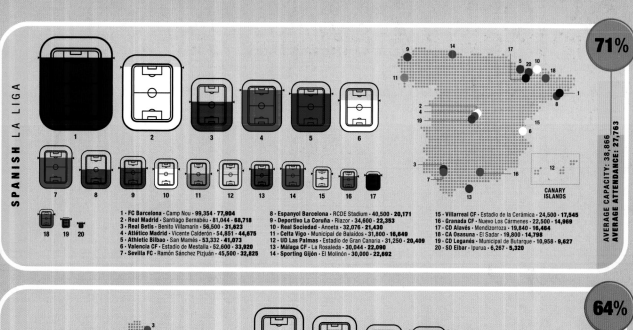

SPANISH LA LIGA

71%

AVERAGE CAPACITY: 38,866
AVERAGE ATTENDANCE: 27,763

CANARY ISLANDS

1 **FC Barcelona** · Camp Nou · **99,354** · **77,904**
2 **Real Madrid** · Santiago Bernabéu · **81,044** · **68,718**
3 **Real Betis** · Benito Villamarín · **56,500** · **31,623**
4 **Atlético Madrid** · Vicente Calderón · **54,851** · **44,675**
5 **Athletic Bilbao** · San Mamés · **53,332** · **41,073**
6 **Valencia CF** · Estadio de Mestalla · **52,600** · **33,920**
7 **Sevilla FC** · Ramón Sánchez Pizjuán · **45,500** · **32,825**
8 **Espanyol Barcelona** · RCDE Stadium · **40,500** · **20,171**
9 **Deportivo La Coruña** · Riazor · **34,600** · **22,353**
10 **Real Sociedad** · Anoeta · **32,076** · **21,430**
11 **Celta Vigo** · Municipal de Balaídos · **31,800** · **16,649**
12 **UD Las Palmas** · Estadio de Gran Canaria · **31,250** · **20,409**
13 **Málaga CF** · La Rosaleda · **30,044** · **22,090**
14 **Sporting Gijón** · El Molinón · **30,000** · **22,692**
15 **Villarreal CF** · Estadio de la Cerámica · **24,500** · **17,545**
16 **Granada CF** · Nuevo Los Cármenes · **22,500** · **14,969**
17 **CD Alavés** · Mendizorroza · **19,840** · **16,464**
18 **CA Osasuna** · El Sadar · **19,800** · **14,798**
19 **CD Leganés** · Municipal de Butarque · **10,958** · **9,627**
20 **SD Eibar** · Ipurua · **6,267** · **5,320**

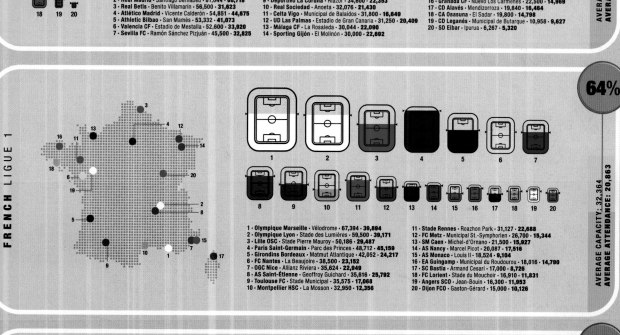

FRENCH LIGUE 1

64%

AVERAGE CAPACITY: 32,364
AVERAGE ATTENDANCE: 20,863

1 **Olympique Marseille** · Vélodrome · **67,394** · **39,894**
2 **Olympique Lyon** · Stade des Lumières · **59,500** · **39,171**
3 **Lille OSC** · Stade Pierre Mauroy · **50,186** · **29,487**
4 **Paris Saint-Germain** · Parc des Princes · **48,712** · **45,159**
5 **Girondins Bordeaux** · Matmut Atlantique · **42,052** · **24,217**
6 **FC Nantes** · La Beaujoire · **38,500** · **23,152**
7 **OGC Nice** · Allianz Riviera · **35,624** · **22,949**
8 **AS Saint-Étienne** · Geoffroy Guichard · **35,616** · **25,792**
9 **Toulouse FC** · Stade Municipal · **35,575** · **17,068**
10 **Montpellier HSC** · La Mosson · **32,950** · **12,356**
11 **Stade Rennes** · Roazhon Park · **31,127** · **22,688**
12 **FC Metz** · Municipal St.-Symphorien · **26,700** · **15,344**
13 **SM Caen** · Michel-d'Ornano · **21,500** · **15,927**
14 **AS Nancy** · Marcel Picot · **20,087** · **17,516**
15 **AS Monaco** · Louis II · **18,524** · **9,104**
16 **EA Guingamp** · Municipal du Roudourou · **18,016** · **14,790**
17 **SC Bastia** · Armand Cesari · **17,000** · **8,726**
18 **FC Lorient** · Stade du Mouchoir · **16,910** · **11,831**
19 **Angers SCO** · Jean-Bouin · **16,300** · **11,953**
20 **Dijon FCO** · Gaston-Gérard · **15,000** · **10,126**

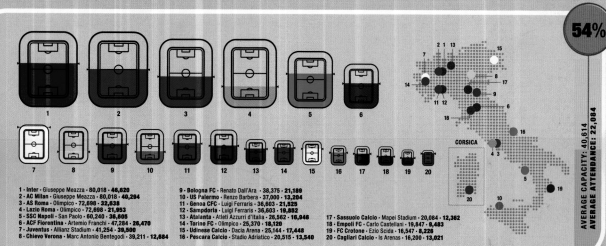

ITALIAN SERIE A

54%

AVERAGE CAPACITY: 40,614
AVERAGE ATTENDANCE: 22,084

CORSICA

1 **Inter** · Giuseppe Meazza · **80,018** · **46,620**
2 **AC Milan** · Giuseppe Meazza · **80,018** · **40,294**
3 **AS Roma** · Olimpico · **72,698** · **32,638**
4 **Lazio Roma** · Olimpico · **72,698** · **21,953**
5 **SSC Napoli** · San Paolo · **60,240** · **36,605**
6 **ACF Fiorentina** · Artemio Franchi · **47,284** · **26,470**
7 **Juventus** · Allianz Stadium · **41,254** · **39,500**
8 **Chievo Verona** · Marc Antonio Bentegodi · **39,211** · **12,684**
9 **Bologna FC** · Renato Dall'Ara · **38,375** · **21,189**
10 **US Palermo** · Renzo Barbera · **37,000** · **13,204**
11 **Genoa CFC** · Luigi Ferraris · **36,603** · **21,525**
12 **Sampdoria** · Luigi Ferraris · **36,603** · **19,852**
13 **Atalanta** · Atleti Azzurri d'Italia · **26,562** · **16,946**
14 **Torino FC** · Olimpico · **25,370** · **18,120**
15 **Udinese Calcio** · Dacia Arena · **25,144** · **17,448**
16 **Pescara Calcio** · Stadio Adriatico · **20,515** · **13,540**
17 **Sassuolo Calcio** · Mapei Stadium · **20,084** · **12,362**
18 **Empoli FC** · Carlo Castellani · **19,847** · **9,483**
19 **FC Crotone** · Ezio Scida · **16,547** · **8,226**
20 **Cagliari Calcio** · Is Arenas · **16,200** · **13,021**

GOALS PER GAME PER DECADE

Watch any major European match this year and you can expect to see around 2.5 goals. The goals-per-game ratio has declined steadily from four per match in the late 1950s to its current level, but has shown signs of rising again in the era of Messi, Cavani, and Aubameyang. You'll need to head to Puerto Rico, Taiwan, or Bermuda to have a good chance of a four goal top-flight match, while games in Tanzania, Lesotho, and Jordan struggle to register two.

*German Bundesliga not formed until 1965.

"If you want to have fun, you should go to the circus." With these words Juventus coach Massimiliano Allegri defended his club's safety-first approach. Italian teams' reputation for defensive football is borne out in the tables below as *Catenaccio* and defensive prowess took hold from the 1950s. But there are signs of change—in 2016–17 there were 2.88 goals per game in the league, the highest since 1951, backing up claims of a transformation of Serie A football into an often end-to-end entertaining spectacle.

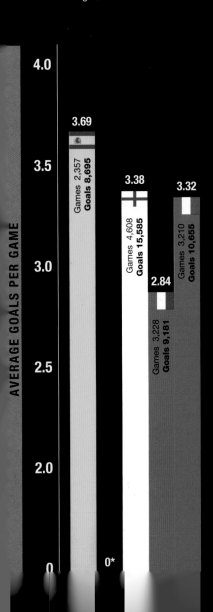
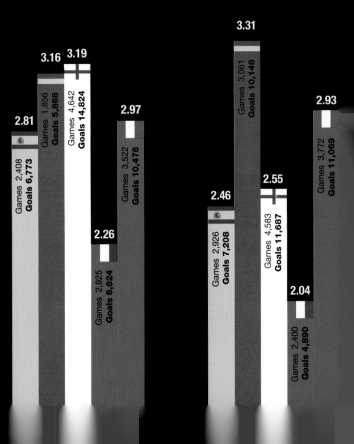

AVERAGE GOALS PER GAME

4.0

3.69 — Games 2,357 — Goals 8,695

3.5

3.38 — Games 4,608 — Goals 15,585
3.32 — Games 3,210 — Goals 10,655

3.0

2.84 — Games 3,228 — Goals 9,181
2.81 — Games 2,408 — Goals 6,773
3.16 — Games 1,856 — Goals 5,868
3.19 — Games 4,642 — Goals 14,824
2.97 — Games 3,522 — Goals 10,476
3.31 — Games 3,061 — Goals 10,146
2.93 — Games 3,772 — Goals 11,069

2.5

2.26 — Games 2,925 — Goals 6,624
2.46 — Games 2,926 — Goals 7,208
2.55 — Games 4,583 — Goals 11,687

2.0

2.04 — Games 2,400 — Goals 4,890

0

0*

Robert Lewandowski, the Bundesliga's greatest modern-day goalscorer. The Polish striker has passed 151 league goals for Borussia Dortmund and Bayern München since 2010.

Source: Opta (May 2017)

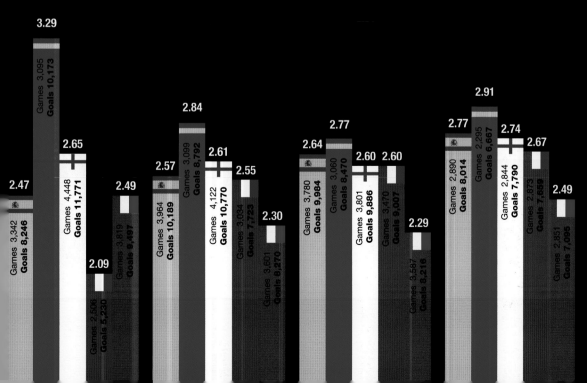

3.29
Games 3,095
Goals 10,173

2.65
Games 4,448
Goals 11,771

2.09
Games 2,506
Goals 5,230

2.47
Games 3,342
Goals 8,246

2.49
Games 3,819
Goals 9,497

2.57
Games 3,964
Goals 10,189

2.84
Games 3,099
Goals 8,792

2.61
Games 4,122
Goals 10,770

2.55
Games 3,034
Goals 7,723

2.30
Games 3,601
Goals 8,270

2.64
Games 3,780
Goals 9,984

2.77
Games 3,060
Goals 8,470

2.60
Games 3,801
Goals 9,886

2.60
Games 3,470
Goals 9,007

2.29
Games 3,587
Goals 8,216

2.77
Games 2,890
Goals 8,014

2.91
Games 2,295
Goals 6,667

2.74
Games 2,844
Goals 7,790

2.67
Games 2,873
Goals 7,659

2.49
Games 2,851
Goals 7,095

LONGEST UNBEATEN RUNS

AC Milan

58 Games

Run started on May 26, 1991
0–0 vs Parma FC

Bayern München

53 Games

Run started on November 3, 2012
3–0 vs Hamburger SV

Arsenal

49 Games

Run started on May 7, 2003
6–1 vs Southampton

Real Sociedad

38 Games

Run started on April 29, 1979
1–0 vs Valencia CF

FC Nantes

32 Games

Run started on July 29, 1994
1–1 vs Olympique Lyonnais

"The Invincibles" was a nickname first given to the 1880s Preston North End team when they won the first "Double", completing the season unbeaten with just four draws. Arsenal would inherit the title in their unbeaten (12-draw) Premier League-winning season of 2003–04. In Europe, Juventus, AC Milan, S.L. Benfica, FC Porto, AFC Ajax, and others have all completed an unbeaten campaign, and in 2017, Celtic's now famous "Infrangibles" became the first Scottish team to manage the feat since the nineteenth century. However, no Ligue 1, Bundesliga, or modern-era La Liga club have yet run the course of the season without defeat.

Source: Opta (May 2017)

Run ended on March 14, 1993
0–1 vs Parma FC

Run ended on March 29, 2014
0–1 vs FC Augsburg

Run ended on October 16, 2004
0–2 vs Manchester United

Run ended on May 4, 1980
1–2 vs Sevilla FC

Run ended on April 8, 1995
0–2 vs RC Strasbourg Alsace

> **"It's not impossible [to go through the season unbeaten] as AC Milan once did it but I can't see why it's so shocking to say it. Do you think Manchester United, Liverpool, or Chelsea don't dream that as well? They just don't say it because they're scared to look ridiculous, but nobody is ridiculous in this job as we know anything can happen."**

Arsène Wenger in 2002, a whole year
before Arsenal's "invincible" season

STAYING POWER

Promotion to the top league presents a wonderful opportunity to establish a club in the top flight. The lucky ones such as TSG 1899 Hoffenheim in the Bundesliga or AC Monaco in Ligue 1 thrive, usually helped by big money backers. Some, like US Pistoiese 1921 (Serie A, 1980–81) or Barnsley (Premier League, 1998–99), are immediately relegated and never seen again. More often they are "yo-yo" teams like FC Nürnberg, Middlesbrough, Real Betis, or FC Bari 1908, doomed to eternally oscillate between promotion and relegation.

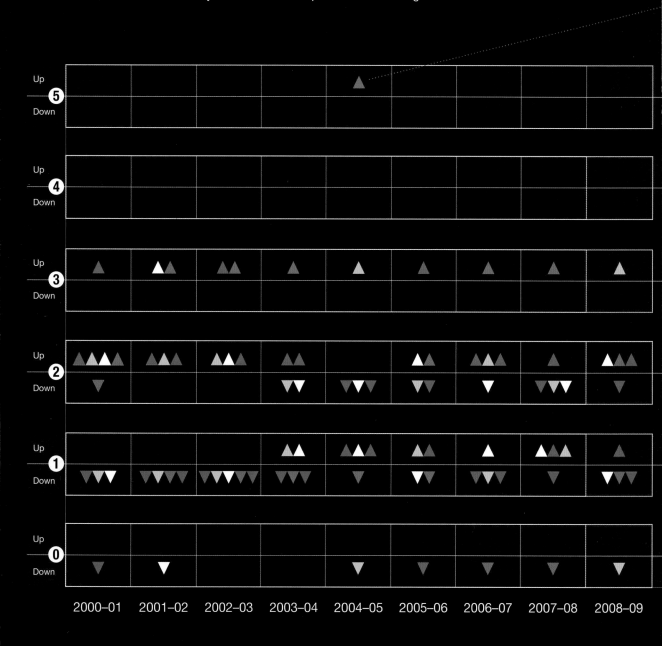

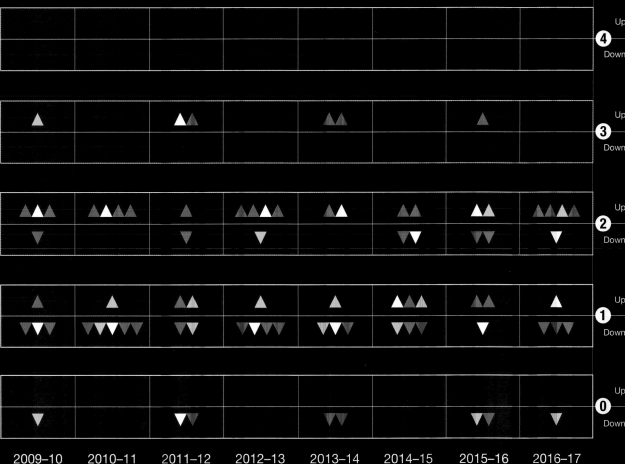

FIFA WORLD PLAYER OF THE YEAR WINNERS

In 2010, the Ballon d'Or merged with FIFA's World Footballer of the Year award, the two competitions having run concurrently since 1991.The Ballon d'Or (Golden Ball) is the award given to the soccer player rated by FIFA as the best player in the world. The coach, team captain, and a media representative of every nation selects their top three players (awarded five, three and one point, respectively) from a 23-man shortlist devised by FIFA. The top three players in the world are decided by combining all of the points awarded.

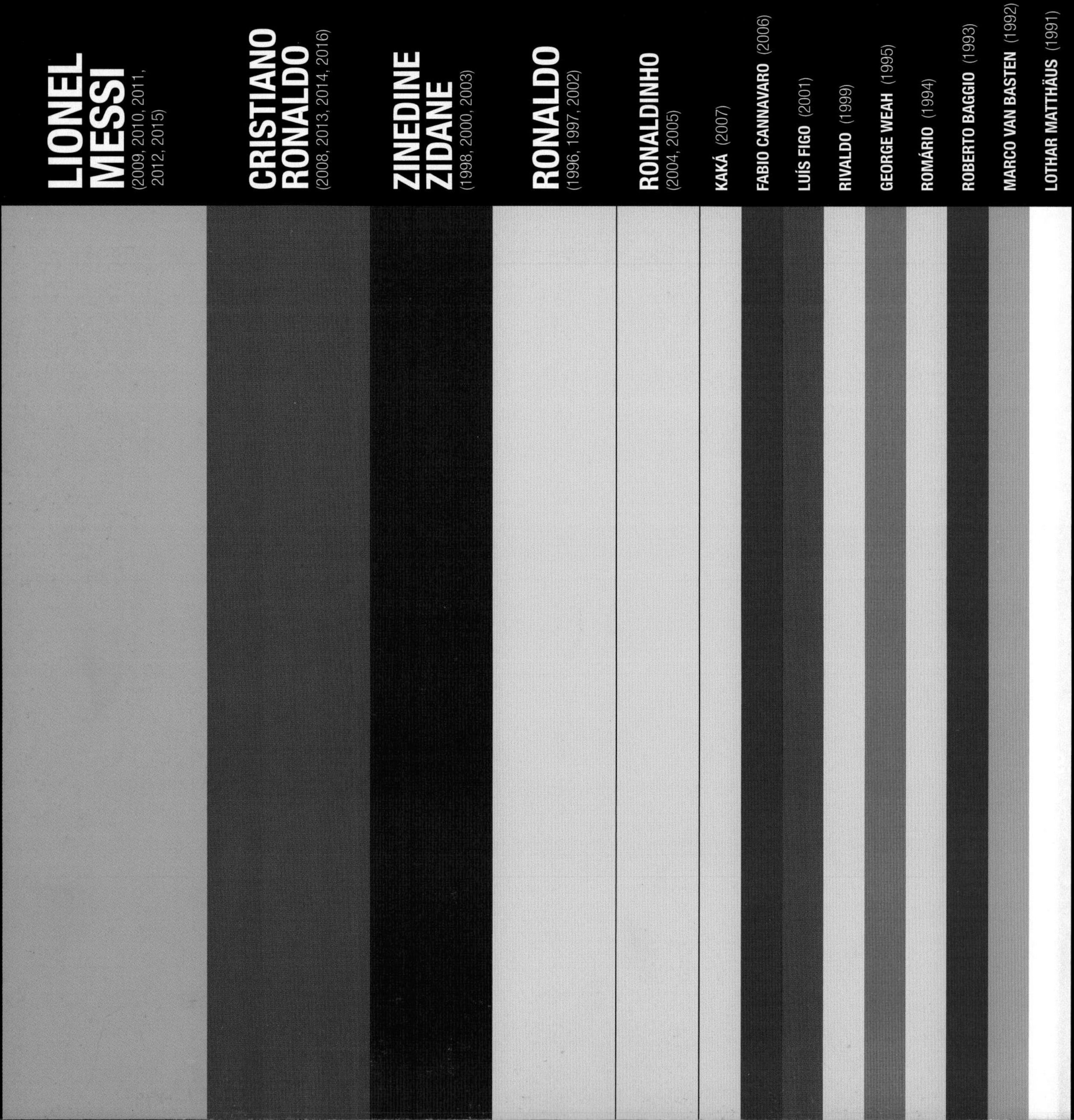

LIONEL MESSI (2009, 2010, 2011, 2012, 2015)

CRISTIANO RONALDO (2008, 2013, 2014, 2016)

ZINEDINE ZIDANE (1998, 2000, 2003)

RONALDO (1996, 1997, 2002)

RONALDINHO (2004, 2005)

KAKÁ (2007)

FABIO CANNAVARO (2006)

LUÍS FIGO (2001)

RIVALDO (1999)

GEORGE WEAH (1995)

ROMÁRIO (1994)

ROBERTO BAGGIO (1993)

MARCO VAN BASTEN (1992)

LOTHAR MATTHÄUS (1991)

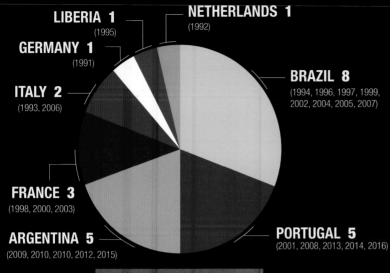

LIBERIA 1
(1995)

GERMANY 1
(1991)

ITALY 2
(1993, 2006)

NETHERLANDS 1
(1992)

BRAZIL 8
(1994, 1996, 1997, 1999,
2002, 2004, 2005, 2007)

FRANCE 3
(1998, 2000, 2003)

ARGENTINA 5
(2009, 2010, 2010, 2012, 2015)

PORTUGAL 5
(2001, 2008, 2013, 2014, 2016)

BY NATION

" The only bad thing about Ronaldo's life is Messi. If it was not for him, Ronaldo would be the best player in the world for five years in a row.**"**

Filipe Scolari, former coach of Portugal

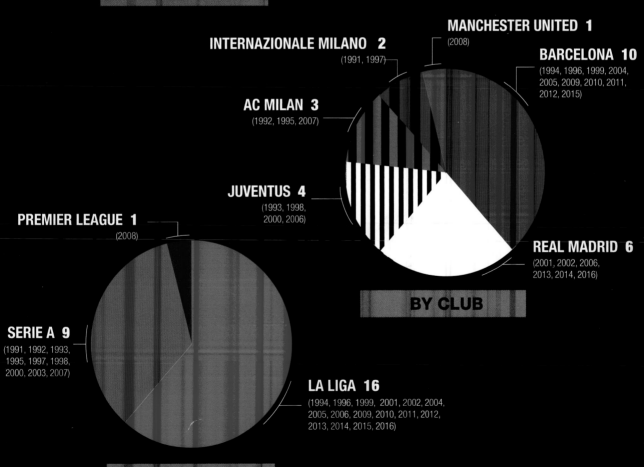

MANCHESTER UNITED 1
(2008)

INTERNAZIONALE MILANO 2
(1991, 1997)

BARCELONA 10
(1994, 1996, 1999, 2004,
2005, 2009, 2010, 2011,
2012, 2015)

AC MILAN 3
(1992, 1995, 2007)

JUVENTUS 4
(1993, 1998,
2000, 2006)

REAL MADRID 6
(2001, 2002, 2006,
2013, 2014, 2016)

BY CLUB

PREMIER LEAGUE 1
(2008)

SERIE A 9
(1991, 1992, 1993,
1995, 1997, 1998,
2000, 2003, 2007)

LA LIGA 16
(1994, 1996, 1999, 2001, 2002, 2004,
2005, 2006, 2009, 2010, 2011, 2012,
2013, 2014, 2015, 2016)

BY LEAGUE

Source: Opta (1991–2017)

THE FLAIR LEAGUE

We all love a wow moment; those demonstrations of skill that are worth the ticket price alone. When it comes to individuals, EA Sports' *FIFA 17* listed its best dribblers as Messi (Barcelona) and Neymar (Paris Saint-Germain). Real Madrid's Ronaldo tops their most powerful shot list, but the top 10 also includes Hull City's Tom Huddlestone, Schalke's Naldo, and Piti from Rayo Vallecano. Take a look at these comparison charts and see where Europe's mazy masters and hot shot kings ply their trade.

Chelsea's often unstoppable Eden Hazard boosted the Premier League's stats by attempting more than 150 dribbles in the 2016–17 season.

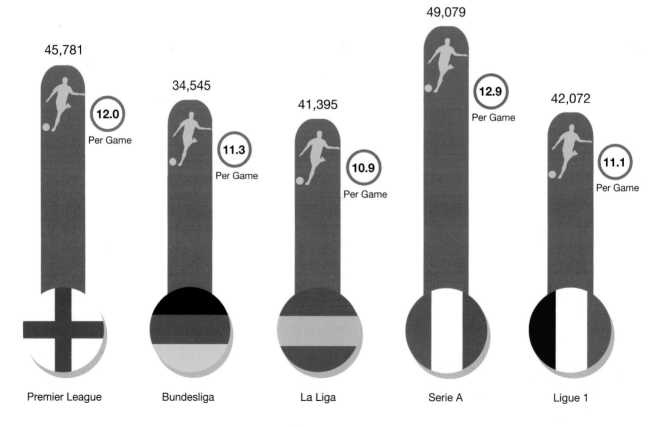

League	Total	Per Game
Premier League	45,781	12.0
Bundesliga	34,545	11.3
La Liga	41,395	10.9
Serie A	49,079	12.9
Ligue 1	42,072	11.1

LONG SHOTS

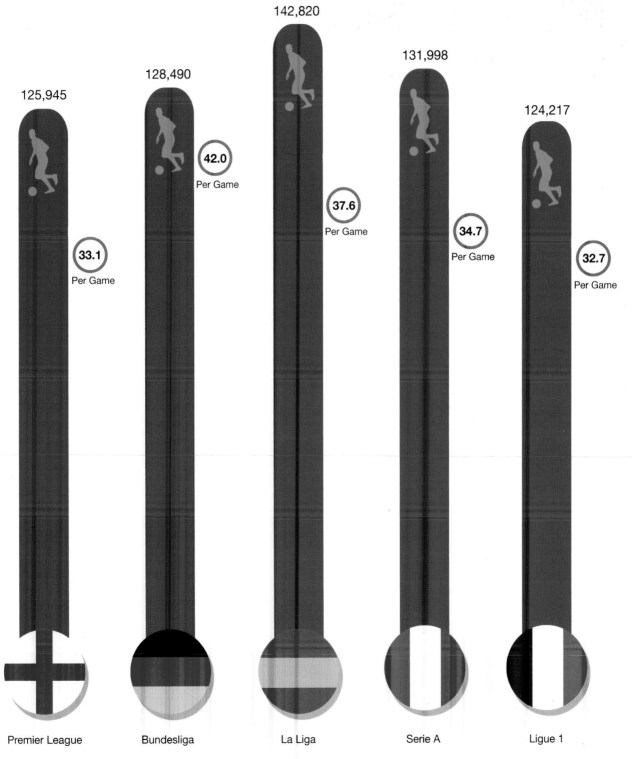

125,945

128,490

142,820

131,998

124,217

33.1
Per Game

42.0
Per Game

37.6
Per Game

34.7
Per Game

32.7
Per Game

Premier League

Bundesliga

La Liga

Serie A

Ligue 1

DRIBBLES

THE FOREIGN LEGION

The quest to build the best team in Europe now involves searching the globe for the best players. While cultural links still explain many of the sources—England picking the best Welsh, Scottish, and Irish players, Germany looking to Switzerland and Austria, with Italy and Spain seeking out South American talent—all major clubs are now prepared to look further afield. Brazil is the leading provider of expatriates to Europe, with French players being most in demand across their own continent.

Source: Opta (August 2016–May 2017)

KEY:
- UEFA
- OFC
- AFC
- CONMEBOL
- CONCACAF
- CAF

Total number of players

Average number of appearances

ENGLISH PREMIER LEAGUE

177 ENGLISH PLAYERS

18.8 AVERAGE APPEARANCES IN SEASON • **3,333** TOTAL APPEARANCES

347 FOREIGN PLAYERS — 232 · 53 · 44 · 8 · 5 · 5

SPAIN	FRANCE	BELGIUM	NETHERLANDS
36 / 22.4 / 807	30 / 18.0 / 540	21 / 26.3 / 553	20 / 20.0 / 399

FRENCH LIGUE 1

303 FRENCH PLAYERS

18.7 AVERAGE APPEARANCES IN SEASON • **5,652** TOTAL APPEARANCES

256 FOREIGN PLAYERS — 126 · 79 · 42 · 6 · 3

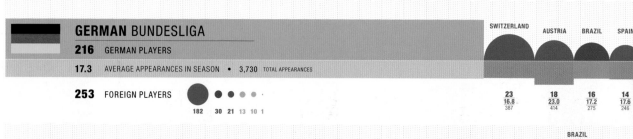

GERMAN BUNDESLIGA

216 GERMAN PLAYERS

17.3 AVERAGE APPEARANCES IN SEASON • **3,730** TOTAL APPEARANCES

253 FOREIGN PLAYERS — 182 · 30 · 21 · 13 · 10 · 1

SWITZERLAND	AUSTRIA	BRAZIL	SPAIN
23 / 16.8 / 387	18 / 23.0 / 414	16 / 17.2 / 275	14 / 17.6 / 246

ITALIAN SERIE A

240 ITALIAN PLAYERS

17.9 AVERAGE APPEARANCES IN SEASON • **4,301** TOTAL APPEARANCES

320 FOREIGN PLAYERS — 175 · 99 · 38 · 4 · 3 · 1

BRAZIL
37 / 16.0 / 593

SPANISH LA LIGA

301 SPANISH PLAYERS

19.6 AVERAGE APPEARANCES IN SEASON • **5,904** TOTAL APPEARANCES

240 FOREIGN PLAYERS — 106 · 93 · 27 · 10 · 3 · 1